BODIES IN EVIDENCE

Bodies in Evidence

Race, Gender, and Science in Sexual Assault Adjudication

Heather R. Hlavka *and* Sameena Mulla

NEW YORK UNIVERSITY PRESS

New York

NEW YORK UNIVERSITY PRESS
New York
www.nyupress.org

References to Internet websites (URLs) were accurate at the time of writing. Neither the author nor New York University Press is responsible for URLs that may have expired or changed since the manuscript was prepared.

Library of Congress Cataloging-in-Publication Data
Names: Hlavka, Heather R., author. | Mulla, Sameena, author.
Title: Bodies in evidence : race, gender, and science in sexual assault adjudication / Heather R. Hlavka and Sameena Mulla.
Description: New York : New York University Press, [2021] | Includes bibliographical references and index.
Identifiers: LCCN 2021003072 | ISBN 9781479809639 (hardback ; alk. paper) | ISBN 9781479809660 (paperback ; alk. paper) | ISBN 9781479809653 (ebook) | ISBN 9781479809646 (ebook other)
Subjects: LCSH: Sex crimes—Law and legislation—United States. | Evidence, Criminal—United States. | Sex discrimination in criminal justice administration—United States. | Discrimination in criminal justice administration—United States. | Forensic sciences—United States.
Classification: LCC KF9325 .H53 2021 | DDC 345.73/0253—dc23
LC record available at https://lccn.loc.gov/2021003072

New York University Press books are printed on acid-free paper, and their binding materials are chosen for strength and durability. We strive to use environmentally responsible suppliers and materials to the greatest extent possible in publishing our books.

Manufactured in the United States of America

10 9 8 7 6 5 4 3 2 1

Also available as an ebook

This book is dedicated to Ibo and James,
for making it all worth it.

اَللّٰهُمَّ اَخْرِجْنِيْ مِنْ ظُلُمَاتِ الْوَهْمِ وَ اَكْرِمْنِيْ بِنُوْرِ الْفَهْمِ

اَللّٰهُمَّ افْتَحْ عَلَيْنَا اَبْوَابَ رَحْمَتِكَ وَ انْشُرْ عَلَيْنَا خَزَآئِنَ

عُلُوْمِكَ بِرَحْمَتِكَ يَا اَرْحَمَ الرَّاحِمِيْنَ

CONTENTS

Introduction

Imagining and Witnessing Sexual Assault Adjudication

A Typical Case

By the first Monday of October 2013, we had been conducting fieldwork in Milwaukee's felony courts for almost six months. On the way into court that day, the air was brisk and chilly. Leaves were beginning to fall from the trees lining the plaza in front of the Milwaukee County Courthouse Complex. We passed through the metal detectors and made our way to Judge Colin's courtroom located in the adjacent Safety Building. Several jury trials were stacked that morning, but only the *State v. Craig Anthony* case was ready to go forward. Compared to the streets, Judge Colin's courtroom was warm and still. It was also spacious, austere, and open, and we and our research assistants frequently referred to it as the "church." Some of the other courtrooms were more ornate and featured wood carvings on the jury box and judge's bench, but not in Judge Colin's court. Sometimes when we referred to the courtroom as "church" we were being facetious, and at other times it was a slip of the tongue. The long wooden benches, pewlike in their appearance and arrangement, and the natural light flooding the court from the towering windows, the slow-turning ceiling fans, and the solemnity of Judge Colin and the judge who had previously occupied this courtroom contributed to the church-like aura. High above the city, screeching seagulls sometimes flew by the windows, reminding us that the shores of Lake Michigan were only a mile and a half east of the courthouse. That Monday, the courtroom was busy as Judge Colin and her staff prepared for *State v. Craig Anthony*. Unlike most sexual assault cases, the *Anthony* case was not resolved with a plea, and so the attorneys readied for the jury panel to be summoned to the courtroom.

Our daily routine consisted of weekday trips to the Courthouse Complex, which included three interconnected buildings: the Milwaukee County Courthouse, the Safety Building, and the Criminal Justice Facility. The courthouse and Safety Building housed the 47 branches of the county court system, the Offices of the District Attorney, and sundry other public services. The courtroom was usually teeming on Monday mornings. Multiple jury trials were often scheduled on the same day and time, because the judges and attorneys knew that most of the trials would vanish, rescheduled for procedural reasons or resolved by plea bargain. Nevertheless, all participants were required to present themselves at the scheduled hour in court. Attorneys and court personnel could circumvent the long security lines. People new to the court system were wise to give themselves extra time to navigate the court's maze of offices and courtrooms. The court system was generally overwhelmed with high caseloads and too few personnel. Case processing and speedy adjudication were oftentimes impeded by these limited resources. In July 2013, only three branches of the court tried felony sexual assault and homicide cases, and when a fourth was added in August, it seemed to do little to speed up case resolution.

Following jury selection and opening statements by both attorneys in *State v. Anthony*, the prosecutor called the first witness to the stand, Regina Crane. For the prosecutor, Regina was the victim-witness in the case, though the defense would refer to her as the "complainant" or "complaining witness." For almost an hour, Regina testified about her experience of sexual assault, going into painstaking detail about how her assailant, who she thought was her landlord, abducted her from the street, brought her to his home, and assaulted her. Regina detailed what led up to the assault, what she was wearing, where it took place, and how the defendant pushed and pinned her down. She shared that during the assault he ripped her shorts and laughed at her when she asked, "Why are you doing this?"

He was like, "Why are you crying?" Like, "What's wrong? You knew this was gonna happen." After, he threw my shorts at me. I just hurried up and put them on as I was, like, trying to run out the room to the door. And I still couldn't open it because there were no, like, handles or deadbolts to, like, open it.

The defense attorney theatrically waved those same shorts in front of a 13-member jury at least seven times during trial according to our field notes. Both the prosecutor's direct examination and the defense attorney's cross-examination required Regina to repeat many details of her experience from the stand. The more details Regina shared about the afternoon, the more defense counsel quizzed her memory. "How long was the intercourse?" she queried. "It certainly was not a long, drawn-out process, right?" The day she testified, Regina responded that she thought it might have been about five minutes, maybe less.

> DEFENSE: You told the cops it was 15 to 20 minutes. Do you remember that? So, was it less than five minutes? Or was it 15 plus a couple minutes to 20 plus a couple minutes time?
> REGINA: It was, like, in between.
> DEFENSE: So, it was more than five but less than 23ish?

Immediately following this exchange, defense counsel returned to the subject of Regina's shorts. She walked toward the prosecutor's table, motioning for him to pass her a large brown paper evidence bag.

> And then, after it's all done, you told us how you got your clothes on. Did you realize at that point in time the zipper was broken? 'Cause I've got to show you Exhibit No. 2. These were the shorts you said you were wearing, right?

Reaching deep into the bag, defense counsel gingerly lifted up a pair of faded cut-off denim shorts and dangled them high in the air for the first time. She held them pinched lightly between her thumb and pointer finger as she approached the witness stand. We documented how she held the shorts as though they were soiled, wrinkling her nose with faint disgust. When Regina confirmed that the shorts were hers, defense counsel continued, "And were the shorts tight on you?" Prosecution did not object, and Regina answered, "They are Daisy Dukes, so yes, and no."

This case was no more or less distressing than other cases we observed in the Milwaukee County Courthouse. Most of the trials we witnessed were tedious and exacting, with rare moments of high drama or dazzling legal rhetoric—quite unlike the television shows with which many of us are accustomed. Instead, we moved between four courtrooms, watching cases at different stages of adjudication, tracking last-minute changes to the court calendar, and following attorneys from courtroom to courtroom. The combination of chaotic disorder and courtroom tedium, as well as the endless anticipation that infused our time in the courts, cannot truly be represented in one case. How can one ethnographic vignette represent a typical case and the quotidian representation of sexual violence as neither remarkable nor exceptional? No individual case could ever wholly embody the multitude of seemingly trivial, oftentimes trifling, but always distressing details that emerged in each of the 688 court hearings (including 34 trials) we observed. *State v. Anthony* stood out among the hundreds of court hearings we observed in part because of defense counsel's calculated display of Regina's shorts. This gesture seemed relatively "low-tech" in contrast to the prosecutor's case, which included a forensic nurse examiner, who had examined Regina following the assault, and the crime lab's analysis of the DNA recovered. "She's waving the shorts around again," we whispered to each other in the gallery. In many ways, the juxtaposition of all these elements—a forensic examination, a positive DNA identification, and the crude gestures calculated to shame the victim-witness with her clothing—drew attention to the staying power of rape myths and the emotional and rhetorical potential of technoscientific interventions in sexual assault cases.

As *State v. Anthony* continued, the defense attorney implied that the sex had been consensual, explaining away the DNA evidence. She further intimated that it was transactional. "You didn't have any money did you, for rent?" defense asked as she shook her head and thrust the shorts in the air once again, snapping them as if to remove wrinkles. In the quiet courtroom, the snapping sound of the shorts commanded attention. As she continued to cross-examine Regina, the defense attorney posed with the shorts against her own waist, turning around in a semicircle toward the judge, the jury, and the gallery. Sitting in the gallery, we were separated from court personnel by bulletproof glass. Defense counsel was taller than Regina by several inches, though it was difficult to judge from a distance through the divider. Against defense counsel's demure, just-below-the-knee black woolen dress, the denim cutoffs seemed especially scant. The gesture also called attention to Regina's body on the stand. Just like most of the attorneys and judges in

Milwaukee's felony courts, defense counsel was white. The majority of adjudicants—including defendants, victims, and other witnesses—were Black and brown. Regina was a young Black woman in her early twenties and curvier than the defense attorney. Was the jury being directed to imagine how those shorts would hang on her body? "And were the shorts tight on you?" defense asked a second time. Regina explained that she had gained some weight since then. It was, after all, more than four months since the assault, and it had been a challenging time for her.

Since that trial, we have often wondered whether it was this gratuitous gesture alone—the repeated snapping and waving of the cutoff denim shorts—that led the jury to return a not guilty verdict despite the wealth of evidence presented by the state. There were numerous witnesses to Regina's abduction in front of her home that day. Regina text-messaged her cousin "I'm being kidnapped" before the defendant took her phone and removed its battery. Returning home after the assault, Regina then went to the hospital and endured multiple hours of a forensic examination. During the examination, the sexual assault nurse examiner (SANE) recovered DNA that matched the accused. Regina called the Milwaukee Police Department and made a report. Regina's actions that day—an immediate call to the police and participation in a forensic examination—are rare among sexual assault victims. In fact, delayed reports of sexual assault are the norm, so collection of forensic evidence is exceptional. Most sexual assaults have no witnesses and leave no visible injuries. And yet, in a court of law, corroboration is often expected and required, and evidence of physical injury and eyewitness testimony are used to convince juries of the victim's credibility. On the stand, Regina testified about the details of what happened to her that day, and her testimony was supported by material evidence and corroborated by a SANE, a patrol officer, and a sensitive crimes detective. The prosecutor argued that, although the defendant's DNA was found, "that's not the issue. The issue is consent, and the most important part of this trial will be what people have to say and whether you believe them." Defense counsel argued that the case was "a he said, she said situation," and while there was no question that Mr. Anthony, the defendant, "had sexual contact with [Regina] on that day, the ultimate question [wa]s whether or not Mr. Anthony had consensual sexual contact, sexual intercourse, with Ms. [Regina Crane] or whether it was nonconsensual." Though Regina insisted that she had not consented to have sex with Craig Anthony, defense counsel argued otherwise, spinning a tale of how Regina exchanged sex for rent money. From the defense attorney's perspective, Regina had fabricated the entire story and endured the indignities of a forensic examination, police investigation, and trial as an elaborate cover for a transactional sexual encounter. The defense attorney's prominent display of the Daisy Dukes, and her obvious disgust as she handled the unwashed denim, implicitly proclaimed them to be some type of sex worker's uniform.

This book is about sexual assault adjudication in the age of forensic intervention and the ways in which expertise is imagined and practiced in the day-to-day operations of a court of law. We show how, time and again, forensic technology and science fail to resolve questions of guilt and innocence. In fact, in cases where the defense is one of consent, as was the case in *State v. Anthony*, the DNA evidence can merely be stipulated to by the court, and therefore witness testimony remains central to establishing the facts of sexual violence. Expert testimony and corroborating material evidence, including forensics, are often included in trials simply because attorneys believe that jurors expect it. And so, the vast amount of time and energy spent on explaining the presence or absence of DNA to the jury effectively reproduces localized, cultural narratives about rape, race, sexuality, and respectability. Making credibility assessments is part of the jury's charge, and its members are instructed to consider the evidence presented as it applies to their everyday "common sense." This common sense often includes how juries think about race, sexual violence, and gender. In a postforensic age in which criminal justice investigation almost always includes the use of forensic technologies, we examined the role of technoscience in courtroom processes, both in terms of its persuasive power and its emotional and affective heft. In this way, technology interweaves with cultural narratives about sexual violence and contributes to the ways in which cultural narratives are reproduced in a new era of sexual assault adjudication. By integrating technoscience into legal processes and the persuasive practices of the court, sexual assault adjudication becomes another realm in which racialized populations are "fixed in place" (Benjamin 2016, 151). And though prevalence rates of sexual assault are distributed across all racial groups, sexual assault adjudication disproportionately involves Black victims, witnesses, and defendants in Milwaukee. In the criminal justice system, racialized populations are fixed in place by imprisoning Black defendants, obligating witnesses to testify in court, and generating permanent court records that document narratives about race, crime, and sexuality.

In the modern courtroom, forensic technology has transformed the ontological practices and the phenomenological experience of adjudication. By "ontological practices," we mean that sexual violence is understood within historical and cultural contexts that govern the categories through which we understand it. Put differently, our collective interpretation of sexual violence is based on broader narratives and experiences shaped by when and where we are living. The conditions of our living delimit how we understand and interpret sexual violence. Race, gender, sexuality, and place are among those collective narratives that emerge in our shared worlds and make their way into how evidence is presented and interpreted in the courts. By "phenomenological," we invoke the realm of experience, in particular the experiences that trial participants may draw on to interpret and understand the court's processes. While research shows that forensic evidence has little impact on sexual assault trial outcomes, we demonstrate how courtroom adjudication and its reliance on science and expertise are crucial sites of cultural reproduction. In this book, cultural reproduction captures the ways in which specific ideas about sexual violence, the law, race, and gender are sustained or augmented through legal processes. In fact, our research reveals how courts are sites of knowledge-making practices that draw from normative cultural narratives about authentic victimhood, credibility, and expertise. In the course of criminal legal adjudication, these narratives are bolstered by the aura of authority attached to them by the forensic.

As interdisciplinary collaborators trained as a sociologist and an anthropologist, we have taken an ethnographic approach and framed our study around fieldwork within Milwaukee's courts. Much sociolegal research relies on court records and case law. While this is a productive avenue for some research, it obscures the day-to-day reality of the court's operations and the experiences of participants. Cases that adhere to precedent rarely find their way into case law, which typically only represents cases that escalate to the appellate level. We focus here both on the commonly anticipated forms of expertise in sexual assault adjudication, including forensic examination and DNA analysis, and also on developing a frame for the myriad other forms of expertise wielded by courtroom personnel. While popular interpretations of forensic expertise privilege the technological and scientific, the term "forensic" itself refers to law. Thus, our research engages a range of expertise and modalities as it exists within contemporary sexual assault adjudication, including the rhetorical strategies honed by prosecutors and defense attorneys, the role of judges in administering hearings and trials, and the skills of practiced witnesses who take the stand again and again.

Our focus on the everyday realities of the court revealed many unpredictable constraints that impacted its functions and practices. For example, that October in 2013 we also sat in courts where judges discussed how Milwaukee's pretrial monitoring program had an inadequate supply of GPS-enabled ankle bracelets and thus could not comply with orders for pretrial GPS monitoring of defendants.[1] In the absence of adequate technology, defendants were jailed as they awaited trial and gained release only if they could afford bail. These material conditions further impacted cases that had reached resolution. During our field research, we attended many hearings in which Department of Corrections officers testified that sentenced sex offenders were unable to participate in court-ordered sex offender treatment programs. Long waiting lists for treatment, with further limitations for Spanish-speaking offenders in the absence of Spanish-speaking therapists and interpreters, meant that many sex offenders were unable to meet their probation requirements. Failure to comply with court-ordered treatment regimes meant imprisonment for some and delays for many. The predicaments of the ankle bracelets and the treatment programs' long waiting lists also illustrated the differential impact of crisis on participants; delays and lack of access to resources resulted in trauma and imprisonment for some and merely inconveniences for others. That these shortfalls in resources would result in the imprisonment of overwhelmingly Black and brown men is also a feature of cultural reproduction in the court system, whereby technoscience is linked to criminalization. These disruptions to the operations of the court and criminal justice system contrast with the ways in which the court of law occupies a powerful presence in the cultural imaginary (Ewick and Silbey 1998). Judges and attorneys navigated these tensions, deploying law as rational and unbiased, but were frustrated by an inadequately resourced system. Their critiques of case law, legal statutes, and state legislation were recorded in our field notes and often in official court transcripts.

Throughout this book, we show how court professionals adjudicate sexual assault given these strained resources and how forensics intersects with cultural understandings about rape, race, gender, and sexuality. As a result of the development of DNA testing and the admissibility of forensic evidence in court, biological evidence recovered from the crime scene or materials derived from the human body have taken on new significance. Analyses of saliva, skin tissue, blood, and semen can now be used to link individuals to crimes and have become an established part of criminal justice procedure. However, the slick technology and boundless resources of fictional forensic units and crime labs depicted on many popular television series has oriented the public to a fantasy version of the world in which sexual assault adjudication takes place. Indeed, discussions about the "CSI effect"—a phenomenon that posits that juries have expectations of the nature of legal evidence based on media representations—are a reflection of the perceived power and certainty of scientific evidence in the justice system (Lynch et al. 2008). Research on the CSI effect, however, reveals little evidence that such media influences trial outcomes (Cole and Diosa-Villa 2009). While entertaining viewing, the glossy version portrayed in television dramas is a far cry from the reality of the court system. Adjudication occurs in a modest setting limited by public resources. The technical and highly skilled work of adjudication in Milwaukee County unfolds in an under-resourced, overtaxed, and frenetic environment similar to many urban courthouses across the United States. As in the case of *State v. Anthony*, the linking of a suspect to a crime vis-à-vis DNA does not address the questions of force or consent that are often central to sexual assault adjudication. Many scholars have demonstrated that forensic evidence is hardly the magic bullet it was anticipated to be by its early adopters in the criminal justice system. Several studies examining the impact of forensic evidence on case outcomes have shown little correlation between the inclusion of forensic evidence and arrest rates, charges, acquittals, or guilty verdicts (Du Mont and Parnis 2000; Quinlan 2017; Sommers and Baskin 2011), a trend that invites reconsideration of the resources poured into forensic technology and case processing.

The place of forensic evidence in sexual assault adjudication calls into question the use of expertise in investigating and prosecuting sexual violence. In this book, we consider the court of law as an authorizing domain that not only relies on expertise but also arbitrates what constitutes expertise. At the same time, the court of law authorizes and reproduces hierarchies of race. We examine the socialization practices and normative structures of evaluation and validation by the expert. In doing so, we problematize the institutionalization and naturalization of the routine activities of the courts and the knowledge they produce (Carr 2010, 18). This knowledge bears on the domains of sexual violence, race, gender, and sexuality. The highly charged nature of sexual assault cases makes them explosive theaters for the production of knowledge about race and inequality. Anthropologist Carolyn Nordstrom described rape as a public secret and wrote: "Public secrets tend to coalesce around matters of power and its abuse. They are thus generally imbued with relationships of domination, contestation and resistance" (1996, 147). Sexuality and race both comprise fields of domination. The authoritative institutions and voices through which law exercises discipline over its subjects intersects with the world of medicine, statistics, and scientific specialization (Foucault 1980, 93; Foucault 1973; Jasanoff 1995). Writing about statistical indicators, legal anthropologist Sally Merry (2016a) noted that they "are indeed seductive in their promise of providing concrete knowledge about how the world works, but they are implemented most successfully when paired with context-rich qualitative accounts grounded in local knowledge." Scholars of policing, such as Jonathan Wenders, have argued that criminal justice research ought to be considered a form of cultural *poesis*, or cultural production. This approach privileges contextualizing "the ontological foundations of the human condition" such that "police-citizen encounters cease to be reducible to abstract 'problems' or 'data'" (Wenders 2008, 3). By rooting our interpretation of the role of police and other actors within the trial, we reveal, once more, the categories through which sexual assault is understood and parsed in our legal system. We extend this analysis beyond policing practice during investigation or on the beat, entering into the space of the trial. Attending to the process of forensic technology and expertise in the court of law unpacks the "aura of objective truth and scientific validity" that Sally Merry argues constitutes a form of power, while analyzing the myriad ways that sexual assault adjudication is itself a form of cultural *poesis*.

Given that forensic evidence and expertise are so routinely incorporated into criminal justice, our research focuses not on case outcomes but on the changing terrain of adjudication processes. We show how the court itself has participated in sustained knowledge-making practices, has drawn on well-worn tropes to interpret and describe sexually violated and violating bodies, and has served as a site of experience for those participating in the trial (Baxi 2005; Foucault 1978). In other words, we think about the court epistemologically, ontologically, and phenomenologically. While court actors and law enforcement weather the storm of changing technologies and practices, victims of crime and defendants who navigate the system are also impacted by new strategies and expectations. These costs are not equally borne, and by many reckonings it is the defendant's rights that are privileged in the process (Flood 2012; Lees 1996; Matoesian 1993). Victims, by contrast, are not plaintiffs but are witnesses for the state in criminal trials ("victim-witness" or "complaining witness"). This important distinction means that, from the outset, the interests of the state may or may not coincide with the interests of the victim. For example, the feminist political scientist Rose Corrigan found that the rape kit examination itself was used to vet the victim's commitment to the investigative processes by submitting to invasive procedures. Corrigan (2013b) termed this phenomenon "the new trial by ordeal." Anthropologist and coauthor Sameena Mulla (2014) also found that forensic nurses deployed similar notions of "good" and "bad" patients based on their compliance with therapeutic regimes in emergency rooms. These regimes enter the court of law via the victim-witness, and the noted anthropologist Veena Das has highlighted such tensions between victim subjectivity and "judicial verification." She (2003) has argued that a victim's speech is "pitted against her body" and that therapeutic and juridical processes work against one another. For the trial, the victim is expected to perform trauma, bracketed as what can be culturally read as credible, acceptable, and palpable (Konradi 2007). The spectacle of the court may exacerbate that trauma, while therapeutic practice is recognized as successful only when victims are able to transcend trauma (Das 2003). The presentation of forensic evidence by expert witnesses must engage the appropriate range of affective or emotive qualities as well, conveying knowledge, authority, objectivity, and reason. These qualities are cultivated both over time and within the space of the courtroom, drawing our attention toward the emotional labor of all courtroom participants. Emotional labor is found not only in the ways that witnesses manage their own affective composure but also in how they contribute to affective sensibilities of the court (Hochschild 1983). Ethnographic research in the courtrooms reveals the human costs borne by all these participants in sexual assault adjudication, and it demonstrates how a priori assumptions about sexual violence, race, gender, and sexuality are reproduced or challenged in courtrooms within and beyond the United States.

The *Nomos* of Sexual Violence

Just as the realities of the underresourced, beleaguered court contradict the dominant cultural imagination of a court of law, so too does the sexual assault trial itself. In *A Theory of the Trial*, legal scholar Robert Burns (1999, 11) argued that this normative view of the trial assumed its power and importance, its factual accuracy, and its truth and that it actualized the rule of law. Burns noted, however, that while this view of the trial is important, it is "so partial as to be a serious distraction of what the trial has become." The cultural imaginary of law, of the courts, and of the rape trial itself now relies heavily on forensic technology and expertise. But it is the law that mediates the modes through which medical and scientific expertise become legal artifacts through court records and case law (Baxi 2014). These investigative and adjudicative processes are steeped in culture and norms, or what the legal theorist and jurist Robert Cover (1983) termed *nomos* in his iconic essay on how law is informed by interpretive commitments and narrative forms. In the context of sexual violence, medicolegal and forensic expertise are informed by cultural norms and dominant narratives, what we term the "*nomos* of sexual violence" (Hlavka and Mulla 2020). Cultural narratives remain crucial to understanding sexual assault adjudication, especially during moments of "shifting terrains of knowledge" (Harper, Kelly, and Khanna 2015, 3) that promise a populace that courts are objective gatekeepers of truth and justice. Rather than eliminating these interpretive commitments, this book shows how they are transformed, reproduced, and repackaged under the guise of scientific authority. These processes are not abstract but instead grounded in the lived and embodied realities of trial participants, who tender their bodies and their voices in service to the courts.

From an institutional standpoint, the myth of the infallible techno-scientific court is revealed in its cultural norms and practices. When we consider the cultural contexts through which we make sense of and understand sexual violence, we recognize that pernicious rape myths represent part of this cultural context. In the modern classic *Rape and the Culture of the Courtroom*, legal scholar Andrew Taslitz (1999) boldly claimed that rape law reform was a failure. Rape shield laws were a legislative response to rape reform movements in the 1970s and 1980s that challenged the legal system's reliance on stereotypical myths that codified "real rape" (Estrich 1987). "Real rape" was constructed as that which occurs only between strangers; as impossible if the victim adequately physically resisted; and as an assault that left unmistakable signs of physical and emotional damage to the body and psyche (MacKinnon 1979). As researchers replaced these discourses with more nuanced realities about sexual violence, reformers promoted further legal reforms to secure victims' rights in investigation and adjudication processes. Recognizing that rape victims were treated with suspicion and deep distrust in the criminal justice system, reformers demanded legal changes to the definition of rape to include a series of graded offenses. They changed the standard for consent by eliminating the requirement that the victim show proof that she physically resisted her attacker; by eliminating the requirement for corroboration of the victim's testimony; and by restricting evidence regarding the victim's sexual past.

However, Andrew Taslitz is not the only one to submit that these reforms have been ineffective in the courtroom (Ehrlich 2001; Konradi 2007; Matoesian 1993). Research has demonstrated how defense attorneys continued to emphasize victims' characteristics, drawing on cultural stories and stereotypes of women and their sexuality and demanding that they justify their own behaviors. Cultural stories are at the root of jurors' unconscious prejudices. According to Taslitz, juries apply their existing stories to witness testimony, converting evidence into familiar tales and filling in the gaps where needed to create a coherent "common sense" narrative. Stories create our world of meaning; they are the lens through which we view all of life's events. Many of these stories tend to channel the political and economic power that our society most values to men and to privilege male perceptions of reality (Taslitz 1999, 7–8). These patriarchal rape tales are embedded in paternalistic conceptions of sexuality and gender roles. As sociolinguist Gregory Matoesian (1993) revealed through rigorous analysis of rape trial transcripts, courtroom talk is sequenced in a particular manner to effect persuasive arguments that result in "legal domination" of the victim-witness. Legal domination within court practices, of course, reflects the intensities and norms of domination and oppression outside of the courts. Gendered and racialized ordering in the courts is intimately tied to such ordering beyond the courthouse walls.

Legal Ethnography: Race, Racism, and Carceral Feminism

Ethnographic studies of courts have highlighted important questions about the authority of the law and the ways in which the law mobilizes to codify narratives of sexual assault in relation to the realities beyond courthouse walls, especially those that draw on shared understandings of race, gender, class, and sexuality. Courtroom ethnographies within legally pluralistic settings, such as the legal anthropologist and jurist Justin Richland's work on Hopi courts, draw attention to the differential sovereignties of legal systems within the same cultural space. In Richland's (2008) case, he demonstrated that Hopi law held a differential status from U.S. criminal and civil law, and while this differential treatment is not codified, it is easily identifiable within processes of adjudication. In the Milwaukee courts, differential status emerges in a unitary criminal law system, and though participants are not explicitly granted rights in relation to their race, class, gender, and sexuality, adjudicative processes effectively grant adjudicants differential rights and obligations in practice. These inequalities are compounded especially when gendered vulnerabilities intersect with racial and ethnic identity (Crenshaw 1991; Merry 1996). In her 2016 postscript to her earlier research in Hawaii, Merry noted that

> the intriguing feature of this trial, as in the anti-gender-based-violence movements I studied subsequently, is the role that law plays both as an

instrument of power, supporting the interests of dominant groups, as well as a mechanism for challenging power by weaker groups. In both cases, there is a mobilization of law to challenge forms of behavior that are sanctioned by law—to attack injustices that are themselves part of the way state legality operates.

In this way, Merry indicated how trials themselves were engines for legal domination. She also recognized that gender-based violence in Hawaii was resourced and took a different shape depending on the racial and ethnic communities in which it took place. Communities had very different relationships with law enforcement and criminal justice institutions that made legal intervention differently fraught (Merry 2016b). Merry drew a direct connection between her observations in Hawaii and the work of groups such as INCITE! who critique the treatment of Black communities and other marginalized populations in criminal justice systems and advocate for justice from gender-based violence outside these systems.

While the dynamics of racial stratification and oppression are always particular to a specific setting and context, anthropologist Mindi Lazarus-Black's work in Trinidad and Tobago identified court rites in domestic violence hearings that appeared to hover outside of racial and class differences, a so-called race-neutral claim that is frequently invoked in legal procedure. Her meticulously documented work showed, however, how race and class and the ways in which they are tied to sexual politics were intensified in the course of courtroom adjudication (Lazarus-Black 2007). As in the court rites Lazarus-Black described, the routines of prosecution that we observed in Milwaukee did not need to explicitly name race or economic vulnerability for them to de facto play a role in racial or sexual domination. Markers of class, access to courts, and differential familiarity with court processes created an unequal playing field for adjudicants. In Lazarus-Black's work, the court's investments in marriage and the appropriate gender roles of husbands and wives contributed to the social reproduction of sexual respectability. This was demonstrated in the courts' commitments to reconciling couples after complaints of abusive and violent incidents. While Milwaukee felony court judges did not explicitly evoke reconciliation in sexual assault cases, they had much to say about ideal households, family dynamics, and appropriate sexuality, often thinly veiling the racism of these comments when they were explicitly about Black families. In her research on sexual assault prosecution in Ayacucho, Peru, the legal anthropologist Laura Bunt (2008) similarly argued that indigenous identity was brought to bear on witness credibility. Attorneys in Milwaukee similarly deployed markers of racial identity as proxies for victim credibility (Powell, Hlavka, and Mulla 2017).

Many of the sexual assault cases we observed included evidence of entangled and complex marriages, partnerships, and divorces. The more cases we witnessed, the more apparent it was that marriage and sexuality were themselves employed in the court's project of racialization, as particular configurations of marriage and care were cast as healthy or as abhorrent, violent, or pathological. Marriage and bids for its dissolution are the focus of the anthropologist Srimati Basu's 2015 legal ethnography *The Trouble with Marriage: Feminists Confront Law and Violence in India*. Basu's fieldwork in Kolkata's courts, alternative dispute resolution programs, and women's police stations shows that many interventions and reforms that resulted from feminist advocacy resulted in reproducing oppression even as they gave rise to different subjectivities within these institutional locations. Her fine-grained investigation locates these new subjectivities on the bodies of adjudicants, who she shows are formed in relation to sectarian and class identity. The meticulous ethnographer Pratiksha Baxi (2014) presented many distinctive iterations of how these sectarian and class identities are localized in her groundbreaking work on sexual assault trials in Ahmedabad. For Baxi, the sexualized spectacle of the rape trial is shaped by genealogical relationships to colonial jurisprudence and sweeps up participants in relation to these colonial legacies. Baxi's work particularly informed our own understanding of forensic science as an instrument of statecraft and the ways in which child witnesses are understood through sectarian and racial regimes. Baxi's work further helped us to think about Muslim girlhood in Ahmedabad in comparison to Black girlhood in Milwaukee. The mistrust of the child witness in both instances is rooted in distinctive normative orientations to sexual violence.

In the United States, we thought about these normative orientations of gender and race in everyday life, as well as how attorneys and court personnel deployed patriarchal stories capitalizing on cultural "tool kits" (Swidler 1986). These tool kits of images, representations, and worldviews were used by attorneys to explain gendered, racialized, and classed codes and appraisals. Attorneys deployed cultural frames (DiMaggio 1997) that are often outside of the individuals' direct experience to explain rape, but these cultural frames reference collective understandings that can be reinforced in the process of the trial. They are rooted in historical legacies of racism (Collins 2004) and are tropes so commonly held that they are continually reproduced and repackaged through media and culture for contemporary audiences. Sexual assault adjudication has long relied on the cultural scaffolding of gender and sexuality (Gavey 2005), including heteronormative, patriarchal, and racialized discourses. Scholars have demonstrated how courtrooms across the United States are spaces in which the force of law is disproportionately brought to bear both against and in the name of Black and brown people.

Much scholarship that focuses on race and racism in the U.S. sociolegal context explicitly centers Black-white divides. In the field, the courts mirrored this approach to race, framing issues of race almost strictly in terms of contrasts between Black and white communities. Other racial categories were treated as emergent, grounded in ethnographic realities surrounding the relatively recent growth of Milwaukee's Latino/a[2] and Arab American populations and the court's nascent understanding of how those racial categories come to matter in the courts. Researchers have found notable racial and ethnic disparities in pretrial criminal processing such as bail decisions, pretrial detention, and sentencing (Martinez, Peterson, and Omari 2019; Schlesinger 2005), but much less work has explored how Latino/a identities are targeted for racial oppression within U.S. policing, courts, and legal systems (Gonzalez Van Cleve 2016; Rios 2011; Trinch 2003). In the institutional spaces where we conducted research, men of color were generally perceived as criminals, rapists, "thugs," and "mopes," and these labels are most explicitly leveled at Black men. This phenomenon has been observed in court systems beyond Milwaukee (M. Alexander 2010; Bogira 2005; Gonzalez Van Cleve 2016). The trope of the Black rapist and white victim engages with deep and complex discourses linked to southern lynching histories (Dowd Hall 1993; Frederickson 1971; Sommerville 1995). These discourses can also be localized through histories of northern urbanization, which rested on the integration of European immigrants into categories of whiteness by emphasizing the criminality of Black urbanites and downplaying the crime rates in communities of recent European immigrants (Muhammad 2010). These racial archetypes always have regional and local histories, but we rarely think about how these particular histories and geographies of race, rape, and inequality continue to operate in the present day.

Even as Black men are burdened with histories of vilification and criminalized in the ways that we have outlined, Black women are also burdened with harmful forms of racialization that are bound up in gender oppression. They are subjected to characterizations of sexual deviance (Crenshaw 1991) and depicted as "welfare queens" and "jezebels" (Collins 2004; Flood 2012; Taslitz 1999). These cultural categories are directly connected to the contexts of U.S. chattel slavery and its subjugation of Black women as reproductive laborers tasked with being birth workers in the plantation system (Wilkie 2003) while also living under regimes of sexual violence that forced them to become pregnant and give birth (Collins 2004; Feinstein 2019; Roberts 1997). The globalization of the erotic economy has contributed to the commodification of Black women's sexual labor (E. Williams 2013). With such a broad array of stereotypes to draw on, Dawn Rae Flood (2012) and Kimberlé Crenshaw (1991) show how attorneys appealed to jurors' racist and sexist sensibilities by invoking notions of the promiscuous lying woman. These indignities are the specific ways in which sexual assault adjudication functions as a public "racial degradation ceremony" (Gonzalez Van Cleve 2016). In our work, we approach questions of credibility within a broader cultural *nomos* from a feminist and intersectional lens to consider how medicine and forensics make sexual violence legible. We identify cultural narratives as shared perspectives of dominant groups and consider how those perspectives "might cause the content of gender and racial stereotypes . . . to overlap in specific ways" (Ridgeway and Kricheli-Katz 2013, 295). The process of adjudication, we argue, is a site of recalibrating culturally animated truths about sexual violence, evidence, and race.

Decades of advocacy for expanded legal rights for victims and survivors, and the call for more resources for criminal justice intervention into sexual violence, have been widely critiqued because they do little to impact social change at a structural level. Scholars and activists—many with an abolitionist perspective—have raised the point that a project once rooted in feminist grassroots organizing for social transformation has become a cry for carceral expansion (Gottschalk 2006). This project of carceral expansion is not aligned with prevention of sexual violence. In her research on movements organizing against human trafficking, Elizabeth Bernstein (2007, 143) termed the phenomenon of feminist advocacy for carceral expansion as "carceral feminism," describing the dynamic as a shift away from feminist advocacy for solutions supported through the welfare state in favor of institutionalizing and enforcing reforms within the carceral state apparatus. Parallel to the normalization of carceral feminist projects is the expansion of mass incarceration in the United States, characterized by its shocking racial disparities (M. Alexander 2010; Hinton 2016). This is especially salient in a city like Milwaukee with an intensely overincarcerated community. Examining the history of how feminist movements with origins in antiracist work transformed into carceral expansion projects, Mimi Kim (2020, 252) writes:

> While recognition of deep race and class disparities inherent in pro-criminalization strategies may have impeded investment in crime control, the suppression of these differences under a gender essentialist framework facilitated the continued adherence to carceral strategies as a central feature of feminist anti-violence movements.

Kim labels this dynamic "carceral creep" and explicitly draws attention to the ways in which gender essentialism promotes carceral expansion, which in turn expands racial domination of Black and brown subjects within the ever-expanding carceral system.

Where does this book enter these debates? First, we do not see the institutional processes of adjudication through a reformist lens. While there may be ways to increase the efficiencies of the courts or to soften the inequities experienced by individual participants, we recognize the overwhelming volition of the courts as an engine of reproduction of racial injustice. In focusing on sexual violence, we see the ways in which gender and sexuality are recruited particularly in service of racial inequality, and we resist the gender essentialism that is central to Kim's criticism. That is, our work shows that men, women, and gender-nonbinary participants are subjected to distinctive forms of racial subjugation and oppression in the courts, and we draw attention to these throughout the book. Sexual assault adjudication is also unique in the way it relies on the forensic imaginary, and so we discuss the ways in which this expertise is mobilized to produce and preserve racial hierarchies.

Method: Ethnography Goes to Court

Milwaukee is the largest city in Wisconsin, the fifth-largest city in the midwestern United States, and the second-most densely populated metropolitan area in the Midwest, second only to Chicago.[3] Ethnographic methods allow us to generate deep insight into the particular configurations of a process such as adjudication. Although urban ethnographers do not aim for generalizability, they operate while understanding that broader issues, like the way that local knowledge about race, place, and forensic science inflect daily adjudication processes, will allow researchers in other cities to identify these mechanisms within many court systems. The inflection points may simply differ, but thinking about courts as an engine of inequality, and understanding how those processes take place, is a project with import that extends well beyond Milwaukee. Like many other cities, Milwaukee's Black population experiences disproportionately high levels of incarceration. Wisconsin has incarcerated over half of the young Black men from Milwaukee County in state correctional facilities, and thousands of men from central Milwaukee neighborhoods have state prison records. Incarceration is a prime example of racial and ethnic disparities, illustrated by the fact that, whereas Wisconsin's population is only 6 percent Black, its prison and jail population is 38 percent Black. Like other midsized cities that once relied on industry, deindustrialization has left many Milwaukee city residents in economic turmoil (Sampson 2009; Wilson 1996 and 2009). As one of the most racially segregated cities in the United States, Milwaukee has long endured problems of "hyper-segregation" (Massey and Denton 1993; Peterson and Krivo 2010; Sampson 2009). Milwaukee is consistently cited as being the most segregated metropolitan area in the United States, and in 2015 it was rated as the "worst city for Black Americans" based on disparities in employment, health outcomes, educational achievement, and income levels (Greer et al. 2013; Kowalik 2018; Levine 2012).

The Wisconsin Department of Justice is no stranger to scandal involving sexual assault policing practices. Two prominent cases involving the sexual assaults and deaths of numerous Black women in Milwaukee brought the policies, practices, and training of Milwaukee Police Department officers under national scrutiny. In March 2010, Gregory Below was found guilty of 29 counts including kidnapping, sexual assault, and stalking in a series of attacks from 2004 to 2009. He was convicted of sexually assaulting eight vulnerable women—including women who were sex workers or had serious drug addictions—on Milwaukee's South Side over a five-year period. Many of the women asserted that they were ignored and mistreated by Milwaukee police officers when they reported that Below had sexually assaulted them. Some complained that, when they came forward, they had been arrested for prostitution. Indeed, internal investigations noted the lack of officer training and sensitivity to victims of sexual assault that resulted in victims' mistreatment.[4] Then, in February 2011, Walter Ellis was convicted after pleading no contest to the homicide of seven Black women on the North Side of Milwaukee over a 21-year period. Ellis's case made national headlines,[5] and the role of DNA was front and center after Chief Edward Flynn and the Milwaukee Police Department admitted to misplacing Ellis's DNA in 2001. In both cases, Milwaukee police were accused of not taking seriously the reports of sexual assault and the murders of sex workers in Milwaukee.[6] The controversy surrounding these cases highlighted the persistent lack of coordination among law enforcement, loss of evidence, poor investigative techniques and evidence collection, and the mistreatment of vulnerable victims, primarily Black women. Case mismanagement and the disregard for women of color affect sexual assault adjudication as well. Exasperated assistant district attorneys often told us about sexual assault cases they had lost when victims were Black women, explaining that defense attorneys deployed the "prostitution defense." "They just say that she was a prostitute," they told us with incredulity.

The Milwaukee County circuit courts are embedded in these local histories and material conditions, and while many court personnel insisted that they simply "processed those cases that the police brought them," research has suggested that, along with police practices, charging decisions and sentencing disparities contribute to Wisconsin's mass incarceration crisis (Davis, Chisholm, and Noble 2019). Into this fray, we located our study on sexual assault procedures, prosecution, and adjudication with a commitment to thinking about the history and context of local policing, sexual assault interventions, and racial inequalities that are magnified through the courts' daily practices. Built in 1931, the Milwaukee County Courthouse, located in downtown Milwaukee, is part of a civic area that includes the Milwaukee Public Museum, the Central Library, the Courthouse Complex, and, a few blocks east, City Hall. Walking to the main entrance on the south end of the building, individuals pass through Clas Park into MacArthur Square—a small green space that leads to a water fountain. Protestors would rally in the courthouse square a few times a year. The high-rise, Neoclassical limestone architecture stands out against an otherwise empty sky. The drone of the I-43 freeway running along the west side of the building mixed with the hustle of loading and unloading bus passengers and the lunchtime clamor of Food Truck Thursday during the summer months. There were at least four public entrances to the courthouse, including the main entrance to the south, two on the west and the north, and one underground that was accessible via the parking structure. The parking structure also served the jail and the museum. At various times during our observations, the main entrance was accessible only to attorneys and members of the media. All others were directed to the underground parking garage (see figure I.1), which was dark, secluded, and hidden from public view. At times, long lines weaved outside the door. The pungent smell of gasoline and motor oil often filtered into the building. Once inside the doors, the air was musty and chilly, like a damp basement, and defendants, families, and children waited as the security lines slowly moved. Only police officers and those court professionals with identification badges were allowed to skip to the front of the security lines.

Criminal statutes defining sexual assault and rape vary from state to state. Similar to other states, Wisconsin statute 940.225[7] outlines four degrees of sexual assault distinguishable by, among other factors, type

Figure 1.1. Parking Garage. Photo credit: Heather R. Hlavka

of charge, bodily harm experienced, violence inflicted, use of a weapon, state of the victim, and relationship between the parties. First through third degree sexual assault were charged as felonies, and fourth degree sexual assault was a misdemeanor.[8]

The statute also defines terms and phrases including "sexual intercourse," "sexual contact," and "consent."[9] Consent includes words or overt actions by a person who is competent to give informed consent indicating a freely given agreement to have sexual intercourse or sexual contact [940.225(4)]. Consent is not cited in cases in which the complaining witness does not have the legal capacity to consent (most commonly because she is a child), and sexual intercourse or sexual contact are the only elements that prosecutors must prove. Child Sexual Assault [948.02] includes first and second degree, repeated acts of sexual assault of the same child [948.025], incest with a child [948.051], sexual exploitation of a child [948.05], and soliciting a child for prostitution [948.08].[10]

According to the Uniform Crime Reports (UCR), in 2013, which was primarily when we were in the courts, 239 forcible rapes were reported to and handled by the Milwaukee Police Department, a 2.6 percent increase from 233 reported in 2012.[11] Of course, sexual assault is notoriously the most underreported violent criminal offense in the United States, so the UCR statistics do not capture the majority of the sexual assaults reported in Milwaukee County.[12]

During our fieldwork and at the time of publication of this book, the Mayor's Commission on Sexual Assault and Domestic Violence, an interagency body made up of appointees from a range of governmental and nongovernmental agencies and community groups supported a coordinated response to sexual assault in Milwaukee. Members included sexual assault nurse examiners, rape crisis advocates, district attorneys, police detectives, and representatives of specialized victim advocacy groups. Milwaukee does not have a stand-alone rape crisis center and embeds services in a variety of nonprofits, such as the Hmong American Women's Association, Asha Family Services, Pathfinders, Sojourner Family Peace Centers, and UMOS Latina Resource Center. The commission meets monthly to discuss a range of issues including sexual assault prosecution, and in 2010 local backlogs in rape kit testing became a primary concern (Polcyn, Fox 6 News, July 25, 2010).[13] Sexual assault nurse examiner services existed at Milwaukee County's two Sexual Assault Treatment Centers (SATCs) at Aurora-Sinai Hospital and Aurora West Allis Medical Center. Both centers serve Milwaukee and much of southeast Wisconsin. SANE programs number over 450 nationwide (IAFN 2007). Nurses collect evidence from victims' bodies, including human tissue and fluids, proof of bodily and anogenital injury to the victim, such as photographs of wounds (Mulla 2011; Rees 2009; White and Du Mont 2009), and trace evidence from the location of the attack such as carpet fibers, gravel, and plant material.

Police and crime scene investigators are responsible for collecting material and evidence from the crime scene itself. During interviews with SATC nurses, they reported that in 2011 the Milwaukee program was the second busiest sexual assault treatment program in the country. The SATC provided victims a liaison service that worked closely with the Sensitive Crimes Unit of the District Attorney's Office. The Wisconsin Coalition Against Sexual Assault (WCASA) is a statewide organization that supports the work of Wisconsin's community-based sexual assault service provider programs and provides Wisconsin statistics on sexual assault, prevention and training tools, police, law, and advocacy updates. For example, in 2012 WCASA[14] reported 2,591 sexual assault victims served by several area advocacy organizations including the Sexual Assault Treatment Center, 977 sexual assault victims reporting to 21 Milwaukee County law enforcement agencies, and 281 convictions in the Milwaukee County courts (142 cases of sexual assault; 139 cases of child sexual assault). The Wisconsin Court System 2013 Caseload Summary Reports document 25 sexual assault jury trials (68 cases plead or were dismissed before trial), 31 child sexual assault jury trials (152 cases plead or were dismissed before trial), and one second degree child sexual assault bench trial.[15]

In 2013, Milwaukee's Sensitive Crimes Division included the Domestic Violence Unit, Sensitive Crimes Unit, and Child Abuse and Protection Unit. At this time, within the Office of the District Attorney there were 43 assistant district attorneys (ADAs), one victim-witness coordinator, and 41 county staff who provided services to crime victims and witnesses on criminal cases, served subpoenas, and completed other processes in criminal and juvenile cases. In 2013, there were 41 total Wisconsin state public defenders.[16] Prior to a trial, there was very modest or light preparation of victim-witnesses by the prosecutor's office. Across the United States, while some prosecution units invest significant time in preparing victim-witnesses, others do not (Konradi 2007). This is not necessarily a function of neglect but rather of both prosecutorial resources and preferences. The typical prosecutor with the Milwaukee County District Attorney's Office carried a load three to four times higher than recommended by the American Bar Association and had little time to prepare witnesses for court. In addition, interviews with prosecutors revealed a desire for victim testimony to be "spontaneous and unrehearsed," thus there was little to no preparation of lay witnesses who took the stand.

Ethnography in the Details

Our collaboration builds on our prior research on sexual violence focused on contexts of the forensic, in the emergency room (Mulla

2014), and at a child advocacy center (Hlavka 2013, 2014, 2017). By the time the spectacle of the forensically examined body emerges in court, many processes have already taken place. Aware of this context, as well as the interagency collaboration required to coordinate among law enforcement, health care and social services (Corrigan 2013a), and crime laboratories (Kruse 2016), this book draws on our combined backgrounds in these areas to examine the space and practices of the courtroom, documenting how expertise becomes naturalized, normalized, and codified.

Psychologist Jerome Bruner (2002, 37) described "storytelling" as the heart of legal practice. Cultural narratives are crucial to understanding trials and legal outcomes. Witnesses, attorneys, judges, and jurors participate in storytelling as narrators and audience members (Ewick and Silbey 1998; Polletta et al. 2011). Depending on these discourses, attorneys work to provide the legally compelling narratives that convince jurors and judges of the victim's credibility (Ewick and Silbey 1998; Schafran 1995; Taslitz 1999). Attorneys tell stories about evidence—what it means, what it does, and does not, show. These stories are taken from a variety of powerful cultural narratives that are likely to resonate with jurors, and they "invoke emotion, moral and political values while telling of motives, behaviors, actions, and intentions" (Burns 1999, 28). In the 1990s, medicolegal and forensic evidence played a minor role in a court's representation of the facts of the case and was rarely included within scholarship on rape trial discourse (Ehrlich 2001, 37). In the context of new policies and sexual assault investigative practices that have emerged since roughly 2000, this book takes a renewed look at medicolegal and forensic evidence in sexual assault cases, investigating the ways in which such evidence reanimates cultural narratives of sexual assault. Forensic evidence, too, must be worked into legal stories (Jasanoff 1995). These stories are animated by the attorneys and witnesses who speak them into existence in the courts. The juries who share the world of the courts with these actors (Hlavka and Mulla 2018) are shaped by collective perceptions and understandings of race and racism, even as they actively contribute to them.

In 2010, we met with the chief judge and discussed the court's openness to place student observers in the courtroom. Our students were welcomed, and for three years between 40 and 60 students would conduct observations in the courts each semester, noting basic characteristics of the proceedings. We located students in various courtrooms, observing different types of hearings so they might gain an appreciation for the distinctive approaches to adjudication. Each semester, we joined them, learning how to navigate the court complex, the calendar system, and the general ethos of the courthouse. Our presence in the courts made us a regular fixture of the site. Our students were often invited back to chambers to learn more about the legal system and had opportunities to ask questions of judges and commissioners. Students also documented, discussed, and commented on the deeply lopsided racial dynamics of criminal justice. From outside the courthouse walls, it was easy to imagine a magisterial and rational system, but within the courts, the messiness of adjudication was apparent.

In May 2013, we began daily observations in the courthouse. During fieldwork, we observed 688 court hearings and appearances representing the gamut, from full trials to initial appearances, pretrial motions, plea negotiations, sentencing hearings, doctors' reports, and probation reviews. A total of 364 distinct defendants accounted for these 688 appearances. Our observations included a total of 34 full jury trials, and we purchased 22 complete trial transcripts and 54 sentencing hearing transcripts. One of our students, Amber Powell, joined the team in May 2012 and conducted fieldwork with us through the duration of the project. Another student, Sophia Torrijos, joined our team in the summer of 2014. We compiled their field notes along with ours to enrich the data, and their observations and insights also represent part of the data that we analyzed.

People of color, particularly Black men, were disproportionately represented as defendants in the hearings and trials we observed (see table I.1). As displayed in table I.1, whereas Black residents represent 27.2 percent of Milwaukee County's population in 2018, they make up 57 percent of the total unique defendants whose court appearances we recorded in the study. The inverse relationship can be observed with white defendants, who represent 24 percent of the defendants included in the study while accounting for about 50 percent of the county's overall population.

TABLE I.1. Defendants by gender and racial/ethnic characteristics

Racial/Ethnic Group	Men/ Women	Total defendants	% of all defendants in study	% of Milwaukee County population*
Black Men	199	206	57%	27%
Black Women	7			
White Men	82	86	24%	64%
White Women	4			
Latino Men	61	63	17%	16%
Latina Women	2			
Asian/Asian American Men	7	7	1.5%	5%
Asian/Asian American Women	0			
Arab/Middle Eastern Descent Men	2	2	.5%	**
Arab/Middle Eastern Descent Women	0			
TOTALS	364		100	

* Based on July 2019 census estimates, www.census.gov/quickfacts/milwaukeecountywisconsin.
** Data unavailable (conflated with category Asian and White in census data).

The duration of jury trials varied, generally lasting between two and five days. Each jury trial included 12 deliberating jurors (and one or two reserve jurors depending on the judge's preference), representing a wide range of races, ethnicities, ages, neighborhoods, and professions. Our field notes were descriptive, reflexive, interpretive, and analytic. Detailing attorneys' narratives required paying close attention to each stage of the trial, including admissions of evidence, sidebars, jury selections, preliminary and final jury instructions, opening statements, presentations of the evidence, and closing arguments. Visual supports often accompanied verbal testimony (Jasanoff 1995) and were included in our field notes. Court transcripts supplemented courtroom observations and extensive field notes that documented dialog, tone, gazes, gestures, silences, appearances, interactions among courtroom actors, and, of course, evidence displays. Court transcripts reflected only on-the-record discussion, and there were numerous slippages between our notes and the records. We were attentive to these slippages and divergent accounts, following Ranajit Guha's (1988) historiographic instruction on counterinsurgencies, in which he urged scholars to critically examine the source of documentary evidence and the perspective from which official records were recorded. While his instruction to read between the gaps and exclusions referenced peasant uprisings in the context of colonial India and cast doubt on the record of the colonial government, this method was useful for thinking about law courts and their inscribing authority. Our field notes accounted for the "bodily modes of expression that asserted themselves in the courtroom" and that "paradoxically became a visible supplement that was invisible to the official transcript and the legal record" (Salamon 2018, 11). In addition to erasing gesture and embodied expressions of race and gender, trial transcripts also erased time and emotion. Thus, our field notes tracked, to the extent possible, these lost moments and inflections that were disappeared from the official court records.

The court record is, over time, an official archive of precedent-adhering law. In our analysis, we also queried the ways in which the record functioned as a form of official marking and of racial surveillance (Browne 2015). As such, we amplified our field notes, focusing on the gaps between official and unofficial records, capturing short jottings of conversations and statements, off-the-record sidebars, or casual meetings in the hallways and elevators of the courthouse (Emerson, Fretz, and Shaw 2011). Following cases over their entire trajectory from initial appearance to resolution captured the workflow of a courtroom located within the local and historical context of time, space, and place.

Our mixed-methods qualitative design was embedded in ethnographic fieldwork, gathering additional data from pre- and postcourt observations including archival documents and semistructured interviews with sexual assault nurse examiners, attorneys, judges, victim-witness advocates, forensic scientists, and several jurors who agreed to be interviewed following trials. We asked SANEs and forensic scientists about the technical and legal aspects of their work, best practices, training in new technologies, local resources, and the frequency and nature of expert testimony. We asked courtroom personnel about pretrial preparations and courtroom workgroup relationships, common case dynamics, and experiential understandings of the social life of sexual assault adjudication, including their use, understandings of, and familiarity with medicolegal evidence such as photos, drawings, video and social media, GPS tracking, trace evidence, and forensic evidence. We also attended training events hosted by the Wisconsin chapter of the International

Association of Forensic Nurses, in addition to continuing education courses on domestic and sexual assault for the Milwaukee Assistant District Attorney's Office. We also interviewed personnel in the Wisconsin Department of Justice Office of Crime Victim Services. Along the way, we gathered archival and supplemental sources such as court documents and forms during observation and through court records retrieved and tracked using the Circuit Court Calendar (PROTECT interface) and the Consolidated Court Automation Programs (CCAP interface). We rarely asked direct questions about race and racism. At times, our research participants would raise these issues themselves, but direct questions about race often resulted in awkward silences or responses reflecting what we think the respondent thought we might like to hear. Instead, we allowed the work that race, racialization, and racism did within the courts to emerge as a process grounded in daily practices.

Our work provides unique comparisons across sexual assault cases regarding the type, role, and impact of medicolegal evidence in order to disentangle distinctive properties from cases including extralegal factors such as race, gender, sexuality, and relationships between parties (Beichner and Spohn 2005). Information from interviews with courtroom personnel and experts situates the local and structural factors related to training, presentation, and modes of knowledge regarding the collection and use of medicolegal and forensic evidence. Thus, these multiple nodes of understanding expertise in the trial capture the communicative and interactive details of settings "as scenes in which reality-construction work is taking place" (Holstein and Gubrium 2008) while simultaneously making use of participants' subjective understandings to fill in explanations about that which might not be visible. Staller and Vandervort (2010, 7) note that "legal narratives—particularly the opening and closing arguments of counsel—utilize preexisting components familiar to their constructors from stories they have read, heard, watched or told." Moving beyond the question of case outcome, we analyzed both the specific content of narratives and the narrative practices that reproduce inequality throughout the trial process (Choo and Ferree 2010; Polletta et al. 2011; Plummer 1995). We do not dispute or confirm the factual findings of sexual assault trials but rather expose how attorneys produce narratives to establish legal guilt or reasonable doubt, as well as how the court serves as an engine of cultural reproduction and racial calibration.

Team Ethnography: Collaboration in Court

We have conducted this research as a collaborative ethnography grounded in feminist praxis, blending together anthropological and sociological approaches to produce a complex understanding of the courts. We recognize the strength of collaborative ethnography to provide "a richer description, [highlight] perceptual inconsistencies [while also] recognizing the influence of ethnographers' personal and intellectual backgrounds on the collection and recording of data" (May and Pattillo-McCoy 2000, 65). We set out to develop a reflexive research design that combined our methodological and analytical strengths in qualitative research, including institutional ethnography and discourse analysis (Mulla 2014; Hlavka 2013, 2014, 2017). A core tenet of feminist epistemology is to "grapple with power relations," seeking to understand "how social structures organize relations of inequality and how diverse people relate to those social structures" (Rosenberg and Howard 2008, 677, 682). Part of our feminist praxis means thinking intersectionally—that is, focusing on various ways in which our research participants are rendered vulnerable in the world of the courts and thinking deeply about the conditions under which each subject might be fully liberated. For us, it has meant finding an ethical way to include defendants within our research without decentering the harms experienced by victim-witnesses; to take seriously racial prejudice and the role it plays in sexual assault prosecution; and to question whether justice is what unfolds in a courtroom. A guilty verdict and ensuing sentencing of a defendant does not, in this study, necessarily translate into liberatory conditions for a victim, as the process in which she participated may still have reinforced a racist and sexist cultural dynamic in her own community and familiar geographies. As U.S.-based ethnographers with different biographies and training, we recognize how our race, ethnicity, gender, culture, and social positions result in differential treatment and visibilities, often reaffirming the social positioning of all actors within the courtroom (Gonzalez Van Cleve 2016). We privilege reflexivity in our everyday lives and in our research practice, and we continue to interrogate how our standpoints produce situated knowledge (Collins 1990; Harding 2004; Dorothy Smith 1990).

We have thought carefully about the "epistemic object" in studies of sexual violence and written on gendered violence and research ethics elsewhere in the sense that every study of sexual violence focuses on some specific subject of study. "Sexual violence" is itself too sweeping and broad to constitute a single specific scope of inquiry (Mulla and Hlavka 2011). Our views on the victim as ontological subject interrogate issues of temporality and duration of victim status. As feminist scholars, we approach the issue of language and labeling individuals as "victims" or "survivors" from a variety of perspectives. We intentionally use the word "victim," and occasionally interchange this with the terms "complainant" or "victim-witness," not as a paternalistic term or in any way to diminish the agency of individuals. We identify the term to be most accurate given the setting, as legal institutions constitute victim-witnesses and complainants, not survivors. We also understand victimhood within an ethnographic context, in which members might simultaneously elect and be coerced to participate. We also found that, in both formal interviews and everyday conversations with courtroom personnel, including defense attorneys, "victim" was the most commonly used identifier. We have diligently worked to maintain the confidentiality of our participants and subjects in court cases, including victims, defendants, and attorneys. Of course, the courtroom is a public space open to observation, and CCAP provides extensive, oftentimes intrusive, personal information about defendants that can sometimes be linked back to victims, especially in child sexual assault cases because most are intrafamilial. We used pseudonyms for all participants and subjects observed, occasionally drew on multiple cases to create composite cases, and often altered distinguishing features of participants, aside from a few high-profile cases involving public figures. It is also important to note that, as of this publishing, most of the prosecutors and judges we observed during our fieldwork have rotated out of the felony homicide and sexual assault branches.

Our daily research rhythms were shaped by the court schedule. We entered the courtroom with bodies that were perceived in a particular way, and our own gendered and racialized identities often inflected our experiences in the courts. Guards flirted with members of the team whom they perceived as Black and brown, and civilians often perceived white team members as courthouse personnel. Assumptions about whether we were adjudicants ourselves often attached to our research assistant Amber, who, as the sole Black woman on the team, was frequently assumed to be a member of the defendant's or victim's party. Men frequently asked Amber for her phone number. Wearing skirts and dresses, as Sameena did, often garnered attention from men waiting to check in during pretrial monitoring. Both Amber and Sameena were often hissed at or catcalled while walking around the courthouse, and Heather was most likely to be mistaken for an attorney or clerk, though sometimes Heather and Sameena were mistaken for social workers or victim advocates. One early morning after waiting in the damp basement security line, a familiar guard greeted Heather and Sameena with a smile, "You ladies again?" As he proceeded to take our bags and wave the screening wand over our bodies, he grabbed Heather's waist and firmly slid his hands up and down her ribcage. The feigned security check at the hands of a gatekeeper for the court made Heather feel trapped and upset. How many victims had experienced the same while walking through those security lines on their way to hearings? We avoided that security line for weeks, later choosing different entrances, often with longer lines. Events like these never allowed us to slip into the fiction that we could transcend our own gendered, racialized, and sexualized flesh as we conducted this project. We were ethnographers in the courts, in a city we called home. The courts were not simply a distant site but were an extension of our sense of our city and of our communities.

As we have noted, our community was one experiencing a crisis of mass incarceration. We committed to approaching our work with sensitivity to those carceral projects. For so many feminists, it is when addressing gender-based violence that the inner (or sometimes outer) carceral feminist emerges, and our research becomes a prescription for intensifying the capacity of the state to incarcerate—particularly to disproportionately incarcerate members of Black and brown communities (Whalley and Hackett 2017). In studying the processes of the criminal legal system, we rejected a commitment to optimize its capacities and efficiencies and categorically questioned the claim that criminal justice institutions are engaged in producing a just world. If we do not attribute liberatory transformative processes to criminal justice practices, we can then explore the forms of social reproduction in which adjudication is heavily invested. This is simultaneously a methodological and ethical practice that takes seriously the witnessing of violence. Even in the gravest of moments—some of them shared in this book—we strived not to distance ourselves from the field, a common coping strategy for researchers working on gender-based violence as well as for many professionals working in the system. Bearing witness to the intimate forms of the impact of interpersonal violence on many lives is essential to our shared analytical decisions throughout this book and our collaborative approach. Bearing witness also meant accounting for our own vulnerabilities in the courthouse (Behar 1997) and supporting each other and our research team in working through what were both analytic and also deeply felt experiences. As fieldworkers, we acknowledged that, as Veena Das has so lyrically phrased it, the eye that sees is also the "I" that weeps (Das 2000). We were also attentive to our emotional responses to fieldwork experiences, rejecting the framework of emotion as unreason and embracing instead a perspective that posits that emotion is a form of knowing or intellection (David Smith 2008). If Heather, Sameena, or Amber had strong feelings about a scene, a case, an utterance, or an occurrence, we understood that this phenomenon demanded additional scrutiny, analysis, and unpacking.

Every Monday, we downloaded court schedules, noted trials and proceedings that were of interest, and decided who would be located where. We often aimed to place at least two of us in a single courtroom to capture the expansive space and the many side conversations, providing multiple perspectives on the same ethnographic scene. Court budgets and a disciplined professional regime dictated a strictly enforced lunch break and ending time. While all personnel clocked out at lunch, we gathered in the courthouse café and debriefed about the morning's proceedings. This daily debriefing focused our observations such that we identified and embedded our sensitizing concepts into our fieldwork itself. Bringing the team together daily was also a grounding ritual that allowed us to ask questions, express discomforts, and process the scenes we had witnessed in the morning and the previous afternoon sessions. Practically, it was one way we collectively mourned all of the harms, injustices, and inequities we recorded in our field notes (Rushing 1993). Biweekly emails served as our memos, and when we finally drew our fieldwork to a close in April 2016, our data was expansive, rich, and complex. Wading through the transcripts of trials, sentencings, interviews, and the pages upon pages of field notes, we elected to frame our analysis through the process of the trial itself. As a site of knowledge-making, the sequences of trials revealed the way we make or unmake truths in layers in an adversarial justice system. There was no neatness or simple resolution to most cases, and it gave us an opportunity to weave in data from the sentencings we had observed and to include other cases that did not result in a trial or a plea. Writing was also a collaborative process; we share joint credit for this work and chose to list our names alphabetically as authors who are equal contributors to this project. We have framed each chapter to cumulatively draw readers into the operations of the court to reveal its potential as a space for creating historical and cultural knowledge through sustained narratives about sexual violence.

Expertise and Sexual Assault Adjudication

The chapters of this book are organized to track the order in which sexual assault trials typically unfold, beginning with the jury selection process and then centering on each of the witnesses who commonly testified. With such expansive and rich field observations, we felt this conceit makes the complexities of the process more legible. Each chapter demonstrates the many forms of legal storytelling by both fact and expert witnesses, as well as how these modalities conform to or defy the expectations of jurors, prosecutors, criminal defense attorneys, and the public seated in the gallery.

Chapter 1 examines the most common ways in which attorneys introduce jurors to ideas about sexual violence, trauma, victim disposition, forensic science, credibility, racism, truthfulness, and fairness. Judges and attorneys began each trial with strategic selection of a jury during the process of *voir dire*. According to attorneys we spoke with, in an adversarial court system, jury selections had at least two functions: attorneys sought jurors whom they believed would be persuaded by their arguments, and they also rely on *voir dire* to "educate the jury," framing the case by focusing on information the jurors would likely draw on during deliberations. Jury selection was both a formal procedure to vet jurors on their presumed impartiality and an opportunity to assess jurors' positions and cultural commitments to matters relating to the case. Typically, attorneys' questions referenced many preconceived ideas about sexual assault, stereotypes about gender and race, as well as medicolegal and forensic interventions. If jurors' expectations and common-sense notions of trial derived from depictions of courts of law and forensic evidence on popular television dramas, attorneys disabused them of such false versions of reality. The courtroom is a heavily racialized space wherein most of the defendants, victims, and families are people of color and the jury pools and courtroom personnel are overwhelmingly white. The fragmented, adversarial nature of the trial intensifies the gendered and racial prejudices entrenched in Milwaukee, and attorneys can draw on these cultural and historical narratives as they construct case arguments. Anticipating the testimony to come, attorneys referenced cultural narratives through which jurors could frame the evidence. In the collective exercise of jury selection, attorneys posed questions to panelists, gauging their attitudes about criminal justice prosecution, sexual assault, and evidence. These questions also potentially activated normative frameworks that an empaneled jury could use to interpret evidence and decide a case.

Attorneys also built cases through the careful selection of witnesses. In case after case, the court created and sustained knowledge-making practices in its orchestration of who testified and in what order. Almost all the cases we observed opened with the testimony of the victim, called the "complaining witness," the "victim-witness," or "alleged victim" in legal parlance. Chapter 2 therefore opens with an examination of the voices of victims in the context of the trial. We approach testimony as heterogeneous and variously embodied modes of expressing the harm that one has suffered as a result of sexual assault. Prosecutors and defense attorneys mobilize strategies embedded in the cultural narratives introduced during *voir dire* to examine witnesses. The veracity of the victim's narrative is always front and center (Estrich 1987; Flood 2012), and chapter 2 demonstrates the distinct approaches defense attorneys take to discredit the testimony of women, children, and adolescents. These strategies are grounded in many of the cultural commitments addressed and cultivated by attorneys during *voir dire* including distrust of women's testimony. The spectacle of victim-witness testimony unfolds at the intersection of gender and race. This trope reappears when discrediting child victims, who are often cast as under the influence of untrustworthy and manipulative women. The adolescent witness bridges the category of woman and child. The victim's account is tied to her embodied testimonial practices, and both prosecution and defense offer contentious interpretations of the victim's practice of voicing and framing the content of her testimony, her gestures, and her affects.

Typically, law enforcement was called to testify following the victim, as police investigation is one of the key techniques upon which adjudication relies. The police witness is a prototypical example of the fluidity between the category of fact witness and expert witness. Chapter 3 examines the role of the police officer in the sexual assault trial, distinguishing between the work of the uniformed officer and the detective. Formally called as a fact witness to report on the details of investigation, law enforcement personnel take on the dual role of expert witness when they are asked to give opinions based on their professional experience. Legal analysts find that judges are often satisfied with nothing more than the prosecutor's assertion that officer expertise is relevant in a case (Blinka 2014). In addition to offering expert insight into police procedure, chapter 3 illustrates how skilled police mobilized a charismatic and authoritative performance when they testified, producing images of authority, rationality, competency, and credibility. The masculinity of routine police work stood in contrast with the detectives' more feminized forms of investigation. In addition, even when officers were in error, their testimony was held up as authoritative at the expense of nonpolice witnesses. Casting the police witness as infallible, the prosecutors and defense could corroborate or challenge nonpolice testimony simply based on whether it deviated from the police testimony. We also show that, when the police officer was the defendant, race asserted itself to affirm the whiteness of policing, which otherwise operated more subtly when the police officer simply testified as a witness in a case where the defendant was a civilian.

If the victim has participated in a medicolegal sexual assault examination, the sexual assault nurse examiner takes the stand. Like the police officer, the SANE brings expert testimony to the trial, also reinforcing distrust in victim's voices by demonstrating that others must corroborate their stories. Chapter 4 argues that the trial draws on medico-legal imaginaries and expert knowledge to construct the raped body, largely to explain the absence of evidence. This same expert knowledge is silent when it comes to narratives of the victimizing body, which is physically present throughout the court case in the person of the defendant. His body may become the subject of testimony of lay witnesses, such as the victim or defendant himself, and is also commented on by the defense attorney. When nurses take the stand, they rely on clinical practices transported into the legal realm in order to render the raped body legible to the jury. Culturally potent categories such as virginity are contested through medicalized narratives. While the nurse generates a sense of the raped body as resilient and capacious, the perpetrating body is frequently cast in an able-ist framework. Defense counsel gestures to cultural investments in masculinity, emphasizing the inability of a masculine body to rape due to physical limitations or casting the male body as unrapeable. Nurses testify to the resilience of the female body in order to counter one of the most common rape myths—that of the presumption of injury. Experts further objectify the body using heterosexual reproductive norms that construct the vagina as always already penetrable and capable of giving birth and, therefore, resistant to injury. These reproductive imaginaries collide with the racialized gendered body, often cast through tropes of Black women's resilience.

Sexual assault forensic nurse examiners also testify to the presence or absence of DNA in the body of evidence they have collected. The discovery of DNA requires the testimony of the forensic scientist. Chapter 5 examines the testimony of these forensic scientists, variably described by attorneys and judges as "crime lab personnel" or "DNA analysts" or self-described as "forensic scientists." The successful presentation of DNA evidence is as dependent on the perception of its scientific rigor as it is on the expert ways in which it is made accessible to jurors. Performative techniques of expert self-presentation may include the use of specialized language, reference to professional experience, training, or education, and strategies that invoke neutrality or objectivity (Carr 2010; Voss and Van Dyke 2001). Just as prosecutors might coach victims to convey affective demeanor on the stand—namely, avoiding anger (Konradi 2007; Sanday 1996)—expert witnesses presenting evidence must engage the appropriate range of affective sensibilities that convey knowledge, authority, objectivity, and reason. The authoritative place of the forensic scientist's knowledge is bolstered by the introduction of statistical probability in a series of figures that appeal to the jury. The selective invocation of weighty correlations stands in contrast to the decontextualized account of racial genomics within the courts, tapping into and naturalizing taken-for-granted interpretations while emphasizing the quality of the techniques of DNA identification. Chapter 5 illustrates how the forensic scientists who present the evidence put as much care into their scientific technique and quantitative literacy as they do into their self-presentation. We highlight how a seamless performance of expertise may come undone when the trial preparation is revealed during testimony. The trial, therefore, serves as a practice that affirms public investment in reifying erroneous biological ideas of race while establishing several positions from which the expert witness may speak about sexual assault and DNA evidence.

It is rare for defendants to take the stand, as most are advised by their attorneys to exercise their constitutional right to remain silent. Chapter 6 explores the strategies and cultural narratives engaged when defendants testify and when others represent them. We argue that many defendants resist the prosecution's efforts to cast them as monsters and rapists by tapping into the potent cultural role of father, particularly as it intersects with race. The prominence of the paternal role is attached both to the overwhelming number of cases in which victims and perpetrators are members of the same family or networks, as well as to the constrained social scripts surrounding hegemonic masculinity (Connell and Messerschmidt 2005). The court also weighs fatherhood heavily in sentencing, casting it as a social obligation. As such, fatherhood can become the grounds for leniency and mercy or punishment and discipline. Whereas the prosecution paints perpetration as a violation of paternal responsibility, defendants (and their counsel) position themselves as paternalistic protectors, highlighting their respectability and credibility through fulfillment of paternal duties. The defendant, therefore, invokes hegemonic notions of fatherly love, emphasizing his breadwinner status and cultural position as disciplinarian who has recourse to violence. These narratives, too, are racially scaffolded, and parallel the paternal role of the state under the guise of the court (Donzelot 1977), that intervenes to regulate the (Black) family and the failures of the (Black) father (Gonzalez Van Cleve 2016).

In the conclusion, we widen the frame of analysis from a single actor to the broader context of adjudication, focusing on the immense human costs of participating in the routine operations of the trial. We draw out the tensions between the forms of harm that the court recognizes as legible versus those forms of harm that the court does not. The process of adjudication is itself a reproduction of violence, and the court is unable to account for the harm it visits upon participants and their families during the process of adjudication. At the center of the analysis is one woman and the powerful and palpable trauma she conveyed through her marathon testimony. Juxtaposing the phenomenological immediacy of witnessing her testimony with the strategic and tactical responses to her testimony, we demonstrate how the jury is asked to rely on their knowledge of local geography as well as myriad forms of expertise to form their judgments. Engaging the role of trauma in the courts, we focus on a common defense narrative: that victims are, in fact, prostitutes and that the defendants were clients. We argue that these narratives particularly imperil Black women, objectifying their bodies and sartorial compositions while also criminalizing their families and their neighborhoods. By asking the jury to consider local racialized geographies, the process of adjudication reproduces the precarious landscape of Milwaukee. These processes unfold in real time but are also transformed into court records and transcripts that endure long after the trial ends. Unsettling the forms of sexual, gender, and racial inequalities that become part of judicial practice and record requires us to think about abolitionist possibilities. We invite the reader to think along with us about the court's participation in violence and its reproduction of oppression as we move through each chapter and each witness testifying during the sexual assault trial.

1

Common Sense and the *Nomos* of Sexual Assault

Selecting and Sensitizing Jurors

[The sexual assault trial] is just so much more open to people's own biases and societal beliefs than if I had evidence . . .
you're just free to pull in anything you want from your life
experience and apply it. . . . If my final argument is always
about credibility and who's more believable, and if the jury
instruction tells you that you are to use your own experience
in real life to determine credibility, because that's what the
jury instruction says. It says you don't come in here and just
leave your common sense at the door as a juror. You bring
in all of your experiences of life as to who's telling the truth
in very serious matters, right? . . . So of course you're going to get all of their biases and everything they believe just
smacked on top of your victim and your case. And that's really tough.
—Assistant District Attorney Anderson, Interview

After months, and in some cases years, of investigation, hearings,
motions, trial postponements, and preparation, the sexual assault trial
would begin. The first stage of the trial is formally termed *voir dire*—
the process of jury selection. As described in the introduction, the law
is highly dependent on "shifting terrains of knowledge at particular
moments in time" (Kelly, Harper, and Khanna 2015, 3). The norms and
cultural conventions through which potential jurors interpret and relate
to sexual violence is what we term the *nomos* of sexual assault, defined
as "the cultural contexts of rape and sexual assault as epistemological
objects embedded within interpretive commitments that privilege legal
interpretations as they are intertwined with the medicalization of the
harm of rape" (Hlavka and Mulla 2020, 232). In jury selection, attor-

neys reveal the *nomos* of sexual violence—or how publics understand sexual assault, forensic investigation, and the law itself. Given the emotionally fraught nature of sexual violence within U.S. cultural mores, attorneys and judges would lay the groundwork for interpreting credibility and evidence during *voir dire*, offering strategies for navigating personal experiences and feelings about sexual assault. Jury selection also provided attorneys with the space to examine how members navigate racism and racial ideology in Milwaukee. It served not only as a procedure for vetting fair and impartial jurors but also for framing the relevant knowledge terrains about sexual assault, criminal investigation, forensic intervention, and attitudes about race and gender. Throughout the jury selection process, judges and attorneys attuned jurors to sexual assault and the law, introducing language and ideas that might inform their eventual deliberations. Signs in the hallway indicated where jurors should stand (see figure 1.1) and deputies ushered them through designated doorways. Each stage of the jury selection process offered jurors a filter for understanding and orienting to all the facets of the case. These filters were not mutually exclusive but cumulatively informed one another. Judges often explained to jurors that *voir dire* literally translated into "to see and tell" and described the process as a question-and-answer period designed to give the judge and attorneys the opportunity "to see, to hear, and to learn" about individual jurors' backgrounds. It was clear from comments made by the attorneys that jurors were expected to be honest both about what they thought and how they felt.

Having cleared their morning schedules, judges often began trials in the Milwaukee County Courthouse on Monday afternoons. Following a review of case updates and evidentiary motions, jury selection lasted hours, often carrying over to Tuesday mornings. As researchers, we were privy to many of the pretrial motions and court appearances, including information about prior criminal records of the defendant and other trial witnesses. So, while we, and the courtroom staff, were familiar with the long case histories, this information was not shared with the jury members. We talked with attorneys and judges pre- and post-trial, inquiring about their concerns around particular cases and their perceptions of jury panels. In some cases, we spoke to jurors following trials, learning about the conversations that drove trial deliberations. In contrast with our knowledge base as researchers, most jurors came to the

Figure 1.1. Signs for the Jurors. Photo Credit: Heather R. Hlavka

trial with little firsthand experience of the judicial system and no information about the case in question.

Jury management required jurors to appear at the courthouse at 9:00 A.M. Sometimes delayed by long security lines, jurors made their way to the jury assembly area of the courthouse and were greeted with an orientation video. Some sat in the jury area all day, snacking from vending machines, giving blood to the local blood bank, and distracting themselves on laptops or cell phones courtesy of free wi-fi access. Before the jury entered the courtroom, judges and attorneys settled outstanding motions and agreed on some of the basic jury instructions. Before closing arguments, jury instructions might be amended if the need arose. During the annual juror appreciation week, the courthouse was decorated with banners (see figure 1.2) and jurors were treated to a few extra amenities in the jury pool room.

Those who were selected for a jury panel lined up based on their randomly assigned numbers and were led by a sheriff's deputy to the courtroom. Each jury panel was roughly 30–40 individuals, of which 13 or 14 would be selected to hear a trial, depending on the judge's preferences. Once jurors were selected, they were repeatedly told not to do outside research or to discuss case details prior to deliberations, even with other jury members. Some judges ordered jurors to relinquish their cell phones during trial, returning them at lunch breaks and at the day's end. While jurors' cell-phone use was closely monitored, attorneys hustled through hallways from courtroom to courtroom often with their eyes glued to their own cell phones and even used their devices during trials (Hlavka and Mulla 2018). Many judges gave welcoming speeches, during which they thanked the panelists for their participation, touting how jurors were the foundation of the American judicial system. Following the completion of the evidence stage of the trial and before deliberations began, the judge would dismiss one or two alternates. These alternates were selected only at the end of the trial, so that all jurors conducted themselves as if they would decide the case.

The jury was tasked with evaluating the credibility of witnesses and the reliability of other forms of admitted evidence, "guided here by its common sense, construed as a reservoir of judgements of the relative probability of events' occurring this way or that in the real world, under the circumstances established by the most reliable evidence presented" (Burns 1999, 7). Scholars have drawn attention to flaws in "common sense" instructions, revealing the contradictions between a community's knowledge and the requirements of legal rules, expertise, and material evidence. Thus, credibility assessments were "deliberately relegated to the amorphous realm of lay common sense and life experience" (Blinka 2010, 359). For prosecutors and defense attorneys, jury selection was central to sexual assault adjudication because, as one prosecutor put it, "the more you know about your jury, the better chance you have of winning your case." Assistant District Attorney (ADA) Ray lamented that juries were often composed of those who said nothing during *voir dire*: "I think the silent person is usually the dangerous one." ADA McClain concurred that silent jurors might give attorneys the impression of being "normal and fine" but worried that selecting them resulted in "having stealth crazy people" on the jury. Thus, many attorneys approached jury selection with the goal of getting every panelist to speak. The silence of potential jurors emerged as the first absence with which attorneys had

Figure 1.2. Juror Appreciation Week. Photo Credit: Heather R. Hlavka

to grapple. It is important to note that the judge and attorneys did not seek to eliminate every juror who revealed that they held a particular opinion or admitted that sexual violence was a difficult subject for them. Rather, the jurors were cast as a body that could be disciplined and re-oriented. Judges would formally "instruct" jurors on how to proceed, and warnings, such as those surrounding cell-phone use, were formally termed "admonishments." Judges and attorneys discussed their desire to "rehabilitate" jurors who revealed a prejudice, often asking jurors if they could put their prejudice aside and conduct themselves as instructed by the court. Those who agreed to make such efforts were often selected. In fact, early in the process, judges asked potential jurors about past jury experience. Had they previously been selected to deliberate? Was it a criminal or civil case? Were they the foreperson of the jury and did the jury reach a verdict? In interviews, attorneys told us that they valued jurors with experience but avoided those who might have been a foreperson. Attorneys prized the ability to make decisions, but they did not seek out leaders and were wary of members who had been part of a hung jury.

During *voir dire*, prosecutors were often concerned about the application of jurors' common sense and how members might assess credibility. For ADA Anderson, the conflict between credibility and common sense lay at the heart of the sexual assault trial. When pointing to "societal beliefs" in the epigraph of this chapter, ADA Anderson was referring to false beliefs about sexual assault that were widely held. Her statement echoed decades of feminist contentions that the "common sense" instruction provided to jurors acts as the portal though which rape myths enter jury deliberations (Cossins 2010; Ellison and Munro 2009; Temkin and Krahé 2008; Temkin 2010). During interviews, prosecutors regularly discussed the deleterious effects of rape myths on sexual assault adjudication. ADA Anderson lamented that rape-supportive attitudes had not diminished over time but instead remained ubiquitous. Feminist scholars have argued that "common sense" disguises the ways in which rape myths affect trial processes and verdicts (Beichner and Spohn 2005; Frese et al. 2004; Konradi 2007; Spohn and Horney 1993). These same scholars have demonstrated that sexual assault cases are vulnerable to cultural explanations that discredit victims' allegations of rape.

Milwaukee's prosecutors agreed that many persistent myths about sexual assault remained commonplace and impacted the cases they prosecuted. They were frustrated that so many jurors believed that "real rape" left physical injuries necessitating medical interventions and, at the very least, extreme emotional trauma (Ehrlich 2001; Estrich 1987; Powell, Hlavka, and Mulla 2017), and they would work to disabuse jurors of this falsehood. Prosecutors also remarked that jurors persistently believed that women and children simply made false rape accusations, despite the fact that false reports are low and no more or less common than in other types of violent crime (about 2 percent) (Lisak and Miller 2002; Lonsway 2010). Potential jurors were also likely to believe that a delayed report of sexual assault indicated "untruthfulness." One tension associated with this minefield of rape myths was that, while jurors often entered the courtroom with misinformed notions about sexual violence, these myths could be introduced and reinforced during the trial itself. Jurors even elaborated on rape myths during jury selection, reinforcing the *nomos* of sexual assault in such a way that their applicability to a particular case appeared rational and commonsensical (Ehrlich 2001). Both prosecution and defense allowed these myths to remain intact in service of their cases. For example, defense could argue that a lack of physical evidence introduced reasonable doubt, capitalizing on the myth that sexual assault always left indelible physical signs on a victim's body. But in another case, prosecutors might argue that the presence of an injury was more significant than a victim's testimony, reinforcing the same myth about rape and injury.

For prosecutors, *voir dire* served as a starting point for assessing the jurors' generalized cultural beliefs and their emotional disposition toward rape that might "serve to deny, downplay, or justify sexual violence" (Bohner 1998, 14). Once these attitudes were revealed or suspected, attorneys and judges could work to mitigate or reinforce these prejudices within the jury panel. This chapter draws attention to the ways in which judges and attorneys framed narratives of rape, race, gender, sexuality, and technology during *voir dire*. We argue that a careful examination of the process of *voir dire* reveals how the *nomos* of sexual assault is evidenced by attorneys, judges, and jurors in the act of anticipating, eliciting, imparting, interpreting, and privileging certain characteristics and "common knowledges." We approach jury selection as a dialogical process grounded in a question-and-response conversational style within an adversarial system that assumes individuals share enough social and cultural common ground so as to have compatible orientations toward a "common sense" approach to sexual violence. Because many jurors were nonresponsive, we also analyze the demonstrations, performative content, and framing that judges and attorneys engaged in as they selected jury members. The process was both dialogical and pedagogical, with attorneys introducing relevant language that the jury itself could rely on once the trial was under way.

In the trials we observed, judges admonished jurors again and again that "there is no magic way for you to evaluate the testimony. Instead, you should use your common sense and experience." Moreover, judges and attorneys unanimously insisted that sexual assault trials were uniquely sensitive and highly emotive. Attorneys therefore attempted to reconcile common sense together with presumed discomfort. Judges read pattern jury instructions to jurors, advising them to use matters of common knowledge and their observations and experience in their everyday affairs of life (WIS J1-Criminal 195) while simultaneously requiring jurors to "free your minds of all feelings of sympathy, bias, or prejudice" (WIS J1-Criminal 190). Our field research demonstrated that attorneys and judges explored sympathy, bias, and prejudice during *voir dire,* often filtering jurors' common knowledge of sexual violence.

In the descriptions of the jury selection process that follow, readers will be able to understand how judges and attorneys imagined and engaged myths and stereotypes that largely focused on witness credibility and cultural tropes of rape, race, and common (mis)understandings of the criminal justice system, especially as it related to forensic evidence. Judges and attorneys benchmarked the various emotional labors of sexual assault prosecution for jurors, in effect staging an inventory of likely responses jurors might have to witness testimony—qualities like sensitivity, shame, disgust, and bias. We argue that attorneys and judges, ultimately, cultivated a particular affective sensibility toward sexual assault cases by the way they orchestrated jury selection. By doing so, jurors could justify any set of emotional responses they experienced by drawing on contemporary understandings of crime and criminal justice. At times, the goals of prosecutors and defense attorneys led to the promotion of competing frameworks. The progression of this chapter parallels the progression of jury selection, moving from soliciting basic demographic information from the jurors to posing questions about attitudes related to sexual assault, law enforcement, and forensic technology.

The questions were not arbitrary, and each rested upon and informed localized, cultural narratives. The first section draws together standard demographic questions posed by judges at the start of every jury selection we observed. By soliciting addresses and neighborhood coordinates, attorneys were able to probe the role of geography and race as it intersected with tropes of rape, gender, and sexuality. In the second section, we track the framing of sexual violence through the attorneys' questions. A paradox emerged, as the questions simultaneously cast sexual violence as so deeply troubling that it was nearly impossible to hear about or discuss while also preparing jurors for the practical reality of the language and tone of the testimony they were likely to hear.

In the third section, we show how jury selection engaged legal understandings of "legitimate" and "believable" sexual violence that relied heavily on discourses of rationality and reason, both of which rested primarily on the presence or absence of medical knowledge, expertise, and forensic evidence. While forensic evidence was often ambiguous or even absent, attorneys operated with the assumption that jurors expected it at trial. Thus, forensic intervention came to be both imagined and anticipated (rather than actualized), and this imagined intervention was foundational to adjudication. Prosecutors readied jurors for the absence of DNA, saliva, and documented physical wounds, while defense attorneys emphasized the importance of such evidence, offering competing frames. It was in this cultural context—a *nomos* that depended on a particular understanding of Milwaukee County's demographic realities, politics, and attitudes toward sexual assault—that judges and attorneys provided jurors with sensitizing frameworks for interpreting witness credibility. Both the second and third sections draw heavily on a single trial, *State v. Jones*.

"What's your ZIP Code?" Navigating Race, Place, and Politics in *Voir Dire*

The first filter through which courts asked the jury panel to consider the case was race and place. While the jury pool is drawn from across Milwaukee County, which includes the city and its suburbs, defendants and witnesses are disproportionately from the City of Milwaukee. This translates into dramatically skewed demographics in which African American and Latino/a individuals are overrepresented among defendants, victims, and other witnesses, while jury pools reflect a much more diverse group with a distinctively white plurality. Attorneys and judges were concerned about both the racial makeup of the jury, as well as the racial sensibilities of the jurors. A Batson Challenge can be brought by either attorney if they suspect that people of color have been systematically removed from a jury. Thus, judges often discussed the racial makeup of the jury on the record following formal selection, preempting a potential Batson Challenge. The judge made these statements outside of the jury's hearing, while talk about race before the jury was often more veiled. Judges and attorneys adopted a range of approaches to assess jurors' racial sensibilities. An indirect approach was to extrapolate assumptions about jurors' social worlds and communities from their employment status and home address. One defense counsel (DC), DC Bronson, succinctly explained that "we have such alignment of location, geography, political perspective, and how that political perspective and geography may align itself or intersect with perceptions of inner-city Black people. And that's most of the [defendants] we represent." He continued: "A lot of my clients are Black. Not enough of my jurors are Black." On this, the prosecutors and defense attorneys agreed: court systems in the United States are spaces in which the force of law is disproportionately brought to bear both against and in the name of Black and brown people (M. Alexander 2010; Gonzalez Van Cleve 2016). The techniques used by attorneys and judges operated to pierce the silence that typically accompanies discussions about race and politics, and attorneys relied on their understanding of localities and neighborhoods to inform their opinions about juror sensibilities.

Judges administered general oral surveys at the beginning of *voir dire*, motioning toward posted courtroom signage with which jurors could follow along. Some felony court branches had several 8-by-10-inch laminated question sheets to pass through the jury panel, while others had the questions posted at the front of the courtroom on a large black felt changeable letter board mounted to the wall (see figure 1.3). Judges asked the panelists to provide eight pieces of information: their name, marital status, number of children, residential location, employment, prior jury service, hobbies, and any close contacts with criminal justice personnel such as law enforcement or court personnel. This question-and-answer period seemed to serve as a group icebreaker habituating jurors to speaking up during the process as each panelists took a turn. Overwhelmingly, attorneys agreed that jury selection was often based on conjecture, consisting of "a lot of stereotyping and a lot of attempted psychology." They referred to jury selection as a "crapshoot" because of its reliance on stereotypes made about juror characteristics such as race, gender, occupation, and residence. Despite what may seem like glib self-assessments of their approaches to selecting jurors, attorneys were

Figure 1.3. Married or Single? View from the Jury Box. Photo credit: Sameena Mulla

deeply concerned about choosing a fair and impartial jury, particularly one with the ability to consider the facts of a sexual assault case. Their dismissiveness of their own techniques for assessing jury members existed alongside their experience with past jurors. They relied on personal experience and local knowledge to assess ZIP codes and neighborhood boundaries as stand-ins for important class and political markers, a fact that many attorneys commented on during interviews. Prosecutors and defense attorneys sought very different features when selecting jurors, often mapping onto race and residence. For example, DC Dolan said he typically sought jurors with higher levels of education. In his experience, a college-educated juror might translate into someone with a greater level of skepticism of witness testimony. He also surmised that such individuals would follow the rules when assessing whether the state had met the burden of proof:

> Sometimes I feel, and again, this is a stereotype, but sometimes I feel people who are less educated rather than higher educated go with their gut more, and if they hear something bad they want to blame somebody and [the defendant is] as good as anybody. Some of the suburbs tend to have people who are more liberal, some of them have people who tend to be more conservative . . . sometimes older people, and you get senior citizens on juries disproportionately. Sometimes older people sit home and read the newspaper or watch TV and are scared of everything. And I don't know if I want that on my jury, someone who's scared of everything. So, people who are more worldly, people who are more educated, I like.

DC Dolan's concerns about suburban people who were "scared of everything" indexed his concern that jurors drawn from these regions would project their fears onto his client. DC Dolan admitted: "I have a stereotype that if you are living in Franklin, Wisconsin, maybe you live there because you don't want to live by Black people. Maybe. Maybe not. Again, it's a stereotype." Another experienced public defender, DC Davis, told us during an interview that "I'm mindful of the life experiences of people who are in . . . not racially integrated areas and not economically integrated areas."

Geography was critical to attorneys as they attempted to choose jurors they anticipated might be more sympathetic to or less judgmental of their case. ZIP code and neighborhood, however, could cast the same jury panelist as desirable to the prosecution but risky for the defense, and vice versa. While DC Dolan expressed his aversion to fearful suburban jurors, a prosecutor might find such a juror quite appealing. For example, during an interview with ADA James, she explained that an ideal juror for the state was more politically and socially conservative, or what she called a "law-and-order type." Open with us about her own progressive politics, ADA James laughed: "The people I like most on my jury are the people that I like voting the least. They're like my dad. I want twelve people like my dad to be on a jury." Echoing the numerous comments about the tendency for attorneys to select those jurors who said little, she continued:

> The problem with our jury selection is that it's mostly focused on selecting *out* the bad people. . . . We end up with people we don't know anything about because everyone who hates rapists raises their hands and they're off the jury. So, I haven't figured that out as much. . . . People don't want to talk about [sexual abuse]. Ever.

The court needed jurors to speak, but attorneys found themselves trying to cultivate open discussion among panelists who did not want to talk about sexual violence. Under these circumstances, attorneys relied heavily on demographic information and seemingly innocuous data, such as home addresses, to form a sense of how the jurors would respond to a case.

The courts' concerns that jurors' racial prejudice would impact case outcomes extended beyond their worries that it would handicap Black and brown defendants. Prosecutors were particularly concerned that racial prejudice also affected juror sympathies with the victim-witness. Several of the ADAs mentioned that they had experienced a series of surprising trial losses. As mentioned in the introduction, the consistent thread among these cases was an African American rape victim coupled with defense's instance that the victim was "prostituting." Accusing sexual assault victims of being engaged in transactional sex also raised the problematic notion that sex workers were not rapeable while simultaneously noxiously attaching these ideas to the racially and sexually vulnerable bodies of Black women (Kelley 2017; E. Williams 2013). Even so, prosecutors rarely addressed issues about race during *voir dire*, often citing sexual assault as an "equal opportunity crime" that impacted victims of all socioeconomic and racial backgrounds. ADA Torres worried, in fact, about bringing up race because "you don't want to introduce a race debate in the back of the jury room." Prosecutors were keenly aware of these difficulties and frustrated by the approaches they might take to mitigate the role of racism in sexual assault prosecutions. For example, in an interview with ADA Adams he told us:

> [G]ive us a case with an African American woman as a victim, and re-gardless of age, our odds of losing that case go through the roof. It's 500 times more likely we're going to lose that case. Substitute in any white child—fat, ugly, zit-covered white girl—and I have a much better chance of winning that case than with an absolutely beautiful, clean-cut, wearing perfect clothing, carrying her Bible, Black girl. It's unbelievable.

Here, ADA Adams posited two hypothetical victims, demonstrating, even if insensitively, those features to which he felt a jury was responsive. In his hyperbolic example, religious affiliation, beauty, body weight, cleanliness, and clothing were all outweighed by race. His well-intentioned complaint echoed many of the myths about idealized victimhood and sought to offset the tendency to characterize Black women as libidinous and oversexualized with reference to her Bible-wielding (Miller 2008). This hypothetical example was also borne out by his and other prosecutors' experiences of losing cases. In the modern classic *Rape on Trial*, legal scholar Andrew Taslitz (1999) began his book with the case of a Black victim who was literally returning home from a Bible study group at her church when she was accosted and sexually assaulted. Despite the victim-witness's faith, this trial ended in an acquittal. ADA Adams shared that, when he first began prosecuting sex crimes cases, he was unaware of the existence of "jurors who have a perception that teenage Black girls are fast girls." Sociological research has long documented the limited archetypes through which Black women and girls are interpreted in U.S. culture, particularly through the image of the "jezebel" as described by Patricia Hill Collins (1990). Such images have historically affected how courts conducted rape trials featuring Black women witnesses dating back to at least the mid-1930s (Flood 2012). In our interview, we asked ADA Adams what approaches he considered taking to counter these prejudices, to which he responded:

> We try to counter it. I don't know how good we've been. I guess I haven't had a . . . we've thought of addressing it directly. And I've said things in closing. But I've never used the race— [pausing]. I've never said, "Because she's Black." I've used as a surrogate, "Because she's poor." We still wind up in the same situation. Jurors don't care—at least as much—about Black women.

An analysis of this response must be rooted in what ADA Adams left unsaid. In the middle of his response, he began the phrase "But I've never used the race—" and then abruptly stopped. The dash indicates the awkward interruption in his train of thought before he continued and completed his response. At the time, we both anticipated that ADA Adams was going to use the phrase "I've never used the race CARD." His abrupt choice to select a different word was at once guarded, but it also signaled the predicament of how to overcome jurors' potential racial prejudice without directly accusing the jury of being racist. He admitted that he used poverty to stand in as a substitute for race but lamented that this approach also seemed ineffective. It problematically upheld the locally circulating notion that "Blackness" and "poverty" were interchangeable descriptors.

Our own broaching of the subject of race during the interview mirrored some of the dynamics that the prosecution was concerned might shape jury selection: that the mere mention or posing of explicit questions about race raised the specter of accusation. For example, we did not ask ADA Adams questions about racism in the district attorney's office or the defense bar, yet he voluntarily reviewed the findings of a 2009 Vera Institute of Justice report on fairness and the courts, which he argued absolved the Milwaukee DA's office from any allegations of racial discrimination. His reference to the Vera report paralleled the general courthouse attunement to the crisis of the criminal justice response in Wisconsin. Attorneys and judges all seemed aware that Wisconsin had among the highest incarceration rates of Black men in the country. Statistics and studies about this fact made the local news. The problems of racial prejudice, though identified, were often deemed intractable. As two judges stated: "We can only prosecute the cases that the police bring us." The judges' deflection pointed the finger of blame at the police department, which could, in turn, point the finger of blame to any other number of agencies or individuals (including defendants themselves) that refused to intervene to reduce Wisconsin's crime rate.

In some ways, the tensions between individual strategies, as well as more systematic cultural interventions, inform ADA Adams's sincere frustrations over how to best address racism in sexual assault adjudication. Another prosecutor, ADA Brooks, told us that the Sensitive Crimes Unit had been working together as a team on strategies to combat the so-called prostitution defense. Ultimately, they decided to take it on a case-by-case basis. She explained:

> So, we don't have good answers to "they're just prostitutes." It's very, very sad and frustrating that it seems to be that people can just call Black women in Milwaukee prostitutes, and juries believe them. It's very frustrating.

While ADA Adams relied on substituting the term "poor" for "Black," ADA James joked about taking a direct approach:

> I've threatened [the district attorney] that I'm going to be asking juries if they think women of color are all prostitutes. And he told me that I couldn't do that! (Laughing) I'm just going to go in there like a wrecking ball and we're going to talk about this from the get-go and I'm going to be fired, but. . . . [trailing off]

While ADA James's proposed approach was unusual as a prosecutorial strategy, defense attorneys tended to approach issues of race head-on.

In many cases, defense attorneys' arguments in court relied heavily on racist cultural narratives used against the victim (Hlavka and Mulla 2018). They introduced the trope of the sexualized Black woman and argued that defendants were merely engaged in soliciting sex workers. They depicted the families of sexual assault victims as pathological, suggesting that tensions in the home led to false accusations by child victims (Powell, Hlavka, and Mulla 2017). In contrast, defense attorneys took a strong position against the pervasive and long-standing stereotype of

Black male criminality (Muhammad 2010) and magnified the crisis of Black incarceration. Note, however, that tactics such as arguing that one's client is not a rapist, but simply engaged in a less serious criminal offense such as soliciting a sex worker, relied on jurors' gendered stereotypes as well—solicitation was a behavior that, while perhaps "immoral," was not so criminal and not so outside of the expected behaviors of (Black) men. The tactic allowed jurors to cast the defendant as reprehensible and libidinous, even criminal, but not as a rapist. In interviews, defense counsel was aware of this tension and spoke to how racist ideologies had the potential to both harm and help their clients.

Like prosecutors, defense attorneys also depicted race as the proverbial elephant in the room, an unavoidable topic that was difficult to speak about. In practice, however, we observed defense attorneys making very direct statements about race during jury selection. They told jury panels that questions of racial prejudice, while "unfortunate," were a "necessary" reality in a contemporary court of law. Defense attorneys asked if anyone had a "prejudice against Black men" or would "bend over backwards to not convict him because of [his] race," often apologizing for having to raise such issues. One private defense attorney we observed in court, DC Cahill, seemed to draw on the rhetoric of postracialism, scoffing before majority-white jury panels that even though race was a "dead issue" he was obligated to explore this topic with the jury:

> I bring this up and I almost hate to have to bring up, the issue of race or not. The defendant is obviously Black. You'll find out the person accusing him is Black as well. I'm white. The ADA is white. [The] detective is white as well. I'd like to think race is a dead issue these days. I hope it is, but if anybody has an issue with it or problem with it and we kind of need to know that. . . . I have had people raise their hands, really not because they think themselves to be racist, but some were raised in racist homes and they were concerned. Things of that sort. It shouldn't be a problem here, but if it is, you know, be sure to let us know.

While no one responded to DC Cahill's query, his proclamations reminded jurors of their duty not to be governed by racial prejudice.

One of the few African American defense attorneys we encountered during our study took a rather different tactic. DC Giles attempted to build rapport with the majority-white jury panel by excusing racial animus as "human nature":

> We all have certain gender, racial biases—that's a fact. My question is: Can you put those aside? Attorneys, judges, we all put our feelings aside while we deal with evidence. And we have "PC" today—I don't want 30 people who are politically correct on the jury. I'm not gonna hold your personal opinions against you. Maybe you don't like Black men. It doesn't matter. I get it. It's human nature. I need to know if you can be fair.

Taking the jury panelists into his confidence, DC Giles glibly waved away their racial and gender biases. He used the language of "bias" rather than of "racism," deflecting the jurors from having to admit that they had racist feelings. Rather, he gave them the out of reflecting on their personal biases, proclaiming that such feelings were normal. DC Giles even questioned the need to seek a jury free of any individuals with such biases if they could put their "feelings" aside.

Attorneys adopted a range of techniques for determining the racial sensibilities of jurors. They subtly solicited information about community and neighborhood, extrapolating what they could from jurors' home addresses and occupations. Thinking collectively about their language use, it is interesting to note that issues of race were generally invoked through questions about bias. The only instances in which a specific racial category was mentioned was in reference to anti-Black prejudice. Latino/a identity was largely explicitly excluded from these frameworks. Again, this parallels the general tendency in this country to parse all issues around racial prejudice and racial tensions in the context of a Black-white divide.

We also recognized some of the defense attorneys' questions as provocations designed to trigger self-examination of one's own motives and biases. None of the questions suggested that jurors should have neutral feelings about issues such as race and the criminal justice system but, instead, that jurors could simply reconcile their own feelings with what the court required them to do. We could also consider one other potential effect of these forms of questions: signaling to jurors they should keep their racial prejudices a secret throughout the trial. As with questions around racial prejudices, judges and attorneys expected jurors to have strong feelings about the subject of sexual assault—the second filter explored during *voir dire*.

Feelings and Sensibilities Toward Sexual Violence

Most prosecutors said that there were very few moments to educate the jury about rape myths and legal understandings of evidence but that *voir dire* was one of those opportunities. The attorneys we interviewed unanimously agreed that sexual assault cases were highly sensitive for everyone involved. They expected that jurors would struggle while listening to the proceedings and the visceral descriptions of witnesses' experiences of violence. ADA Howard, told us: "Some jurors, understandably, they're told it's a sexual assault and some of them are like, 'I just don't want to do it' and they'll make themselves known fairly quickly." DC Dolan, a defense attorney, explained how he would often tell jurors that they would be hearing "graphic details of sexual assault" and that they should speak up if that would be "too much for them to handle." The judges confirmed such emotional challenges, adding that an appointment to the felony court bench—which heard both homicide and sexual assault cases—was the least-sought-after rotation. Judges and attorneys agreed that sexual assault cases were the most emotional, time-intensive, and resource-demanding. During jury selection, attorneys were attentive to jurors who claimed they could not manage to deal with the emotional complexity of sexual assault prosecutions.

In this section, we show how attorneys elicited information about sexual assault during *voir dire* in the case *State v. Jones*. (In the passages below, we use the term "juror" and "jurors" when referring to *potential* jurors who are participating in the jury selection process and who may or may not be empaneled for the formal trial.) Following the survey questions during the first phase of jury selection, the judge explained to jurors that the attorneys would now ask some potentially delicate questions but also clarified that the questions were not posed with the intention to embarrass them or to "pry into private lives." The judge offered jurors the opportunity to request privacy if they did not want to answer a question in open court. This customary disclaimer prepared the jurors for what the attorneys assumed would be discomfort—even shock and disgust—with the subject of sexual violence. The various ways in which judges and attorneys addressed the jury served as a type of sensitizing process in anticipation of what was likely to be experienced during trial. The reading of the formal charges further attuned jurors to the specific types of actions and body parts at issue in the case.

In *State v. Jones*, the defendant, Derrick Jones, was charged with second-degree sexual assault of a child in October 2011 in the North Side neighborhood of the City of Milwaukee. The charges were read in a personalized way, using the name of the defendant and the victim as described in the criminal complaint. (Following the reading of charges, two judges we observed in other cases typically inquired whether jurors had "any feelings of bias or prejudice about the case knowing the nature of the charges?" These two judges effectively provided the space for jurors to publicly express their feelings as it related *only* to "the nature of the charges," echoing what ADA Nelson once announced in open court that "just hearing" the charge of sexual assault "can kind of make that hair on the back of your neck stand up.") In *State v. Jones*, four jurors—two men and two women—raised their hands indicating they had responses to hearing the charges. In summary, the two men described their generalized repulsion to rape and discomfort with listening to people describe such acts. The two women, for their part, shared their personal experiences of being victims of sexual assault. Such admissions were common in all the trials we observed. In fact, at least one juror raised the issue of their own victimization in every jury selection observed.

In general during the selection process, jurors' willingness to speak contrasted with judges' opening disclaimers indicating that sexual violence might be somehow "unspeakable." Contrary to these assumptions, jurors consistently expressed a remarkable willingness to speak about their experiences of sexual violence in the presence of others. Furthermore, there was only one occasion during our observation period in which a juror requested to speak to the judge privately. Once a juror disclosed an experience of sexual assault, judges followed up with questions related to impartiality. One judge asked: "Have you gotten, sort of, an emotional resolution on that so you think you could be fair and impartial, or no?" Another inquired: "Do you feel like emotionally, you have enough detachment to separate [your experience] from this case?" A third version of the question was: "Do you feel like you have enough distance, or would that affect your impartiality?" The variants of this question suggested that unresolved emotion could be antithetical to fairness and impartiality. When some jurors responded that they could not be impartial and serve on the case, it demonstrated for the court and to the other jurors that sexual assault was a potential source of lifelong suffering that affected a victim's capacity for judgement and rationality. As judges signaled their own sensitivity to jurors' discomfort and unease, they were among the first court actors to frame sexual violence through cultural norms that imagine it to be so traumatic and so shameful that it is rendered unspeakable and unhearable. Prosecutors, too, used similar questions to frame sexual assault as life-altering and difficult to speak of, even to the extent of reproducing the *nomos* of sexual assault (Hlavka and Mulla 2020).

In both their perceptions and their performances in court, prosecutors marked a "common sense" understanding of sexual assault as shared in experience, sensitivity, and revulsion. Their interest in sexual assault was tied to commitments to root out and assess bias and prejudice as it related to jurors' preconceived notions about sexual violence. In an interview, ADA Ray insisted:

> In sensitive crimes types of cases, it's really important to deal with people's personal experiences because it's a very emotionally charged area. You know, a lot of people have either been, just by virtue of the statistics, either victims themselves, had friends as victims, girlfriends, children. And so I think you really need to address people's experiences, as difficult as it is for them, because otherwise you never know who has got that kind of underlying opinion that could really be judgmental of your witnesses or very fair to the case.

Here, ADA Ray described the paradox of *voir dire* in sexual assault cases, acknowledging sexual assault as a common experience that simultaneously generated silences and tensions. Both sensibilities could inform the jury's "common sense." Familiar with prevalence studies that revealed the high incidence rates of sexual assault but anticipating the cautious orientations of jurors toward open and frank discussion, prosecutors employed carefully worded inquiries. They demonstrated care for the jury, empathetically apologizing as they addressed jurors: "I'm sorry to have to ask, but has anyone been a victim of sexual assault?" Such gestures of apology were commonplace, paralleling defense attorneys' apologies to the jury for posing questions about race we introduced earlier in the chapter. Some prosecutors occasionally meandered as they posed questions about experiences with assault, seeming to linguistically fumble as they trailed on and on:

> Is there anyone who either personally or who has a family member or someone that you are close with who as a child in some way had sexual experiences or acts forced upon them or performed on them—they got pulled into engaging in those kinds of acts?

Hedging questions and stringing together multiple acts and possible victims was often a sign of consideration by prosecutors hoping to soften the delivery of the question. It was also a performative act of emotional labor, signaling both the prosecutor's sensitivity to and distaste for the subject of sexual assault, contributing to rapport-building with jurors. By asking jurors both about their experiences as victims and their familiarity with friends and family who had been victimized, jurors could respond to the query without necessarily identifying themselves as victims of sexual assault. Prosecutors made this possible by embedding the mention of sexual assault within an array of other possible experiences of violent victimization:

> Any victims or witnesses of crimes? Specifically, if there's anyone here who themselves or someone who's close to them, been a victim of either a violent crime, assaultive crime, or victim of sexual assault or abuse of any variety. This would be yourself or someone close to you.

Prosecutors effectively combined "victims" and "witnesses of crimes," carefully inserting the mention of sexual assault among a variety of other violent crimes, potentially removing some of its perceived exceptionalism. By conflating the question of personal experience with that of a friend or family member, prosecutors also subtly suggested that sexual assault had a communal impact. From case to case, many jurors consistently raised their hands in response to such questions. Prosecutors would then ask individual jurors for a few details about their experiences. These details often included their relationship to an offender or to a victim, circumstances surrounding the event, and any feelings of prejudice or bias resulting from past personal experiences. We observed only a single prosecutor, ADA Howard, who did not inquire into the details of jurors' experiences but instead asked jurors to "please keep your hand up if you feel that, because of your experiences, you cannot be impartial in this case." This approach allowed jurors to maintain more privacy about the specific nature of their direct and indirect experiences of sexual assault. It also limited a lengthy and vigorous discussion of sexual assault and its impact in front of the entire jury panel. ADA Howard felt strongly that jury selection and trials should be as short as possible so that jurors remained attentive. He also seemed reluctant to allow lengthy discussions to unfold during *voir dire*, as these discussions might influence the jurors in unpredictable ways. In one trial we observed, ADA Nelson emphatically sighed before telling potential jurors "I think a lot of people would have a little easier time with a dead body and talking about homicide than they would about sexual assaults."

The case of *State v. Jones* is illustrative of these types of approaches to questions about sexual violence. During *voir dire*, ADA Ray questioned the 36-member jury panel:

> And, as you've heard now a few times, this case involves a sexual assault of a child, and I know this may be difficult for some people. But, has anybody on this panel ever been the victim of a sexual assault?

Thirteen jurors on the panel raised their hands in response, and ADA Ray addressed each in succession:

> ADA RAY: Juror No. 2, you said you have been a victim?
> JUROR 2: Yes, I have. I have been molested three times.
> ADA RAY: Was that the same person or different?
> JUROR 2: No, different people.
> ADA RAY: And what was the relationship between you and those individuals?
> JUROR 2: I was the niece of one, my uncle was . . . and I babysat for one. And the other one was my foster father.
> ADA RAY: And how old were you when those things happened?
> JUROR 2: I was between the age of 9 and 12.

ADA RAY: Was anybody ever prosecuted, any of those three people prosecuted?

JUROR 2: No.

ADA RAY: Anything about those experiences that would affect your ability in this case you think, to be a juror?

JUROR 2: It might.

ADA RAY: And what do you think specifically would be hard for you?

JUROR 2: I—I don't think I would like to hear it.

ADA RAY: Thank you.

The court eventually struck both Juror No. 2 and a second juror who had raised her hand and disclosed a previous experience as a victim of child sexual assault. The second juror indicated that she was having a difficult time concentrating during *voir dire* due to the subject matter. Both women indicated that "hearing" about the case proved too difficult for them given their past sexual assaults. Another woman explained that her best friend was sexually assaulted, and she felt that she could not be impartial in the current case because no one was prosecuted in her friend's case. She, too, was struck for cause, as were five other women victims of sexual assault who said they felt they could not be "fair" to the case. The women victims who were struck for cause were of various races, including both white-presenting and Black-presenting jurors. ADA Ray then asked the panel: "Does anybody have a close friend, family member, or somebody they know that's ever been *accused* of sexual assault? I see a couple hands." ADA Ray followed up to determine whether these potential jurors could be fair and impartial, asking Juror No. 8 to identify his relationship to the person who had been accused:

JUROR 8: My brother.

ADA RAY: Your brother. And how old was he when he was accused?

JUROR 8: Probably about 13.

ADA RAY: So, a teenager?

JUROR 8: Yes.

ADA RAY: Who was it that he was accused of assaulting?

JUROR 8: A daycare member.

ADA RAY: And was he prosecuted for that?

JUROR 8: Yes.

ADA RAY: Okay, let's see, at 13 he wouldn't be convicted. Was he found delinquent of that, if you know?

JUROR 8: Yes.

ADA RAY: Anything about you now being his brother and having him go through that, would affect your ability to be fair and impartial?

JUROR 8: Yes. Because he was accused, but he didn't do it because he was never around this child. I said yes because he never was around this child and never at the daycare, and it affected my family and my siblings because we couldn't be around my brother.

ADA RAY: Juror Number 14, did you raise your hand?

JUROR 14: My brother.

ADA RAY: And how old was your brother?

JUROR 14: In his twenties.

ADA RAY: And were you pretty involved? Did you know what was going on with that?

JUROR 14: No, not until he went to court.

ADA RAY: Was he convicted of something?

JUROR 14: I think, yes. The girl was 17. She was—I guess she was using someone else's ID at the time saying she was 18.

ADA RAY: Anything about that experience that would influence you here?

JUROR 14: I just think that—I don't know if someone says they're one age and, you know, they're lying about age, how do you know unless you show proof? But then [the] ID wasn't even correct, so. . . .

ADA RAY: Okay. And then any other hands for that?

JUROR 27: My nephew was accused.

ADA RAY: Juror Number 27, you said your nephew was accused?

JUROR 27: Yes, my nephew was accused. He was 17, the girl was 14. And she actually gave her diary to a friend to give to him and his attorney, so that they could see where she wrote in her diary that she was going to approach him to have sex with him. And she refused to testify at the hearing, and her parents are the ones that brought the charges.

ADA RAY: Thank you.

Juror Nos. 8, 14, and 27 were all struck for cause, as were two other panel members who indicated that they knew someone accused of sexual assault and said that they could not be fair or impartial. The gendered response patterns were glaring, given that those jurors who described experiences as victims of sexual violence all appeared to be women, whereas those jurors who indicated that they knew someone accused of sexual assault all appeared to be men, as were those described as the accused individual (e.g., brothers, nephew). The mere fact of having experienced sexual assault as a victim, or being in the role of supporter of someone who had been accused, was not enough justification to be struck. The court struck the jurors only after they had publicly narrated their stories of suffering and its impact on their impartiality. The trope of the false accuser was a strong feature of the jurors' responses to questions of accusation. In all the instances excerpted above, jurors relied on various features of the false-accuser rape myth, citing concerns about underage girls, fabricated identification, as well as feelings about unjust or perhaps overzealous prosecution. As observers of these cases, we noted the marked contrast in tone between the responses of victims and the responses of supporters of accusers. In their telling, men presented their narratives very matter-of-factly, adopting a mode of reasoning in which they explained their logic and shared the reasons why their relatives had been falsely accused. In only one instance did a juror share the depth of impact that adjudication had on his family, stating that "it affected my family and my siblings because we couldn't be around my brother." Otherwise, the jurors' responses warned of the untrustworthy and oversexed teenager who had entrapped the accused. ADA Ray neither continued to question the jurors about these attitudes nor interrupted and challenged these assumptions in the presence of other jurors. However, the judge in the case, Judge Van, sought to curtail some of the detailed discussion:

> Everybody here has been hearing a lot of conversation in the last few minutes about things that you may have had in your life or your friend's life or sexual assault charges or friends [who] were victims . . . yourselves, and as I said earlier, the lawyers want you to be candid and I want you to be candid and honest. That said, all 36 of you, like the rest of us, lawyers, myself, court staff, all have different experiences in life. . . . And just because you were involved in a case 10 years ago where your neighbor was charged . . . 15 years ago, that's not this case. This is an entirely different set of facts, different people.

Here, Judge Van performed his own juror education, paradoxically deeming jurors' personal experiences and common knowledge as critical to sexual assault *voir dire* but also as individually exceptional and unrelated to the defendant in the case. The judge's emphasis was on the singularity of sexual assault, a position that might push back against rape myth reliance by challenging jurors who present victims in a particular way. Judge Van reminded the jury of the prosecution's burden of proof, thereby separating jurors' feelings about sexual violence from their orientation toward the facts of this specific case. In other words, the judge created a dichotomy between jurors' affective sensibilities versus their ability to rely on rationality and reach a conclusion about the "truth" of the case (Lees 1996; Smart 1989).

As the jury selection continued in *State v. Jones*, ADA Ray returned the jury's attention to sexual assault, this time exploring the jury's attitudes about a "teenaged" victim's credibility.

ADA RAY: The primary witness in this case, the victim is a teenager, and she'll tell you what happened to her when she was 14 years old. You are going to be asked to judge the credibility of all the witnesses in this case, but her as well. Does anyone feel they would be skeptical of testimony coming from a teenage child, teenage girl? I don't see any hands. If you are told to evaluate someone's testimony even though they are a child, the same as you would if they were an adult witness, does anybody think they would have a problem with doing that? That just because one is an adult and grown up and one is a child, that there would be difference for you? I see one hand. Juror 11.

JUROR 11: My sister was 15 when she got pregnant from a 17-year-old, and they were going to prosecute him. And my parents decide not to, and they've been married for 28 years. So I don't think I could be fair on that because it takes two people to consent, so. . . .

ADA RAY: What I'm asking here is would you disregard somebody's testimony just because they're a teenager or a child? Do you think you would disregard it just because of the age—because they're a teenager?

JUROR 11: Like I said, I don't know. I just know from experience from my sister.

While ADA Ray noted that no hands were raised when she asked about judging the credibility of witnesses in the case, including a young "teenage girl," some jurors hesitated upon further exploration. Given the opportunity later, defense counsel also asked the jury panel if anyone with young children or teenagers would have a problem listening to a young person testify or "have problems if the attorneys have to ask difficult questions?" Marking various preconceptions of children and youth as especially vulnerable, fragile, or incorrigible fabricators (Powell, Hlavka, and Mulla 2017), defense counsel also asked jurors: "Does anyone believe that sometimes kids make up stories?" Indeed, Juror No. 11 had narrated his experience for the court, remarking that "it takes two people to consent" (in his example, a 15-year-old and a 17-year-old) followed by another male juror who asked the judge a clarification question: "Are we to understand credibility the same for everyone?" Judge Van's response to this question in *State v. Jones* was similar to others we observed as he explained that jurors are tasked with evaluating witness credibility in the same way for everyone: "There's no reason that one person isn't more credible than the other, for example a police officer versus a juvenile versus a defendant." The prosecutor then seamlessly and swiftly (lest the judge or jury become annoyed by the length of questioning) attended to a host of rape myths commonly used to criticize victim behavior following a sexual assault:

> ADA RAY: Thank you. Does anybody have an opinion as to how a victim of sexual assault should appear or act when testifying? I see a lot of heads shaking "no," and I don't see any hands. Does anybody disagree, meaning that you had a certain expectation, and if they don't meet that expectation, you're going to hold that against them?

The jurors' heads shook back and forth, indicating their negative response to this question, too. ADA Ray continued:

> Is there anybody who thinks that it is okay for an adult to have sex, sexual contact, sexual intercourse, any type of sex act with a child? I see heads shaking "no." I have to ask that. The victim in this case did not immediately report what happened to her. Does anybody feel that they would discount or disregard her testimony because of that? I see more heads

shaking "no." Is there anybody that thinks that in order to believe what's going on or to find someone guilty that you need an injury? Is there anybody who thinks that in order to be sexually assaulted, you must have fought back or yelled out or had the victim done something in response to stop what was happening? I don't see any hands.

Through this line of questioning, ADA Ray addressed several predominant myths that insisted victims respond homogeneously to sexual assault in prescribed ways. Some of these myths considered victim demeanor before and after the assault, insisting a "real" victim would appear visibly upset, traumatized, or shaken when testifying on the stand (Konradi 1997; Taylor and Joudo 2005). The ADA also challenged skepticism about the victim's delayed reporting and lack of "utmost resistance" to being sexually assaulted. ADA Ray's questions were posed to remind the jury that the victim's behaviors in this case had to be considered specifically, but in practice prosecutors often lauded victim behaviors that did conform to rape myths. Victims who had "normal" or stereotypical responses were consistently heralded as more believable and thus more legally credible in a court of law.

These approaches to vetting juror attitudes toward sexual assault were completely reliant on jurors' willingness to respond to questions. Not all jurors spoke during *voir dire*, however, and some prosecutors thus simply tried to provoke responses by using frank and direct language. ADA Nelson, for example, told us that she assessed whether jurors were upset through visible signs of discomfort with "vulgar" language. During one trial, she told a jury panel:

> This is a fairly extensive set of facts here and so I am going to sort of introduce you to the type of sexual things that we are going to be talking about in this case. You are going to hear directly from [the victim]. She is going to come and testify for you. She will be talking about hand to breast. She will be talking about hand to vagina. She will be talking about finger into vagina. She will be talking about hand to penis, penis to mouth, penis to vagina, penis to anus, and sexual[ly] motivated urination. Is there anybody, and these are the words I use when I talk about these cases. I used the body-language words. She may use those things or she may use more like teenage-type of words. You know, like "blow job" is

a word that people use a lot. Is there anything about the type of acts that we are going to talk about or the language that is necessary to use that you think just knowing who you are, you don't think you could listen to this testimony?

In response to her long list of sexual acts, one juror responded that "I just don't want to hear it. I don't really like sexually suggestive conversation, nor things like that and I don't know—especially coming from a young girl. I don't know if I will be able to be impartial." A second juror then chimed in: "I feel very much the same way the juror to my left did. I can push past it, but I just would feel quite uncomfortable hearing it coming out of young people." Such practices aimed to root out previously silent jurors, but they also functioned to desensitize jurors. Just as forensic nurses are professionalized to set aside personal feelings by substituting emotion for legal criteria (Mulla 2014), jurors were encouraged, by demonstration, to mark their emotional discomfort and then to substitute these reactions with a commitment to remain impartial. If ADA Nelson's rhetorical warning above alerted jurors to the possible rousing of emotions, they were also being asked to set those feelings aside for the sake of the current case. These particularities—and the means to distance oneself from victims' stories of suffering—were simultaneously connected to the stories of forensic evidence. Courts consistently used *voir dire* to introduce jurors to the frame of sexual assault forensic intervention in addition to its realities, potentials, and imagined capacities.

"This Isn't *CSI*": Forensic Imaginaries and the Burden of Proof

The third and final filter that courts introduced to potential jurors during *voir dire* was one of forensic technology and its role in sexual assault adjudication. Rape myths not only informed attitudes about race and sexuality; they also informed juror attitudes about forensic evidence (O. Smith 2018). Since jurors are often skeptical of rape, sometimes "demanding greater proof than for many other types of crimes and demonstrating deep suspicion of victims" (Taslitz 1999, 6), it is little surprise that prosecutors believed "the more evidence you have, the better off you are." Jurors' expectations of material and forensic evidence have permeated sexual assault prosecutions, even despite feminist rape law reforms in the 1970s that eliminated the requirement for corroboration of victim testimony and proof of a "woman's utmost resistance." Prosecutors and judges thus readied the jurors for the reality of a criminal trial that "isn't TV, it isn't *CSI*, and you're not going to have tons of DNA." Judges with a historical perspective on the Milwaukee County courts often told us during interviews that, while forensic investigation had become more enhanced and extensive since the early 1990s, it was only with the diffusion of television series such as *Law & Order* and *CSI: Crime Scene Investigation* that attorneys began addressing their influence on juror expectations. Many prosecutors we spoke with agreed that the expectation for material evidence intimately overlapped with societal misconceptions and rape myths. As ADA McClain explained to us during an interview, jurors stereotypically assumed sexual assault occurred between strangers and false accusations were frequent. Forensic evidence could therefore corroborate witness testimony, and juries expected and desired DNA or documented physical injury:

> I think when it comes down to it, people hold a lot of myths and stereotypes that are . . . about DNA evidence and stuff, too. And I was saying this to a colleague today that I think we have to really spend a lot of time in our trials tying to dispel a bunch of myths that these jurors carry around in their heads about things because they apply that as part of their common sense, but some of it's just myth. Like, if I touch you, oh, my DNA is all over your jacket now? No!

ADA McClain's perspective was informed by her years of prosecutorial experience. She and other experienced court personnel and police officers understood that forensic evidence was never recovered in most sexual assault cases, in part because of reporting that came after the period during which DNA evidence could be retrieved or injuries documented. Delayed reports were especially commonplace in sexual assault cases involving perpetrators and victims who knew each other. These effects were even more intensified with children and youth, who might not identify their victimization as abusive because the assaults occurred at the hands of a trusted or beloved adult. Such cases constituted the majority investigated and prosecuted in Milwaukee County. The narrative of stranger-perpetrated sexual assault cases lent itself much more readily to swift and immediate reporting and subsequent sexual assault forensic investigation.

Because most cases prosecuted involved victims who had well-established relationships with defendants, it was important that prosecutors, much like ADA McClain does in the quote above, clarified the limited role that forensic evidence could play in a sexual assault case. If a defendant and a victim shared a household, for example, the mere presence of a defendant's DNA on the victim's person might be explained away. ADA McClain was also concerned with the popular misrepresentation of forensic investigation, addressing jurors' assumptions that DNA easily transferred from person to person or object to object. (We discuss such misunderstandings and their implications for the testimony of forensic scientists at greater length in chapter 5.) Attorney beliefs that jurors expect forensic evidence in criminal cases align with the "CSI effect." In sociolegal studies, the CSI effect is a much-touted phenomenon that posits juries have expectations of the nature of legal evidence based on representations in popular police dramas. To date, scholars continue to learn about the impact of such media on actual behavior, questioning its impact on actual trial outcomes (Cole and Diosa-Villa 2007; Schweitzer and Saks 2006; Shelton, Kim, and Barak 2006). Instead of directly affecting case outcomes, popular police dramas shape jurors', judges', and attorneys' expectations and orientations to forensic science. We have observed this type of CSI effect in the form of court personnel anticipating the influence of media and television on jurors (Lynch et al. 2008). In fact, most attorneys and judges we spoke with believed that jurors expected forensic evidence in sexual assault trials and therefore the issue had to be addressed. In an adversarial justice system, the mitigation or amplification of such media misrepresentations depended squarely on case details. Prosecutors regularly challenged the occurrence and importance of forensic evidence, and defense attorneys regularly reinforced and deployed the myth. As DC Dolan told us about *voir dire* during an interview:

> Even if it doesn't have anything to do with DNA, I'll be saying, "You notice there wasn't any DNA." . . . Mostly, again, just talking to them, alerting them that these are going to be issues in this case. I'm going to be arguing about the presence or non-presence of DNA.

While prosecutors like ADA McClain worried that juries imagined DNA as omnipresent and available, defense attorneys such as DC Dolan capitalized on these expectations, drawing attention to the absence of DNA evidence in cases in which it would not appear.

The *nomos* of sexual assault has come to rely heavily on medical and forensic knowledge so that forensic intervention is both imagined and foundational to sexual assault adjudication (Hlavka and Mulla 2020). We contend that medicolegal forensic evidence is imagined because it most often does not exist. Yet it is simultaneously foundational, because juries might expect its presence and draw on it to form conclusions about victim credibility and testimony. This helps to explain why it was common for prosecutors to rely upon rape myths even as they challenged them. One of the prosecutors, ADA Brooks, told us they would "play up" DNA and forensic evidence if they had it, essentially activating the myth they sought to challenge during *voir dire*:

> I think jurors are very susceptible to the TV influence and that certain frame of mind. I usually try to do something like, "How many folks here watch *CSI?*" in every *voir dire*, especially if I have no forensic evidence. I guess, the less forensic evidence I have, the more I want to attack that head-on. If I have good DNA evidence or other types of forensic evidence, I might play it up a little bit more. Like, "You're not going to see everything you see on *CSI*, but you might see some type of that evidence."

Here, ADA Brooks highlighted the importance of specific case elements, explaining the practicalities of employing effective ways of convincing the jury beyond a reasonable doubt—even if it meant reinforcing and reproducing rape myths. Because there was rarely forensic evidence to present to jurors in sexual assault trials, prosecutors more often than not navigated the CSI effect by refuting its actual importance in real-world adjudication. This was often accomplished by tearing down two enduring rape myths simultaneously: that of the false accusation, and that of the production of material evidence. This was achieved in several ways. For example, in *State v. Jones*, ADA Ray followed her questions about jurors' past experiences with sexual assault with a turn toward questions highlighting the association between false accusations and material evidence. The excerpt below from ADA Ray during *voir dire* in *State v.*

Jones typifies how Milwaukee County ADAs often introduced and challenged stereotypes related to issues of credibility and evidence:

> Because of [delayed reporting], the state does not anticipate admitting any type of medical evidence or evidence of any injury. Is there anybody that thinks that in order to believe what's going on or to find someone guilty that you need an injury? You need someone from a medical profession to say something happened a certain way? If you do, please raise your hands.

When no one raised their hands, ADA Ray continued:

> Anyone think TV is like real life for police? Anyone thinking this trial will be fast-paced and entertaining? Unlike TV, and there's lots and lots of crime shows and trial shows on TV these days, there won't be any DNA evidence either. So, does anybody feel that in order to say that something happened beyond a reasonable doubt, I need DNA? I need it just to be like it is on *Law & Order* or *CSI* or whatever the latest show is that you must have DNA or medical evidence or something else, fingerprints, blood, in order to find that the state's met its burden? I see one hand.

Juror No. 19 responded: "I might just have a hard time deliberating without, you know, certain facts. So I might have a hard time saying one way or the other." While the absence of forensic evidence was framed by the prosecutor as customary, it was also presented as contrary to the common-sense beliefs and expectations jurors had about policing, sexual assault trials, and evidence. As indicated in the above quotation, ADA Ray blamed the lack of forensic evidence on delayed reporting, linking its absence to the victim's behavior postassault. Medicolegal evidence was presented as inhabiting an imaginary television world and yet was vitally connected to the prosecution's ability to meet its burden of proof. Any available forensic evidence was posited as foundational to issues of witness credibility and corroboration because it was a priori demarcated as an "objective" and "neutral" legal artifact (Hlavka and Mulla 2018; Lynch et al. 2008). When Juror No. 19 raised his hand and explained that he might have a difficult time deliberating without "certain facts," he signaled his normative investment in the availability of such evidence. While the majority of evidence in all criminal trials is testimony, material evidence such as records of injury, DNA, blood, and fingerprints were perceived as "facts." In *State v. Jones*, ADA Ray informed the jurors that they must rely solely on testimony. This admission—made by countless prosecutors in front of countless juries and included in the jury instructions read by judges to jurors—reveals a paradox: that testimony, as the most common form of evidence within a sexual assault trial, is not popularly recognized as such and thus does not constitute the jury's common sense. Because the case relied entirely on testimony, ADA Ray's trial was what many prosecutors refer to as a "testimonial case."

Familiar with the troubles associated with such testimonial cases, and in anticipation of defense arguments, prosecutors told us how they try to dissuade juries from thinking forensic evidence was somehow "more than it was." Knowing how defense attorneys relied on myths of the "prolific forensic," ADA Brooks in response regularly presented information about her family and morning routine to demonstrate the credibility and integrity of testimony. At times however, this tactic faltered:

ADA BROOKS: If we were to get on the witness stand and say my name is Laura Brooks, my husband works at [company], we have two little girls, their ages are two and five and I have two cats, is there anyone who would want more information than me telling you to determine that those items have been proven to you?

JUROR: There really isn't anything to prove it besides your word.

ADA BROOKS: Would you—what kind of more information would you like?

JUROR: If I was involved enough, I need some type of proof of name, picture ID, address verification, some type of proof of employment.

ADA Brooks's demonstration of reliable testimony elicited one juror's mistrust of someone's word and what proof he would require to believe her. Following the exchange above, another man on the jury pool raised his hand and said he, too, would need more details: "You gotta be more thorough nowadays in my opinion." ADA Brooks then asked the jury panel: "What if my husband came into the courtroom, would that be sufficient detail?" A woman on the panel raised her hand, stating she would still require more detail, and another woman noted that she would believe Brooks's initial statement if there was corroborative testimony. In short, several jurors demonstrated their basic mistrust of witness testimony, further cultivating that sentiment among panel members. Unlike testimony, Michael Lynch and colleagues (2008) have found that jurors ascribe powerful authority to DNA and other forensic evidence for either legitimating or undermining credibility and other arguments.

Jury selection—the all-important prelude to empaneling a formal jury for trial—commonly ended with defense counsel asking a final set of questions, most often elaborating on points already raised by the judge and prosecutor. Defense attorneys stressed the absence of forensic evidence, often overemphasizing the "unbiased" nature of material evidence and questioning the accuracy and truthfulness of testimony. Defense counsel consistently reviewed legalistic concepts with the jury such as credibility, the presumption of innocence, and reasonable doubt. To do so, they often began *voir dire* with statements about their client's innocence, emphasizing the idea that the bedrock of the U.S. judicial system was based on the presumption of innocence. They insisted that an accusation was not evidence, and they reminded jurors that the defendant did not need to prove his innocence. Defense attorneys directly asked prospective jurors if they believed in the presumption of innocence, especially in child sexual assault cases, and whether they were able to attribute that presumption to their clients. While prosecutors made statements about the evidentiary importance of testimony, defense attorneys contradicted that position by suggesting how testimony was "just talk." They dismissed the serious tone of the prosecutor's discussion of the case, telling jurors that the charges were merely made-up accusations. They demonstrated a dismissive attitude toward the testimony of sexual assault victims and emphasized the need for more "concrete" corroborative evidence. One private defense attorney, DC Bronson, reasoned thus with the jury:

> Everybody understand that an accusation is not evidence itself? Anybody can be accused! The state is required to prove the case beyond a reasonable doubt. It means people charged with crimes are not required to prove their innocence, for example, anybody think that's wrong?

When no one responded by raising their hand, DC Bronson continued: "The defendant is always not guilty and stays that way unless the evidence changes your mind to a sufficient degree of certainty." Defense counsel often used jury selection to stress the various meanings of reasonable doubt and burden of proof, a practice that at times merited comment from the judges, who reminded the attorneys that under the applicable procedures *judges* instruct juries on how to interpret and apply legal rules and standards. Many defense attorneys capitalized on the rarity of corroborative evidence and rhetorically mirrored jury instructions' use of such language as "hesitation." For example, as DC Dolan explained to prospective jurors:

> The burden of establishing every fact necessary to constitute guilt is on the state and the evidence must satisfy you beyond a reasonable doubt. The judge will tell you that reasonable doubt means "a doubt based on reason and common sense. It is a doubt for which a reason can be given arising from a fair and rational consideration of the evidence or lack of evidence. Such a doubt would cause a person of ordinary prudence to pause or to hesitate when called upon to act in the most important affairs of life." . . . Even if you feel as though he probably did it, you must still reach a not guilty verdict.

Concentrating on the last line of his plea, DC Dolan emphasized how jurors' "feelings" do not meet the burden of proof. Defense attorneys appealed to jurors to maintain high standards of evidence, often by elevating the role of corroborative evidence, implying that testimony was not fact, and urging jurors to employ reason over feeling.

Defense attorneys' appeals, while in the best interest of their clients, contributed to a false dichotomy in which "rationality" aligned with forensic evidence and "emotionality" was associated with testimony. Introduced at every jury trial we observed, these three filters during jury selection—racial sensibilities and prejudice; experiences of victimization and accusation; and forensic expectations—provided jurors with a very complex set of reference points through which to navigate their deliberations over guilt or innocence. The inherent contradictions of such frameworks were magnified by the adversarial nature of the courts, the competing narratives (or "theories") of attorneys, and even the tensions between emphasizing legalistic viewpoints and introducing "common sense."

Conclusion: "Clear-eyed and Clear-headed"

To select a jury during *voir dire*, attorneys and judges relied on honest responses from jurors, but attorneys were also concerned about those who remained silent through the process. By staging demonstrations, introducing relevant and sometimes competing frames of reference, and even provoking involuntary responses, attorneys sought to draw out jurors and prepare those who would be selected for the task of deliberation. While attorneys and judges were generally concerned about jurors' fairness and racial sensibilities, they also used *voir dire* to explore jurors' experiences with, and attitudes toward, sexual violence and forensic intervention. As they posed question after question, they were able to glean some information about the potential jurors while also imparting their own. We have demonstrated how the process challenged rape myths but also left them intact. In the short space and time allowed for *voir dire*, attorney and juror attitudes about rape myths surfaced. The subsequent trial, as a process, then molded and shaped these myths into a much more layered and complex set of cultural narratives about sexual assault (Temkin 2010).

Who was ultimately selected from among the potential jurors? Attorneys told us that they often ended up with a panel full of "middle-of-the-roaders." For prosecutors, the "bad people" were those jurors who held strong opinions toward rape and sexual assault or negative attitudes toward the criminal justice system. Both prosecution and defense agreed that it was usually better to avoid "the ones with a lot of complex history." They gravitated toward those jurors with "some life experience." These experiences would inform jurors' common sense, as would their emotional dispositions toward sexual assault, race, and the criminal justice system. As ADA McClain once told a jury pool during *voir dire*:

> We want you to bring your common sense and your perspective as an
> individual and a community member to bear on this. That's really impor-
> tant, but what we want to avoid is someone who has really rigidly held

beliefs or who's had certain experiences that are very personal, very emotional, very overwhelming, that might make it so their judgment would be difficult when looking at this kind of case so they couldn't be clear-eyed and clear-headed about looking at a case like this and analyzing the evidence.

Through the orchestrating of jury selection in sexual assault trials, the practice of law legitimizes and recirculates rape myths. In this chapter, we have documented how knowledge about rape and sexual assault trials emerged "as social and professional constructions and, further, as authoritative impositions that are instituted and perpetuated by existing knowledge/power relations" (C. Williams 2004, 50).

By introducing relevant frames of reference during *voir dire*, the court primed jurors to rely on their personal experiences, even reanimating myths about sexual assault that could inform jury deliberations. The knowledge/power relations within sexual assault adjudication were always informed by race, class, and gender. We have left unaddressed the ways in which attorneys also relied on racially coded language that emphasized deviant families of color (Powell, Hlavka, and Mulla 2017); subjected Black women and girls to assumptions about hypersexuality (Hlavka and Mulla 2018; Powell, Hlavka, and Mulla 2017); and emphasized Black men as sexually aberrant, absent fathers (see chapter 6). After all, the sexual assault trial is fundamentally shaped by intersectional inequalities, as Kimberlé Crenshaw (1991) demonstrated in her pioneering work on women of color, sexual violence, and criminal justice institutions. Alongside ceremonies of racial degradation (Gonzalez Van Cleve 2016), practices of jury selection were also practices of racial calibration. Racial calibration consisted of asking jurors to consider their own racial attitudes, attorneys' efforts to "map" such attitudes through proxy data such as one's home address, and jurors learning to sort racial attitudes into those stereotypes and ideas that would attach to masculinized defendants and feminized victim-witnesses.

In chapter 2, we will discuss the production of the spectacle of testimony in the court of law and the ways in which attorneys interacted with victims to elicit narratives of sexual violence. It is the victim-witness who most critically shaped the trajectory of the trial, whose story conformed to or challenged the *nomos* of sexual violence, and whose testimony constituted the first set of words and facts that the jury evaluated in its deliberations following the presentation of testimony and evidence. The spectacle of testimony was also a spectacle of suffering, one whose racial logics might prove more elusive to the jury. Therefore, the jury's ability to recognize the victim as a worthy subject of suffering is partly attributable to the work of judges and attorneys during *voir dire*.

2

Permission to Speak

Testimony and the Spectacle of Suffering

[T]he special criteria for establishing our trust in the truthfulness of the confession in ordinary life would lie in the fact
that the person confessing to something is not telling us how
the world is but, rather, how it is with him or her. Yet when
confession enters the expert domains of police practice, law,
or medicine, its truthfulness becomes completely dependent
on the protocols through which the body and mind of the
person who is confessing are read.
—(Das 2007, 330)

Jury selections in sexual assault cases were lengthy. As soon as the jury
was selected, it was common for the trial to begin right away with opening statements from attorneys and then testimony by the first witness,
the victim. Despite attorneys' careful management of juror expectations
during *voir dire*, the reality was that testimony could materialize at trial
in unexpected ways. In her work on trauma and testimony, Veena Das
unpacked the act of confession and protocols of truth-telling within
institutional sites including police practice, law, and medicine. In the
opening quote, Das notes that it is not simply the *content* of testimony or
confession but also "the protocols through which the body and mind of
the person" are read. In this chapter, we show how rape victims' speech
is constituted according to protocols of legal storytelling. In thinking
about constitution, we consider the words of the witness herself, how
they are elicited by attorneys' questioning, and how these interact with
the *nomos* of sexual violence. These stories are not freely told narratives;
rather, they are molded and restricted to fit the adversarial, interac-
tional processes in a court of law, or what Matoesian (1993) called "legal
domination" and Foucault (1980) elaborated beyond the courtroom as

"discursive subordination." In this confessional structure, victims are given permission to speak, but others have the power to set the conditions under which the speech occurs and how to interpret it. During victim testimony, we observed attorneys amplify, pursue, interpret, and disrupt elements of victims' speech in the courtroom, explicitly as they related to trauma, vulnerability, and precarity. The vast literature on testimony as a genre also tells us that, in testimony, "the speaker does not speak for or represent a community but rather performs an act of identity-formation which is simultaneously personal and collective" (Yudice 1991, 15). When testifying in court, witnesses are not always conscious or intentional about which collectives they speak for or are perceived as speaking for. And yet, it was this very notion of collectives that attorneys employed, be they racialized, gendered, classed, or age-related.

In this chapter, we detail instances of victim testimony, demonstrating how testimony about the harms of sexual assault took heterogeneous forms, even in a highly structured courtroom environment. We recognize that, in writing about the spectacle of victims' suffering in court, particularly the suffering of Black women and girls, our ethnography slides into reproducing the spectacle of this suffering. Our intention is to emphasize the suffering imposed by the court process itself and to decenter the acts of rape, which we do not describe in detail. We also know, too, that these moves do not make the descriptions in this chapter less distressing for many readers, including ourselves. We thus endeavor to show how victim-witnesses are subjects of legal storytelling embedded in deeply racialized and gendered scripts.

The act of legal storytelling all but required legal domination (Matoesian 1993) of the victim-witness. Despite what they anticipated, neither prosecutors nor defense attorneys knew exactly what victims might say on the stand. Milwaukee County prosecutors may have met only briefly with the victim prior to testifying, but there was no exhaustive preparation or rehearsal. In fact, prosecutors expressed a preference for "spontaneous" and "authentic" forms of telling. The work of legal storytelling meant attorneys had to reframe, redirect, or amplify specific elements of victim testimony through a dialogic exchange during direct and cross-examination. This mode of questioning often resulted in discomfort for victim-witnesses, as the adversarial system of justice required both prosecutors and defense attorneys to probe the victim's account. Matoesian

(1993, 186) described such conditions—the ability of attorneys to interpret reality and to determine the legitimacy of accounts—as "courtroom disciplinary regimes and patriarchal modes of domination." Attorneys, therefore, were the primary drivers of these disciplinary regimes.

Historically, women and children have rarely been accepted as authoritative interpreters of their own lives (Campbell 2003), even while their bodies, especially Black women's bodies, continue to be circulated and consumed by a white, predominantly male public (E. Alexander 1994). The courtroom is yet another space of consumption wherein the suffering and speech of sexual assault survivors have been "absolutely prohibited, categorized as mad or untrue, or rendered inconceivable . . . and therefore could not exist within dominant discourses" (Alcoff and Gray 1993, 265–66). In fact, the testimony of sexual assault survivors rarely conformed to these dominant discourses, or the *nomos* of rape, in any straightforward way. In this chapter, we discuss victims across three age ranges: an adolescent woman, an adult woman, and a child. By placing these cases side by side, we invite the reader to note how the court projected and reproduced expectations about the socialization of women and men into mores of sexual consent and trauma across the life course. The affect, self-presentation, and interpretive reality of a "credible" victim varied based on how cultural norms and collectivities were attached to race and age. We have written elsewhere in some detail about how attorneys constructed the credibility of children and youth (Powell, Hlavka, and Mulla 2017). Young children were not necessarily expected to cry or express grief while testifying, but adult women were consistently cast as noncredible if they did not visibly demonstrate profound and spectacular trauma. Adolescent youths were not statutorily required to demonstrate nonconsent, as the law categorized them as children. However, attorneys regularly appealed to the specter of the adolescent's liminal state between childhood and adulthood. Defense attorneys, in particular, conjured images of dawning adulthood, depicting teenagers as seductive, rebellious, and deceitful. When adolescent Lea testified, for example, the prosecutor told us he was worried because:

> Teenagers are a tough group to sell. They just are. A lot of jurors have teenagers. Teenagers can lie. They do lie. So, with teenagers, the attack [at trial] is often on the teenager themselves.

In all but one of the cases we observed, the victim testified in open court. L'umoya, an adult woman whose case we discuss in greater detail in the conclusion, shuddered, wept, and heaved throughout hours of labored testimony. Lea had a similarly difficult time, breaking down in sobs on multiple occasions and appearing to experience flashbacks while she testified. Tamee, another adult woman, was angry, while middle-aged Mary was matter-of-fact about her sexual assault. Mary teared up once but otherwise responded calmly and directly to the questions she was asked. Pamela, a young woman in her early twenties, seemed angry and a bit incredulous. Jacob, age 12, and Asia, age 14, had a hard time testifying at all, and when they were unable to speak, the prosecutors in both cases proposed that they could write down the answers to some of the direct questions. Maya, a 10-year-old whose case we end with in this chapter, cried once or twice and sometimes smiled sweetly at the prosecutor over two days of testimony in open court. Zoey, age 17, was stoic and forthright, while Jorge, age 13, Jasmine, age 14, and Sofia, age 15, were all quite composed as they testified even though sometimes they seemed bewildered or confused. When asked how particular forms of nonconsensual sexual contact made them feel, Asia, Jasmine, and Sofia all described it as "weird." Among the many victim-witnesses were many different forms of testimony.

Testimony was indeed a public spectacle, taking place in an open courtroom before a gallery full of strangers, including researchers in this case and perhaps some supporters. Courtroom attorneys used various techniques to elicit, amplify, disrupt, or challenge the veracity of victims' narratives (Estrich 1987; Matoesian 1993). These techniques were based on common cultural understandings of rape and behavioral expectations for victims, expectations that attorneys themselves delineated in the process of jury selection. One of the most historically distinctive iterations of the cultural trope of rape trauma is the emotionally compromised and visibly upset feminized subject. Still, one's expression of trauma may be unique and may even be met with skepticism by those who find an overly traumatized witness to be irrational, disturbed, and noncredible (Alcoff and Gray 1993; Brison 2002). Sociologist Amanda Konradi's (2007, 5) work demonstrated how "cultural ideals of competent witnesses and 'rape victims' establish parameters for survivors' courtroom behavior." These cultural ideals "require women to do more than construct convincing answers to questions. As a result, most women seek to moderate what they are feeling, what feelings they express, and how intensely they express them when in court" (Konradi 2007, 5). Even as prosecutors were critical of common rape tropes because they departed from the diverse modes of experience prosecutors saw on the witness stand, they were also concerned with how victims would testify. They wanted the emotional expressions of victim-witnesses to fit with cultural constructions of trauma presumed to best resonate with jurors. In her work, Konradi found that prosecutors encouraged victims to perform gendered, racialized, and classed scripts by preparing witnesses to dress in respectable clothing and to temper their anger while testifying. Such scripts, however, also varied in relation to age. Our observations revealed that, for child victims, shame and grief often gave way to confusion or disgust. Their language did not reveal knowledge of their bodies or comprehension of the mechanics of sexual acts or the emotional mastery of sexual desire. Therefore, where prosecutors focused on demonstrating and amplifying the harm that adult women victims experienced, they instead aimed to show that the child was an able, credible narrator.

U.S. courts of law require victims to speak, but adversarial systems also privilege certain ways of speaking. By focusing on the testimony of Lea, Mary, and Maya—a Black adolescent girl, a middle-aged Black woman, and a young Black girl, respectively—we present a picture not only of the ranges of affects and various forms of vulnerability they embody but also the juridical protocols required for legal storytelling. For example, for adult witnesses, modern juridical practices "require a notion of a forensic self who is able to testify to the reality of past events of abuse and their consequences for present identity" (Reavey and Brown 2006, 185). The juridical act necessitated establishing blame for sexual assault and therefore required the victim not only to recall past events "accurately" but to also exemplify an innocent, passive victim (Haaken 1999). In the cases we observed, victims were expected to demonstrate and perform trauma in the present, in front of the court. Adult victim-witnesses were thus expected to embody a fusion of past, present, and future suffering. The child witness, by contrast, was not expected to have similar reflexive and narrative capacities related to their past and present identities. Instead, prosecutors often implied that they would one day retrospectively recognize sexual violence as a traumatic rupture to their identities.

The forensic notion of time, memory, and identity further suggested universalized experiences of trauma and victimization. The courts expected that both Lea and Mary could recount the details of their sexual assaults in a linear fashion. They both had to navigate appropriate cultural expressions of shame with the judicial requirement to remain collected and rational during testimony. With Maya, the child witness, the prosecutor painstakingly worked to differentiate discrete events of abuse from a single tangled memory of sexual victimization by way of "normal" childhood recollections like school, trips, special occasions, where one lived, or even the weather. This approach to legal storytelling often sought to link single instances of sexual assault with psychological or physical pain in a literalist interpretation of violence (Lamb 1999; Reavey and Brown 2006). Of course, the stories that emerged were far more complex and spoke of harms characterized not simply by physical wounding but also through social failures. These social failures carried great weight in cases with younger victims, and prosecutors wove intense stories of vulnerability through narratives of family and institutional breakdowns. When adult victims shared similar institutional forms of vulnerabilities on the stand, these realities were rarely amplified; instead they were used by the defense as evidence of immorality and poor decision-making by adult victims. Such realities were often contextualized through racial othering, invoking the deficits of Black women navigating violence, precarity, and impoverished communities. The experience of sexual violence was often socially and historically contextualized by a variety of cultural factors, but these were considered mitigating in one case and irrelevant to another.

In the following three sections, we show how prosecutors and defense attorneys tapped into normative cultural frameworks of sexual violence during direct and cross-examination of victim-witnesses. The victim's voice—here inseparable and inalienable from her racialized and age-identified body—was a contested sign within adjudication, with at least three parties struggling to claim the most authority over the emergent narrative: the prosecution, the defense, and the victim herself. Therefore, we focus on the myriad ways in which victims narrated their experiences of vulnerability and pain and the techniques that attorneys used to amplify or to challenge the victim's conformity to the *nomos* of rape trauma.

Lea: The Spectacle of Trauma

Defense counsel routinely proposed that authentic victim testimony must be highly emotional and visceral. As one defense attorney put it during *voir dire*: "There are few crimes as emotionally charged as sexual assault. Not to be glib, but there's a reason there is no *Law and Order: Auto Theft*. There is no interest there. These cases are very emotional." Thus, when the victim presented as the expected visibly traumatized subject, prosecutors argued for their authenticity. Defense counsel, however, would then question whether a traumatized subject was able to narrate the past reliably. Lea was only 15 years old at the time the case against Melvin Harris went to trial. Lea's testimony conformed in many ways to the expectations of traumatic narrative. As mentioned, she had a terribly difficult time responding to the attorneys' questions, required significant breaks, froze and wept while on the stand, and appeared to experience a flashback at one point during her testimony. The jury was often visibly concerned for her, watching her intently with worry on their faces, or otherwise glancing at the judge and attorneys to gauge how the court officials might respond to Lea's visceral pain.

Participating in the sexual assault trial was a heavy burden for Lea. Such hardships were often noted by judges during sentencing hearings as well. At sentencing, judges often stated on the record that making the victim testify in open court was an aggravating factor, contributing to a lengthier sentence for the defendant. In fact, when the trial concluded with Melvin Harris's conviction, we discovered that he was just recently released from prison and still under supervision. A Department of Corrections officer tasked with evaluating whether Harris should be revoked to serve out the rest of his sentence in custody had sat near us in the courtroom through much of the trial. In our conversations, he told us that the state was in the process of revoking Harris. If Harris was still required to adhere to conditions of supervision by the Wisconsin Department of Corrections, why was the sexual assault trial even necessary? At the trial's close, Harris's defense attorney seemed unsurprised when we discussed this information with her, remarking to us that her job had been to ensure that Melvin Harris "lost fairly."

Judge Colin presided over the courtroom. From the beginning of her testimony, Lea was very soft-spoken. The prosecutor asked her to please keep her voice up and speak into the microphone, and Judge Colin offered her several glasses of water. Lea's head hung low on the witness stand. She avoided eye contact, and her hair partially obscured both sides of her face. The prosecutor began by asking: "Are you ready?" and "Are you okay?" Lea's voice quivered as she replied, "I'm scared." Though Lea was on the brink of tears, the prosecutor asked her if she knew why she was in court that day.

> LEA: Yes. Because I was sexually assaulted.
> PROSECUTOR: Do you see that person today?

As Lea replied affirmatively to the question, she began to weep on the stand. Her body trembled as she sobbed into her hands, then forcefully rubbed her eyes for over a minute. The courtroom fell silent, and several jurors glanced back and forth between Lea and the prosecutor.

The prosecutor did not intervene as Lea cried. When her tears subsided, he again approached the witness stand to continue direct examination. Haltingly, she described the sexual assault that took place in the basement of her best friend's grandmother's house. During her description of the assault, her voice grew quieter as her head dropped further forward toward the microphone on the witness stand. She explained why she was not able to fall asleep at her friend's grandmother's house in the early morning hours:

> PROSECUTOR: Why not?
> LEA: I felt a touch.

Lea began to cry again and wiped her face with a tissue.

> PROSECUTOR: On what part of your body?
> LEA: My thigh. (crying)
> PROSECUTOR: What happened?
> LEA: I was scared.
> PROSECUTOR: Who was it that touched you?
> LEA: Melvin Harris.

In between her tears, Lea repeated several times that she did not know what to do. When the prosecutor again asked what happened, Lea began to weep and moan, taking loud, deep breaths. She shook so actively that the top of her head hit the microphone. The amplified hollow sound of Lea's head striking the microphone startled the jury and those seated in the gallery.

In this case, the prosecutor had to make very little effort to emphasize Lea's emotion. As she became more distraught on the stand, however, he seemed concerned by the display. Later, he told us that he feared Lea might not be able to relay her full story to the jury. The prosecutor thus continued his questioning with very simple, open-ended statements such as "What happened then?" and "Then what?" When Lea explained that she felt afraid, he asked her why she was scared. In response, Lea abruptly stopped crying, and her face became very still. "Because I knew what was about to happen and there was no one there to help me," she uttered, disappointed. As she went on to describe the act of assault itself, Lea wept, shook, and trembled once more, seismic tremors causing her body to move involuntarily around her seat on the stand. This time she did not stop, and her wails grew louder and louder. Over the sound of Lea's gasping and sobbing, Judge Colin announced she was excusing the jury so that Lea could have a moment to compose herself. As the jury members began to exit the courtroom, Lea's cries grew more forceful, and her breath became loud and rapid. With exhaustion in her voice, Lea shouted "No! No! I don't want them to leave!" Her words drew attention to the reality of the trial, the jury's presence, and the difficulty of testifying. Co-counsel for the prosecutor visibly wiped tears from her eyes, and the victim's advocate approached the witness stand to comfort Lea. The advocate guided Lea, who seemed to have trouble walking without assistance, to the judge's chambers. Lea held her hands over her face. Once the door closed to chambers, court personnel, the defendant, and the gallery fell silent. There was a heavy stillness hanging over the courtroom and a feeling of uncertainty as Lea's wails poured out of chambers for another two minutes.

Thirty minutes passed before Lea finally returned to the witness stand with a bottle of orange juice and a box of tissues. The prosecutor offered no further questions, and the defense attorney proceeded with cross-examination. Invoking the myth that "real victims" remember a sexual assault in painstaking detail and respond accordingly, the defense attorney peppered Lea with questions:

Where's the guest bedroom in the house?

You're sure that *he's* the one that told you to go into the basement?

You didn't try to leave the house?

You didn't go to find your friend?

You didn't tell your family for a while afterward?

You didn't call your mom or dad?

You told the police you'd been forced and you *think* you'd been threatened?

The defense's rapid succession of directive questions probed Lea's account of the assault, aiming to introduce victim blame and confusion (Matoesian 1993, 104). Defense counsel also asked Lea whether she had lied to police officers, introducing skepticism about Lea's account of violence. In her initial report, Lea told the police that Melvin Harris had hit her when he sexually assaulted her. Later, she revealed that she lied about being hit by Harris because she feared her complaint would not be taken seriously by the police without including physical violence. During closing arguments, defense counsel amplified this point for the jury and suggested that Lea was a liar and was mistaken about who had assaulted her. The jury deliberated for only 20 minutes, returning a guilty verdict against Melvin Harris.

Mary: Trauma as Past

If the overwhelming quality of fear and pain marked Lea's testimony, Mary's testimony was more typical of the range of affects and forms of telling communicated by many adult victims we observed at trial. Overall, Mary appeared timid and gloomy on the stand. At times, she seemed sad, puzzled, or disappointed. She was, however, both earnest and matter-of-fact about the violence she had experienced at the hands of her former partner, Jerry Jordan, who was also the father of her six-year-old child. The story she told was upsetting and harrowing, but it featured a violence that scholars have marked culturally "customary" (Stanko 1985), "ordinary," or "normalized" (French 2003; Hlavka 2014). It was not a spectacular tale of assault—the type that one might hear about on television—and the testimony was complex and subtle in its delivery and tone. There were few tears as she answered question after question posed by the prosecutor and the defense attorney. The prosecution produced many witnesses who corroborated Mary's story and told of her unraveled and upset state following the events, yet the jury ultimately acquitted Jerry Jordan of sexual assault.

This trial was held in Judge Dean's courtroom, which had a different look and feel from Judge Colin's churchlike setting. The wood fittings had a weightiness and were carved with floral patterns that were the most ornate in the courthouse. There was little natural light, so artificial fluorescent lighting gave the old-fashioned furnishings a strange appearance. Judge Dean himself encouraged attorneys to conduct court business swiftly and did not have much patience for complicated, intricate, or extended affairs. Nonetheless, the complicated details of Jerry and Mary's relationship emerged during trial, which is not uncommon in cases involving adults and questions of consent. At the time of the trial, Jerry Jordan was in his early fifties and Mary was about a decade younger. The prosecutor established that Mary and Jerry were no longer in a relationship together, though they shared responsibility for parenting their six-year-old child. Mary also had been assigned as a home health care worker to assist Jerry in accomplishing day-to-day tasks, and she was the designated payee for his Social Security payments.

Disability is a complex issue in the courts, and while the home health care worker and the payee relationship were disclosed, not much else was articulated about Jerry's condition warranting such care. None of the attorneys or witnesses used the word "disability" during the trial, although Jerry's attorney discussed some of his client's mobility restrictions due to arthritis in his arms and hands. Lest the notion that two people who were once romantically involved should end up in a caregiver and charge relationship strike readers as atypical, these formalized relationships between kin and former kin are often the standard for care within social welfare interventions. In foster care for example, placing children within their existing kinship network has long been the ideal among child welfare agencies. There is an assumption that the needs of the child can be more readily met by someone familiar with her situation. This model is also employed within home health care and payee relationships, as most caregiving is dispensed by sick individuals and their family members in the first place (Kleinman 1988). Such relationships can be formalized when there are licensed health workers within the kinship network. Thus, Mary provided Jerry with assistance, and while they were no longer dating, she planned to visit him regularly in this new role.

Although sexual assaults most often involve two parties known to one another, as prosecutors reminded jury panels during *voir dire*, these relationships continue to defy juror expectations. Attorneys told us many times over that intimate relationships complicate prosecutorial strategies. As a result, when working with victim-witnesses, prosecutors often appealed to emotion to combat expected juror skepticism. For example, one ADA explained:

> I've started to tell victims before we start at trial, especially adults, that this is the second time I've met you and you seem to me to be very strong. And I believe that you're telling the truth, and now we're going to go and tell a jury what you experienced. I'm going to ask you a lot of detailed questions and you may feel nervous. You may start to feel—and usually this is the time when they start to get emotional in the talk, and I'll tell them, and they'll just grab a quick tissue and try to pull it together, but I'll tell them when you're on the witness stand, this is not the time to be strong. Because if you feel like crying, you need to show the jury how much this has affected you. This isn't about you being strong or weak. This is about showing the jury what he did to you. So, if you cry, let it out. And I sometimes even say, "And if you feel like crying, it's often very helpful to show the jury that this was really terrible." I mean, putting on a brave face is what you have to do to live with something like this, I can only imagine. And a trial is not the time.

If vulnerability is key, what forms must testimony take to convey vulnerability to the jury? Was Mary's account of sexual violence somehow inauthentic because she could tell her story without breaking down on the stand? The general contours of Mary's precarity—her status as a home care worker, for example—revealed one type of gendered vulnerability, as did her status as a single mother. The way she articulated responses to the attorneys' questions, however, and spoke about her emotional state following her assault were, perhaps, not the right "type" of emotions to display (Konradi 2007). For example, Mary consistently spoke of the emotional aftermath of rape in the past tense. The temporality of her trauma became suspect. That is to say that, by being poised and in control of her testimony, Mary did not demonstrate sufficiently how sexual assault had transformed and impacted her in the present. In contrast to Lea's testimony and her physical and emotional collapse during trial, Mary spoke only of past trauma rather than showing it in the present.

When Mary took the stand, the prosecutor began by asking her if she remembered the day in the criminal complaint. Mary testified that this was the first day of her assigned service to Jerry as a home health care worker. She reported for work, removed her jacket, and asked him what assistance he needed that day. Mary told the prosecutor that, rather than responding to her question, he began to talk about sex, telling her that "he was going to get it out of his system." She testified that she began to cry but that he was undeterred and proceeded to push her down on the bed. The prosecutor repeated Mary's own words by asking her what happened "after [she] began to cry." Appearing concerned or worried, Mary's eyebrows knitted together while she recounted being pushed on the bed, straddled, and throttled. Mary gestured to her own body as she testified, and the prosecutor amplified the gesture during direct examination. The exchange was recorded in our field notes:

> PROSECUTOR: I saw you put one hand on one side of your body and one side on the other side of your body to demonstrate he was straddling you.
>
> MARY: I told him that what he was going to do was called rape, but as I was saying that, he put his hands on my throat. He told me shut up or he would smack me upside the head. . . . At the time I was still crying and telling him I was going to call the police.

Whereas Lea's bodily tremors required no interpretation, the prosecutor drew attention to Mary's gestures for the jury. More questions followed as the prosecutor probed for information about body positions, sex acts, and the order in which Mary's clothing was removed. Following each question, the prosecutor stated "I know it is a lot of detail to ask about something so traumatic," thereby inserting the word "trauma" into Mary's narrative. When the prosecutor asked her if she felt pain during the sexual assault, Mary answered: "I do not remember if it hurt because I was so upset."

PROSECUTOR: Were you in shock?
MARY: I was very emotional.
PROSECUTOR: Were you still crying?
MARY: I had stopped talking, but I was still crying.
PROSECUTOR: How did Mr. Jordan come to stop?
MARY: He stopped when he ejaculated.
PROSECUTOR: Did you give consent?
MARY: No.
PROSECUTOR: Did you give consent to take off your clothes?
MARY: No.
PROSECUTOR: Could you have gotten away at any time?
MARY: The gate was locked.
PROSECUTOR: Were you afraid?
MARY: Yes.

Mary's "yes" was uttered in a surprised tone with a noticeably higher pitch, as if astonished to be asked such a question. Given her consistent, stoic character on the stand, the prosecutor focused diligently on pursuing and amplifying Mary's past demeanor rather than her present composure. For example, the prosecutor repeated segments of Mary's testimony, emphasizing time and again Mary's tears of the past: "What happened after you began to cry?"; "Were you still crying?"; "I know it is a lot of detail to ask about something so traumatic"; and "Were you afraid?" The prosecutor amplified Mary's own words, trying to lead her to speak to her emotional state during the rape. The prosecutor, too, reminded the jury that it was very difficult to speak about "something so traumatic" in detail, underlining the myth of rape as an unspeakable crime.

During cross-examination, defense counsel questioned Mary about her relationship with Jerry Jordan. Demonstrating a common tactic in many adult sexual assault cases, defense counsel argued that their relationship was not over and that their home health care arrangement was one that included transactional sex. As we introduced earlier, this defense strategy—on a continuum with the prostitution defense—was common in cases involving Black victims and defendants, often despite their relationship status. Mary seemed bewildered and offended by the defense attorney's insinuation. "Isn't it true you offered to have sex with the defendant for money?" the attorney asked several times over, repeatedly and doggedly pursuing the topic regardless of Mary's response (Matoesian 1993). "No," she answered repeatedly, until she was excused from the stand and the first day of trial came to a close.

In closing arguments, the prosecutor argued that Mary had everything to lose by reporting her sexual assault to police and testifying in court. She was an "absolute genuine victim of sexual assault," the prosecutor argued. "She takes so many risks reporting to the police." By reporting the rape and testifying, she could lose the support of Mr. Jordan and she could lose her daughter. In his closing, defense counsel argued that the state had offered only "parsimonious evidence" of its views of the facts. He asked the jury: "Do you believe Mary to such a degree that you believe her beyond a reasonable doubt?" Claiming he would not speculate about why Mary had lied, but insinuating that she had, defense counsel reminded the jurors that "this group of people are interconnected and interdependent." These entanglements, he implied, would make truth-telling difficult. Perhaps Mary was jealous of another woman, he suggested. The victim was dishonest, he said, and the medical report was "neither here nor there." He further suggested that injuries could have occurred during consensual sex, especially if one of the partners was clumsy.

At this point, closing arguments took an astonishing turn. Much to the surprise of all present, defense counsel dramatically lay face-down on the floor of the courtroom. In order to project his voice, he angled his head toward the jury. Propping himself up into a push-up position, he argued it was improbable that Jerry Jordan would have been able to do the same given his "condition." His argument, it seemed, was that arthritis precluded the defendant's ability to commit sexual assault. Despite his dramatic posing on the floor and his increased volume, the defense attorney drew his arguments to a close by stating: "I'm not going to raise my voice. I'm not going to dramatize. I'm not going to point fingers." Having watched many trials, we recognized this as a common approach to closing arguments used by defense attorneys in sexual assault cases, particularly when the prosecutors were women. It appealed to the popular notion of the overzealous prosecution. It was slightly unconvincing at this juncture in the trial, however, as he announced it while he was still on the floor.

In her closing arguments, the prosecutor implored the jury: "Please don't fall for [defense counsel's] theatrics," and in another surprising twist, the prosecutor took to the floor herself. Striking the defense attorney's earlier push-up position, she asserted "the answer to the question, 'How could the defendant take this position' is that anyone can take this position." In demonstration, she lifted first her right hand and then her left. Standing up and brushing off her blouse and skirt, she asked the jury to weigh Mary's testimony as credible because it was truthful— and to find Mr. Jordan guilty. On the third day of trial, the jurors were excused and began their deliberations that morning. An hour into the deliberations, they sent the judge a note asking what would happen if they were deadlocked. At 2:32 P.M., they returned a not-guilty verdict and the defendant was acquitted of sexual assault.

Maya: A Truth and a Lie

In the previous two cases, the prosecutors elicited testimony from Lea and Mary in similar fashions, even though the way their testimony emerged was quite distinct. When young children testified, however, attorneys regularly pursued different legal storytelling techniques and strategies to elicit testimony fit for a court of law. In our observations of child sexual assault cases, prosecutors often began direct examination with a set of questions about the nature and importance of knowing the difference "between a truth and a lie." Primarily set to establish the child's cognitive ability to discern fantasy from reality, a major concern for the courts, it simultaneously introduced the child's narrative under the pretext of doubt. Prosecutors also routinely featured the "ordinariness" of violence and the character of chronic victimization. So, while prosecutors often argued cases with adolescent and adult victims, such as Lea and Mary, by eliciting or amplifying dramatic narratives of trauma and emotional angst, these were not the qualities associated with cases involving child victims. Instead, prosecutors worked to elicit the quotidian and insidious nature of sexual violence.

While much has been made over the testimony of adult victims of sexual assault—namely around issues of credibility, corroboration, and compliance—child witnesses enter the court of law framed by expectations grounded in normative understandings of developmental maturity, cognitive ability, and reliability of memory (Pipe et al. 2007). Children, too, were required to conform to the *nomos* of sexual violence, particularly one of memory recall and postassault behavior. During our fieldwork, attorneys in only two cases called expert witnesses to testify to children's typical developmental capacities and behaviors. In the absence of expert witnesses, attorneys again invoked a common-sense standard, instructing the jury to rely on their own lives and experiences to judge the credibility of children. Prosecutors worked to achieve this by immersing jurors in a shared, demonstratable experience of memory and behavior with the child victim-witness. These demonstrations were often painstakingly repeated with children on the stand in order to establish consistency and reliability. In short, the prosecutor had to bring 13 jury members into the world of the child. Her interpretations of sexual violence had to be made legible within the conventions of adjudication, or what Lorraine Code (1995) called a "rhetorical space" of meaning-making. Defense counsel, by contrast, routinely argued that children were capricious, imaginative liars who could be manipulated by others.

In late summer of 2013, *State v. Peeples* began in front of Judge Colin, the same courtroom in which Regina Crane and Lea had testified. Leon Peeples was charged with two total criminal counts for repeated first-degree sexual assault of a child and incest. The first charge applies when a defendant commits three or more violations of first- or second-degree sexual assault involving the same child within a specified time period. The second charge was incest with a child to whom the defendant is a stepparent or related by blood or adoption. This meant that, during the trial, Maya's testimony had to convince the jury that she had experienced at least three different assaultive events. The prosecutor's opening statement introduced us to Maya, her father, and the circumstances under which the criminal charges had come to light. The prosecutor first played a short recording of the defendant speaking to his wife on the phone from jail, telling her "the devil made me do it" and "I swear to God, she initiated every time." Rather than being revelatory or shocking, the call itself was of low sound quality and nearly impossible to make sense of without the prosecutor's explicit narration of the recording. "In this case," the prosecutor told the jury from behind a podium, "you will hear the excuses the defendant makes for having sex with his daughter." The devil, he continued, made his wife cheat on him and then, subsequently, the devil made the defendant engage in sexual conduct with his daughter. The prosecutor incredulously repeated the recorded statement, amplifying Leon Peeples's second excuse: that his daughter had initiated all the sexual encounters between herself and her 30-year-old father.

"How did we get here?" the prosecutor asked the jury, and then suddenly, slouching forward and drawing his head toward his chest, he whispered as he mimicked Maya telling a friend at day care: "My daddy has a bug bite on his privates." The statement, in the vast space of the courtroom, was nearly inaudible in the public gallery. He then repeated it loudly in his own voice: "My daddy has a bug bite on his privates." The first witness, a day care provider who had overheard and reported the exchange between Maya and her friend, testified to the same statement. Unlike the prosecutor, however, she did not mimic Maya and instead spoke the words in her own voice. The phrase "my daddy has a bug bite on his privates" was repeated at least four times in the first hours of the trial. This form of corroboration came through the mimetic performance of the prosecutor; it was deliberate and repetitive throughout the trial.

Ten-year-old Maya Peeples was the second witness in the case and took the stand clad in fluorescent pink shorts, a bright tee shirt, colorful barrettes in her dark braided hair, and with a small stuffed animal in tow. We learned that she had named the stuffy, and here we call the stuffy "Elsa." Elsa accompanied Maya for most of her testimony. After Maya was sworn in, the prosecutor approached the witness stand and stood close to her right, blocking Maya from her father's line of sight at the defense table. The jury to her left, however, had a direct view. "Do you remember me?" he asked her. When she responded "Yes," it was hard to hear her, even though she spoke directly into the microphone. Her voice was quiet and husky. She had answered immediately, without pausing to think about her responses: a sure sign she was telling the truth as she remembered it—or so the prosecutor would go on to suggest. After chatting about Maya's family—a means of establishing rapport and easing the jury into the child's life, the prosecutor asked: "What is the difference between a truth and a lie?" Maya responded: "A truth means that when you say something it is not a lie and it really happened or was really said." The prosecutor then moved on to a demonstration, providing

Maya with a scenario and asking her to demonstrate her ability to tell the difference between a truth and a lie. "If a boy took some pens and tells his teacher he didn't, is that a truth or a lie?" he asked her. "A lie," Maya responded immediately, "because he really did take the pens." The prosecutor gave a second, very similar scenario, this time substituting a jar of cookies for the pens. Maya also identified the untruth. The prosecutor then told her that, in addition to telling the truth, the other "rule" of the court was "no guessing." He then staged a demonstration to show that Maya was capable of stopping herself from guessing. He asked her to spell the names of her three brothers, which she did. He then asked her for the date of one of her brother's birthdays. She thought about it and said, "ummm," and after a couple of beats, finally responded, "I don't know." Jury members smiled and laughed, and the prosecutor said, "There you go."

Direct examination of Maya unfolded quite differently from the ways in which Lea and Mary had been questioned. The prosecutor asked Maya about her hobbies and interests, again bringing the jury into Maya's lifeworld. Was Maya a good dancer? "Yes," she answered. Was she the best dancer? She nodded with conviction, and the prosecutor told her that her answers must be oral for the sake of the court reporter: "The lady who has to write down everything you say." "Yes," Maya said. Did she like parties? She liked swimming parties, she said. She liked to swim, dance, write, and sing. She liked to draw horses. And cheetahs. "Basically, I like all animals," she said. The prosecutor asked her to describe her last trip to the zoo. "We start by visiting the penguins, then the gorillas. Then cheetahs." The Milwaukee County Zoo, a common destination in the summertime, was a place that some jurors were likely to have been. The entrance area was indeed just in front of the penguin habitat. Layering Maya's credibility in such a way, the jurors again had occasion to witness her as a reliable narrator, not simply from her demeanor on the stand but also from her description of a familiar public space. The zoo description demonstrated for the jury that Maya was not simply prone to the quixotic sequencing of a child; there was, in her narration, an ordering of events that reliably mapped onto the world in which both the child and the jury existed.

With the child established as a reliable narrator, the prosecutor then asked her: "Do you know why you are here?" Maya responded solemnly:

"I'm here because I have to tell what happened. What happened was—What happened was—my dad did some wrong things." Because Leon Peeples was charged with repeated sexual assault of a child, as previously noted, the prosecutor had to prove the defendant had committed three or more sexual assaults over distinct time periods. A long pause followed Maya's statement, until the prosecutor asked her to describe what she meant by "wrong things." Maya began to cry, and the prosecutor took tissues from the clerk to give to Maya. In the quietest of voices, Maya whispered that her dad touched her private parts. "What does private parts mean?" the prosecutor continued, asking her to describe, in her own words, the relevant anatomy. Maya did not respond. "How many private parts are there?" he asked, carefully avoiding leading the witness or supplying answers himself. "Maybe two," she responded, "In the front and the back" pointing to her own body as she answered. The prosecutor then inquired whether Maya had ever seen "a boy's private parts." In response, Maya told a story about going upstairs with her dad to watch Netflix. His "weewee," she said, touched her "back private parts." The ADA asked her to describe a "weewee." As she struggled to describe her father's penis, she gestured with her hands saying "it is a circle that goes up" and then suddenly exclaimed: "It has testicles on it!" "What are testicles?" asked the prosecutor. "Round," Maya responded. The prosecutor asked her more questions as Maya cried quietly off and on throughout. As the minutes then hours passed, the prosecutor moved from incident to incident. By 5 P.M. on the first day of trial, Maya had testified, in detail, about what appeared to be four different episodes of sexual assault by her father.

The next morning, Maya returned to the stand for her second day of testimony. Again, she swore to tell the truth, and the prosecutor asked her if she would like to talk about what happened with her dad or something else. "Something else," she answered. As they discussed her zoo trips again and the Wisconsin State Fair, the prosecutor's court officer, a sensitive crimes detective, rushed into the courtroom with Elsa in her hand. The judge immediately waved her in, and Elsa, the stuffed animal, was handed to the prosecutor, who then delivered it into Maya's outstretched hands. Once Elsa was safely ensconced with Maya in the witness box, the prosecutor asked her again if she remembered the rules of the court. She answered: "Tell the truth, and no guessing."

The second day of the trial was dedicated to marking each incident of violence as discrete and separate. In the first incident, Maya and her father were watching Netflix. Another time, they were on his bed. Another time her dad used some Vaseline. Detail by detail, the prosecutor made the events stand apart from each other, all the while marking the ordinariness of everyday violence. Maya and her family had moved homes at least once, so the prosecutor referred to incidents in the "old house" and in the "new house." These distinctions tracked the catalog of body parts and sex acts unfolding before the court. The prosecutor reviewed with Maya the words she used for body parts. What is a poopoo? Booty? Cheechees? Several times, he asked if Maya would rather talk to him or to Elsa—another technique common in child interviewing practices—and each time, Maya said she preferred to tell him. The prosecutor asked slowly and carefully about each incident, triangulating the body parts that had come into contact (her father's and hers) at the old or new house, the room in which the activity took place, and Maya's age at the time of each incident—if she could remember it. The prosecutor also used another common technique of presenting options for Maya in a process of elimination: "Did he touch you with his nose? His eyes? His ear? His mouth? You are saying yes to mouth?" Despite his reminder to Maya the day before that her answers must be oral for the sake of the court reporter, the prosecutor often used his own voice to make a record of Maya's responses when she did not verbalize them herself. As Maya's responses grew less and less audible, he urged her to speak directly into the microphone. How did she feel when the incident happened? "Tingly," Maya said. "Did she ever feel tingly before?" "No," she answered. This time, sensation was used to differentiate chronic, assaultive incidents.

Maya's testimony totaled more than five hours between her two days of trial testimony. The cross-examination was brief, however, as the defense attorney asked only several short questions. Had the private part she saw belonged to one of her brothers and not her father? Maya did not deviate from her earlier testimony, and defense counsel moved on. While other witnesses followed her testimony, the bulk of the evidence involved Maya's direct and cross-examination. The state's corroborating witnesses included Maya's friend to whom she'd initially disclosed the "bug bite" on her father's penis; the pediatrician who examined Maya at

Children's Hospital after the police were contacted; Maya's mother; and the detective who conducted the investigation. These other witnesses all testified on the second day of trial.

The next morning, the final day of trial, Judge Colin read the jury instructions just prior to closing arguments. The prosecutor played the recorded phone call again, and the court heard Leon Peeples say once more, "The devil made me do it." The prosecutor stopped the recording and exclaimed: "The Devil did not sexually assault Maya Peeples; this man did!" The prosecutor loudly said the defendant's name as he pointed, his arm outstretched and his pointer finger extended toward Leon Peeples. In a disgusted tone, he told the jury that Maya was "a child who speaks of things that no child should know." Now more animated, he performed for the jury his own disgust as he repeated Maya's language used to describe the defendant's penis and her account of the use of Vaseline, mimicking the same stroking gesture Maya made when she was testifying to the sexual act herself. The prosecutor paused for a moment, signaling revulsion and identifying the gesture as "a motion consistent with adult sexual activity." "Why isn't there more detail in her accounts?" the prosecutor asked rhetorically. "Because if someone asks you to recount the details of your sexual activity with a person and there have been over 20 encounters, all of the details blend together." He claimed that Maya's limited memory was not cause to doubt her word but instead demonstrated the chronic, ordinariness of life and violence. Her lack of details was evidence of truth, for she "speaks of things that no child should know."

Defense counsel's closing called for the jury to examine objectively and rationally whether the state had met the burden of proof. "Consider [the case] without emotion," the defense attorney urged. The doctor's testimony was not conclusive, he noted, and perhaps Maya made up the allegations so that she would have a secret to tell her friend at day care. Defense counsel did not speak for long, simply suggesting that, if the jury examined the evidence void of emotion, they would find his client not guilty. As his attorney spoke, Leon Peeples himself looked miserable, his eyes downcast and tears streaming from his eyes.

Again, the prosecutor took to the podium for his closing rebuttal, this time projecting a picture of Maya on the screen. The picture was a year or two old, and though she was a tender 10 years old by the time she took the stand, the photo of Maya showed her visibly smaller and younger. He asked the jury to return a guilty verdict, emphatically stating: "Now this is this child's only chance to get justice." The judge gave the jury its final closing instructions, and the 12 jury members filed out of the room to deliberate at 9:50 A.M. Less than 15 minutes later, a loud buzz sounded in the courtroom. Few court personnel had left the room yet, and the court clerk jumped in surprise. The jury had already reached a unanimous verdict, and by 10:14 A.M. the judge pronounced Leon Peeples guilty on both counts including repeated first-degree sexual assault of a child and incest.

Conclusion: Testimonial Violence

During our observations, when victims of sexual assault took the stand, they were part of a rhetorical and affective process of legal storytelling. In a phenomenological sense, experience is a complex multiplicity of intersubjective sensations and thoughts, open to multiple interpretations. Feminist philosophers Sue Campbell (2003) and Susan Brison (2002) have each addressed the relational character of trauma, memory, and narrative as an ongoing process of intersubjective interactions through time. Memory is social, and it is always in process, changing in relation to experiences. The temporal nature of memory invokes the idea that our experiences of the past make substantive contributions to our experiences of the present, including affective responses, sensations, and cognitive attitudes (Beauvoir 1969). Arguing that our culture polices rape victims' speech, Linda Alcoff (2018, 70) states how "any given experience of sexual violation is then added to a host of other experiences, contributing an element to a complex and shifting horizon. This sort of approach captures the everyday way in which experience is used to explain, precisely, the *variability* of interpretations." The courtroom was just that: a dialogic construction—a policing of a rape victim's speech that unfolded for the purpose of inciting the spectacle of suffering. The courtroom was not a space for conversation among equals; it perpetuated discursive subordination and testimonial violence.

The experience of sexual violence itself cannot be understood through courtroom testimony. A particular narrative was produced and performed in the courts. Victims were not allowed to tell their stories in their own words. Although victims' testimony differed in content, attorneys used many of the same techniques to elicit, amplify, or challenge their narratives. These techniques relied heavily on common cultural understandings of rape trauma and memory, including that of the distraught feminized subject unable to speak the "unspeakable" events of rape without judicial assistance. In this chapter, we demonstrated how children—not yet privy to the "correct" feelings of shame and disgust—are provided some latitude for these stereotypical expressions, whereas adolescent and adult counterparts were not.

Race, as always, was also part of the subtle calculus of testimony. All three of the victim-witnesses in this chapter were Black girls and women, and each described various forms of social vulnerability and precarity, such as housing insecurity, poor health, or tenuous employment. These vulnerabilities were not uniformly recognized as suffering, however, particularly when voiced by adolescents and adult victims. Reading the cases of Lea, Mary, and Maya as representative of the body of cases we observed, precarity was presented as the individual, personal failures of adult witnesses, a narrative subsumed by the relentless focus on victims' "choices" by defense attorneys. For example, Mary's role as caregiver and the interconnections between Mary and Jerry's households resonated with what the sociologist Beth Richie (2012, 44) has called the "trap of loyalty" experienced by Black women, where commitments to kin reinforce one's vulnerability to victimization. Respectability politics often require resiliency and resoluteness in the face of precarious living, but when Black women present with this same stalwart affect on the stand, they are often received with disbelief and skepticism (Donovan and Williams 2002). In contrast, children were allowed to communicate the collective failure of their social networks and kinfolk without taking on the responsibility and autonomy ascribed to adults and adolescent girls. This collective commitment to child welfare provided child victims more latitude in their telling and voicing of sexual violations. Prosecutors variably elected to either associate adolescents with adulthood or to portray them as more childlike, depending on the details of the case. However, defense attorneys often cast adolescents as able to make meaningful choices and held them accountable for the failures of their families.

Given the different testimonial expectations of Maya, Lea, and Mary, it is worth considering how long Maya has before being fixed into Black womanhood. A 2014 study by Rebecca Epstein, Jamilia Blake, and Thalia González (2014, 1) found that adult research participants "view Black girls as less innocent and more adult-like than their white peers, especially in the age range of 5–14." They further noted that Black girls' adultification was significant in schools as well as courtrooms. When compared to white girls of the same age, participants believed that: Black girls needed less nurturing; Black girls needed less protection; Black girls needed to be supported less; Black girls needed to be comforted less; Black girls were more independent; Black girls knew more about adult topics; and Black girls knew more about sex (Epstein, Blake, and González 2014, 1). They also noted that the perception that Black girls are more knowledgeable about sex lies in "culturally rooted fantasies of Black girls' sexualization" (Epstein, Blake, and González 2014, 5). Such contemporary findings of U.S. racial regimes must be accounted for when considering how jurors orient to Black girlhood and womanhood.

Testimonial violence took on other forms, including the techniques attorneys used to elicit, amplify, diminish, or challenge victims' stories. Attorneys also expended much of their labors drawing out the continuities between the self who was narrating violence in the present and the self who experienced suffering in the past—as if they were not one and the same. In this way, victims were given "permission to speak," but the state produced victim speech as spectacle. Attorneys and judges commanded speech; they defined, interpreted, and allowed for one type of speech over others. Recall the prosecutor's quote in the section addressing Mary, calling not for the victim's strength and fortitude but for her emotional collapse on the stand. It was through this "policing of statements," Foucault (1980) argued, that the speaking subject is normalized and resistance or transgression is eliminated. Bringing an explicit racial analysis to the Foucauldian paradigm, Alexander Weheliye draws our attention to the ways in which bodies are disciplined within institutions. Raced and gendered subjects have everything to lose in both an ideological and material sense, particularly when it concerns the juridical and the biopolitical (Weheliye 2014). Part of this normalization process occurred through corroborating witnesses as well as the variable weight afforded to their testimony versus that of the victim herself. The state routinely called a police officer or sensitive crimes detective to the stand following the victim's testimony in sexual assault trials. It was indeed the expert domains of police, law, and medicine upon which the jurors' credibility assessments became dependent (Das 2007, 330). When victim-witness testimony was outweighed by other institutional witnesses, the disdain and distrust for the victims' collective communities became clear. Chapter 3 thus presents the testimonial practices of uniformed police officers and sensitive crimes detectives, whose mode of testimony contrasts with that of the victim-witness.

3

The Low and the High

Presumption, Power, and Police Expertise

Your two main witnesses are always going to be your victim and your law enforcement agent. Always. And the police investigation can tank your victim; they can make your
victim mad so your victim doesn't want to prosecute. They
can screw up the evidence collection. You know, they have
the case in their hands. . . . The really good cops and detectives can kind of sneak in some of the expertise. "Here's
why victims do that" and get up there and be like, "Well, I
completely understand why the story wasn't fully told to me
the first time." This victim was suffering trauma. That stuff
is like, they probably didn't ask that question, but the detective is getting it all in and saying all that good stuff, and then
you have it. It's out there. It's in evidence, and you can make
those arguments to the jury and it helps them understand
why victims do the things they do, or don't do the things
they don't do that the jury thinks they should have done. So,
that's what's a good detective.
—ADA Rose, Interview

At all the entrances into the Milwaukee County court complex, citizens
were met by uniformed security guards and screening checkpoints.
Signs catalogued the many weapons that the public was banned from
bringing into the courts, including guns, mace, pepper spray, sticks,
knives, scissors, and even knitting needles. Law enforcement, court personnel, and attorneys could circumvent this line, cruising ahead of the
many irate petitioners waiting for their turn to pass through the metal
detector and have their bags screened. Arriving every morning, we were
often asked why we did not seek identification cards ourselves. "Ask the

chief judge. He'll give you one," the guards suggested. "Aren't you tired of these lines?"

One morning, we entered the courthouse behind a frustrated prosecutor who had forgotten his identification card. Forced to wait in line with the rest of us, he was further angered to learn that the spoon he brought to eat his soup with would not be allowed past the screening point. His patience wore thin as the guards remained unmoved by his argument that they knew him and let him pass daily. He eventually relinquished the spoon, though the guards suggested he could return to his car and leave it there. Eyeing the long line, he huffed that he had no time, and he simply handed it over while loudly complaining that it was a wedding gift. Like other courthouse visitors, he could have stashed it with the pepper sprays and pocketknives found under the trees and bushes outside. After months of observation, it became quite clear that what was allowed in and what was banned from the court complex varied from day to day and officer to officer.

After leaving behind the metal detectors and any object deemed to be a weapon, visitors navigated corridors teeming with police officers and sheriff's deputies sporting sidearms, Tasers, and batons. Law enforcement cruised the offices, hallways, and courtrooms with palpable authority and ease, signaling their familiarity and comfort with the space. They snacked in the café and chatted on the benches and spoke with whoever they wanted to in the courtroom galleries. They were not told to be quiet or to leave the courtroom when their police radios interrupted the proceedings. Civilians were denied the same ease and comfort. On many occasions, halls outside of courtrooms were crowded with kin and community members comforting each other or trying to quiet a crying child. United in their grief, the extended family and friends of homicide victims clustered together, their matching tee shirts bearing the visages of beloved relatives pictured below the letters "R.I.P." Sheriff deputies and police officers regularly marched in-custody defendants down these same hallways and into the stairwells, leading them to and from the jail to the courthouse's so-called bullpens to await their hearings. A veritable parade, most of the prisoners were young Black and brown men shuffling in shower shoes and bright orange jumpsuits. "D.O.C." (for "Department of Corrections") was stamped in large black letters across their chests. Despite the heavy metal chains around the prisoners' wrists and ankles, attaching them to one another and creating a grating jangle with each synchronized step, the deputies and officers routinely menaced those in the hallways, gruffly ordering bystanders to step aside to the far edges of the walls for the duration of the spectacle. Even grief was subordinated to police routine. We often noted the uncanny resemblance between the shackled men being marched up and down the hallways and the young men whose faces were printed on the shirts.

The same familiarity that law enforcement exhibited in the corridors extended into the spaces where sexual assault prosecutions were adjudicated. But in the courtrooms, the same police officers, rather than appearing hostile, as they did in the hallways, were friendly with the prosecutors, nodding, chatting, and exchanging fist bumps as they passed. On one afternoon between two hearings, we sat with two uniformed Milwaukee police officers as they jovially chatted with one of the ADAs. Including us in their repartee, they laughed and smiled, joking about patrolling East Side Milwaukee's downtown club area on the weekends. One officer chuckled loudly as he explained they had to "make sure the hood rats stayed away" from the area, which was often frequented by white patrons. He boasted about ticketing the hood rats for jaywalking. His fellow officer seemed to register our blank facial expressions before he looked away. Officers worked with the courtroom bailiffs and smirked at each other while witnesses were testifying. We frequently glimpsed officers in the gallery clutching their shoulder radios, cradling their sidearms, or tugging on their Kevlar vests. These gestures, whether unconscious or deliberate, demonstrated police status and the apparatuses at their disposal. No other performance in the courtrooms so clearly demarcated what Gonzalez Van Cleve (2016) described as "us" versus "them," in which the margins of gender, race, and power aligned with the boundary between civilians and police officers. The mostly white, male, uniformed, and armed officers enjoyed a privileged status, albeit a historically and culturally complicated one.

In her historical study of Chicago rape trials, Dawn Rae Flood (2012) found that, prior to the mid-twentieth century, victims' narratives were central to rape trials and that at least one police officer always testified to the investigative details. During the 1960s, higher courts began to overturn rape convictions, however, asserting that uncorroborated victim testimony was insufficient evidence when the defendant's evidence conflicted with hers in a "clear and convincing" manner (Flood 2012). As a result, corroboration became standardized in rape trials and legislators developed strict regulations, also addressing chain-of-possession and custody procedures in policing practices. Flood argued that, during this time,

> [victims'] trial narratives were disrupted and impersonalized, giving their accusations less judicial credence and thus reasserting the myth that women lied about sexual matters and could not be trusted when they cried rape. (Flood 2012, 107)

In response, prosecutors began to bring in other witnesses to corroborate victim testimony, often including medical experts and crime lab personnel like those described in later chapters of this book. During the 1980s, sweeping reforms spurred by feminist legal scholars challenged the corroboration requirement and, in most jurisdictions, successfully struck the requirement of corroborative evidence (Bevacqua 2000). While the legal statutes shifted, court practices did not. The practice of providing corroborative testimony and issuing challenges based on lack of corroboration persisted across the United States. During our field research in Milwaukee's courts, police testimony was a fundamental form of corroborative evidence.

As we showed in chapter 2, a complicated narrative of precarity and violence was produced by the victim-witnesses and attorneys at trial. The victim's testimony was often a spectacle of suffering, despite its varied forms. Conversely, police witnesses were asked to focus on mundane police procedures and to verify the facts documented in reports. This proceduralism offered the police officer a technical genre with which to narrate sexual violence. The traumatic experience of the victim-witness often appeared as a brief footnote in the police officer's tale. These contrasting narratives were of course prefigured during jury selection, as attorneys repeatedly told jurors that feeling and emotion were to be met with questions of reason and impartiality. Each trial thus reproduced the dialectical tension of a feminized and (often) minoritized layperson— most often a Black woman or girl trying to establish her credibility— with that of a masculine and white-appearing police professional whose very role granted him credibility. The police officer's descriptions of being dispatched to respond to a reported crime, of the reports filed, evidence collected, interviews conducted, and chains of custody maintained, provided an "objective" and authoritative account of the evidence. In contrast to the victim-witness's testimony, the police officers' technocratic accounts sanitized the anguished descriptions heard only moments before.

Testimony from police officers and, in many cases, a Milwaukee sensitive crimes detective were included in every trial we observed. Reflecting the demographics of the policing profession,[1] male police officers regularly provided testimony with a small number of uniformed women participating in trials. More women made up the ranks of sensitive crimes detectives. With few exceptions, the police witnesses we observed presented as white or white-passing. Straddling the roles of fact witness and expert witness, police officers testified about their involvement in the case, the investigations they had conducted, and their observations of witnesses. Embodying more feminized forms of policing, the plain-clothes officers and detectives testified about subtle and fine-grained investigative work—a form of policing labor that was credible because of its perceptive, delicate, and detailed nature, especially in sensitive crimes. In addition, police officers' and detectives' ability to comment on the routine nature of police work, to compare one case to another, and to offer professional opinions based on experience marked officers' drift from fact witness to expert witness. The term "drift" captures the practice of testimony we observed, as there were no Daubert hearings or other on-the-record deliberations qualifying police officers as expert witnesses.[2] These practices were embedded in both case law and statutory law and routinized in the daily mechanics of the sexual assault trial (Blinka 2014, 6). The lack of critical research and commentary about police officers testifying signals that they are viewed as an inherently reliable and believable group. Few have critiqued officers' unquestioned admissions without consideration of their reliability (Schumm 2000).

Our fieldwork took place in the context of nearly daily reports of racialized police brutality in the United States. As we prepared to enter the courts for fieldwork, Rekia Boyd was killed in Chicago by an off-duty police officer, Dante Servin, in March 2012 (Editorial Board, *Chicago Tribune*, April 22, 2015). In August 2014, Darren Wilson killed Michael

Brown in Ferguson, Missouri (Lowery, Leonnig, and Berman, *Washington Post*, August 13, 2014). And as we prepared to complete our field-work, Dontre Hamilton was shot and killed in Milwaukee by police officer Christopher Manney on April 30, 2014, at Red Arrow Park, only blocks away from the courthouse (Talis Shelbourne, *Milwaukee Journal Sentinel*, April 27, 2019). These public killings and discourses inflected our questions. How were the daily forms of police work we observed in the court related to these cases? Was the integrity of police investigation threatened by the police killings that shook communities across the country? In the sexual assault trials we observed, the police rarely participated in egregious racial degradation ceremonies (Gonzalez Van Cleve 2016) but instead contributed to quieter forms of racial and sexual calibration. This included the earlier scene of loudly bragging in the hallway about their hood-rat policing tactics, a way in which police marked and disciplined young Black men by ticketing them in downtown neighborhoods. Police testimony constituted a more routinized mode of producing sexualized and racialized regimes of criminality that cast all civilian participants in a web of suspicion, regardless of their affiliation with the defense or prosecution. For example, attorneys routinely scrutinized pretrial statements and compared them to what was said at trial (Temkin 2000). The use of police witnesses to bolster victim-witness testimony was often, though not always, efficacious for the state. It did, however, reinforce the notion that sexual assault victims required corroboration. This is yet another form of "[naturalizing] the police-community opposition, essentializing the binary that is produced as a performative effect of the processes we need to understand" (J. Martin 2018, 142).

Anthropologist Julia Hornberger has deemed testimony to be a form of police performance that is a front-stage operation, in which police represent their professional expertise and routine processes in a particular way (Hornberger 2011). In the next section of this chapter, we open with a trial in which the victim-witness recanted her testimony, creating a scenario in which many police officers participated in this front-stage operation. The prosecutor in the case called nine different uniformed police officers to testify to the multiple calls and reports filed in order to prove that the victim-witness (who later recanted her initial allegations of assault) had falsified her courtroom testimony at trial. We demonstrate how officers' testimony was presented and accepted as more reliable than that of victims. We then discuss the role that detectives and plainclothes officers played in sexual assault trials, shifting away from the routine forms of policing to focus on how the subtle details of investigative work are shaped and deployed. To illustrate additional possibilities, we then turn to cases in which police witnesses contradicted testimony from other key prosecutorial witnesses. As with the first case and the recanting victim-witness, the testimony of police was presented as more credible than that of the other witnesses in the case, even when those witnesses corroborated each other's accounts. Finally, we raise the specter of police criminality: How did the courts manage the credibility of police witnesses who were implicated in misconduct, charged with crimes, or accused of sexual assault themselves? Police officers formally charged with crimes often threatened the integrity of all investigations in which they played a role. In the cases we observed involving police officers charged with sex crimes, prosecutors moderated the sexual intent of their crimes, oftentimes downgrading the original charges to lesser crimes. The state further emphasized the individualized nature of police transgressions, even in cases where several officers were involved in the same incident. In the courts, "police culture" did not account for the sexual violence of police officers. This is in marked contrast with how the courts subtly (or not so subtly) pilloried Milwaukee's Black and Latino/a communities as cultivating inappropriate forms of sexual and social life, a trope that we revisit in chapter 6 and in the conclusion.

The Recanting Witness: *State v. Morrison*

In *State v. Morrison*, the defendant, Salim Morrison, was charged with second-degree sexual assault and physical assault of his wife, Ayanna Morrison. Like many other women living with chronic intimate partner violence, Ms. Morrison had recanted her initial complaint of sexual assault and refused to testify against her husband during the trial. For many victims of intimate partner violence, calling the police or turning to emergency room services in the short term—while refusing to publicly take a stance against an abuser—is a tactic of survival. Prosecutors understood that victim-witnesses could not afford to anger defendants and that "domestic violence victims may be accurate in weighing the risks to their personal safety that may be compromised by cooperating with the criminal justice process" (Berliner 2003, 668).

In interviews, prosecutors explained to us that, while "one of the worst things to do was to subpoena a victim and force them to come to court," it also let the victim off the hook. Put simply, the victim could say she was forced to appear and testify. Whatever the outcome of the trial, Ayanna Morrison was likely safer if her husband did not see her as betraying him. When she took the stand, Ayanna Morrison gazed affectionately at the defendant and mouthed, "I love you." He held her eyes but did not respond in kind, his face stalwart and composed throughout the trial. Though not surprised, the prosecutor was frustrated with Ms. Morrison's demeanor on the stand. She anticipated that Ms. Morrison would not be a "cooperative" witness and had prepared the jury for this possibility. During *voir dire*, she explained that assessing credibility was "particularly important in this case because I'm not sure what Ms. Morrison is going to say on the stand. I know what she told the nurses. I know what she told the doctors. And I know what she told the police."

The police, as it turned out, had responded to many 911 calls from Ms. Morrison. The prosecutor called a series of officers to testify to a pattern of violence and abuse in the Morrison household and to show that Ayanna Morrison was intentionally lying on the stand. When witnesses are considered "hostile" to the state's case, rules of evidence allow for some flexibility to hearsay exemptions. In a case with a recanting sexual assault victim-witness and a documented history of domestic violence, the prosecutor was allowed to call police witnesses to testify about previous reports and utterances made by others recorded in the reports. Anticipating the array of police witnesses to come, the judge asked the jury panel during *voir dire* whether anyone had a bias in favor of, or against, police officers. "Anyone or any member of your family who's been employed by a law enforcement agency? Local police, state police, FBI, CIA, Homeland Security, Department of Corrections, probation, parole, or anything else that you can think of?" Jurors who raised their hands were asked whether this connection would impact their ability to fairly evaluate the testimony of police officers.

The prosecutor questioned Ayanna Morrison for a full day and a half before calling the first police witness. Direct examination was unlike

other cases we had observed up to this point. The prosecutor systematically asked her leading questions to which she simply replied, sometimes with exasperation, "No," "I don't know," or "I don't remember." Ms.
Morrison's courtroom testimony contrasted dramatically with what was
recorded in police reports and emergency room documentation. She
variously claimed "my body is easy to bruise" or "I can just walk into
a door and hit my head or arm and get a bruise," and several times she
claimed she had self-inflicted scratches, bruises, and red marks to get the
defendant into trouble with police.

> PROSECUTOR: Oh, I understand that. I bruise very easily as well. But
> those were on your neck.
> Ms. MORRISON: Right. And like I said, half the time when I made a
> statement, it was false to where I was trying to get Salim in trouble.
> PROSECUTOR: So, you would put your own hands around your neck
> and squeeze till redness and then call the police?
> Ms. MORRISON: Yes, ma'am.

The prosecutor appeared frustrated during direct examination, her
incredulity palpable. Verging on sarcasm, she asked if all the reports
from service providers were wrong, incorrect, or lies:

> PROSECUTOR: And did you tell the sexual assault—do you recall what
> you told the sexual assault treatment nurse?
> AYANNA MORRISON: No, I don't.
> PROSECUTOR: So, do you recall telling the nurse that the defendant
> said to you, "You are fuckin' someone else 'cause you don't want to be
> intimate with me?"
> AYANNA MORRISON: No, I don't.
> PROSECUTOR: And if she put that in those medical records, would that
> be right or wrong?
> AYANNA MORRISON: Wrong.
> PROSECUTOR: Do you also recall telling the nurse that your pain scale
> at the time was a seven out of ten?
> AYANNA MORRISON: No, I don't.
> PROSECUTOR: And after the defendant had hit you and choked you,
> that your pain was a ten out of ten?

AYANNA MORRISON: No, I don't.

   . . .

PROSECUTOR: And the nurse, the doctor, the police officer, and the
   detective all made false reports?
AYANNA MORRISON: I guess. Yes, ma'am.

Ms. Morrison's voice was low and even throughout her testimony.
Although treated as a hostile witness by the state, she was not defi-
ant on the stand but rather seemed resolved. On the second day of
Ms. Morrison's testimony, the prosecutor painstakingly reviewed with
her the numerous prior domestic violence reports. Given the victim-
witness's consistent responses to a litany of documented violence, the
jury appeared restless, sometimes frowning and sleepy-eyed. At one
point the judge called the attorneys to chambers for a sidebar, later noting for the record that his staff had noticed two or three jurors with their
eyes closed. When the jury returned from break, the judge reminded
them how important it was to stay alert during trial and informed
them that they could request a break for water or to stretch their legs.
When defense counsel began cross-examination, he argued that that
the Morrisons had a mutually abusive relationship—a common strategy used in cases of intimate partner violence. He stated that the couple
were cheating on each other and Ayanna Morrison often self-inflicted
wounds in order to get Salim Morrison in trouble with the police.

Following the direct and cross-examination of Ms. Morrison, the
prosecutor shifted the pace and tone of the trial, submitting police and
medical reports, video footage from the emergency room, and testimony from a variety of witnesses, including six uniformed and three
plainclothes police officers. The jurors seemed attentive during the
first two police witnesses' testimony. By the fourth, they had slumped
back again into their wooden seats with heavy-lidded eyes. The air was
stale, and the sluggish ceiling fans did little to stir the courtroom air.
Some of the uniformed officers taking the stand also appeared sluggish themselves or, perhaps, resentful of the case. Many prosecutors
we interviewed for our study had concerns about uniformed patrol
officers responding to intimate partner violence or sexual assault calls
due to their lack of the specialized skills necessary to investigate such
cases. They worried that patrol officers were not usually as committed

to a case as a detective might be and possessed far too much discretion. One prosecutor told us that "street cops blame the victim. They act . . . kind of like [a] human truth machine." Despite these concerns, prosecutors had to rely heavily on the police for clear and accurate reports and evidence collection. Prosecutors knew that, depending on the jury selected, police testimony could be interpreted as clear and convincing or disorganized and substandard. In *State v. Morrison*, the prosecutor employed the cultural notion of "street cops" as simply responding officers, capitalizing on ideas of the dispassionate, "just-the-facts-ma'am" patrol officer. Each testified in identical dark blue, short-sleeved uniforms with an embroidered Milwaukee Police Department emblem on the left sleeve and a shiny metal badge above the left breast pocket, visible whether their Kevlar vests were on or off. Each wore a police duty belt weighing around 20 pounds and carried an array of firearms, ammunition, Tasers, handcuffs, pepper spray, batons, flashlights, and radios.

The first of the six uniformed patrolmen was asked a series of questions about his employment. Establishing an officer's experience in the field was customary, followed by a point-by-point description of their involvement in the case. Here, the officer had responded to the hospital emergency room to take an initial report from Ayanna Morrison. The excerpt that follows is lengthy, but it demonstrates the ways in which police work was cast as detached, routinized, and therefore depicted as credible.

PROSECUTOR: How are you employed, sir?
OFFICER 1: I'm a City of Milwaukee police officer.
PROSECUTOR: And how long have you been employed in such a capacity?
OFFICER 1: [For] 22 years.
PROSECUTOR: And what's your current assignment?
OFFICER 1: Patrol.
PROSECUTOR: And what do you do in your patrol assignment?
OFFICER 1: Take assignments, calls that come in.
PROSECUTOR: And do you interview witnesses?
OFFICER 1: Yes.
PROSECUTOR: And do you interview victims?

OFFICER 1: Yes.

PROSECUTOR: Would you be considered a first responder?

OFFICER 1: Yes.

PROSECUTOR: And what does that term mean, "first responder"?

OFFICER 1: When someone calls for the police, I'm sent.

PROSECUTOR: You'll be the first person to show up?

OFFICER 1: Right.

PROSECUTOR: Are there times when there would be different people called in, detectives or specialty units that would be secondary responders?

OFFICER 1: Yes.

PROSECUTOR: And approximately how many citizens have you interviewed in your 22 years as a Milwaukee police officer?

OFFICER 1: Ooh, hundreds.

PROSECUTOR: And do you write reports that summarize that interview?

OFFICER 1: Yes.

PROSECUTOR: And what are some things that you're conscientious about when you're writing a report to summarize an interview?

OFFICER 1: Basically the—what they tell you the first time, what happened.

PROSECUTOR: And are you—is it your goal to summarize what a person tells you in your reports?

OFFICER 1: Yes.

PROSECUTOR: Do you ever editorialize or add comments about—or just add comments in your reports?

OFFICER 1: No.

Beginning with the officer's extensive service, the prosecutor described 22 years of practiced responses to emergency calls, to witness interviews, and to detailed reporting. His mild surprise when asked how many citizens he had interviewed and his response—"Ooh, hundreds"—conveyed the routinized nature of police work. The police officer's testimony also called our attention to the authority commonly attached to first responders' reports in criminal investigation. Police and court practices in Milwaukee County largely operated under the assumption that the first report of a crime was the most accurate and reliable, even though scholarship on trauma responses has challenged that notion (Anderson, Cohen, and Taylor 2000; Sue Campbell 2003; Petrack and Hedge 2002). First reports are touted as the most reliable in part because they are assumed to be free of social contamination by others, be they friends, family, or additional investigators and medical personnel. Of course, such cultural notions and practices can undermine the later accounts and testimony of victim-witnesses.

Small technical details such as assigning incident numbers to reported crimes were reviewed in painstaking detail, demonstrating that establishing a chain of evidence was policing-as-usual:

PROSECUTOR: When you write a report, does the computer system
    from the Milwaukee Police Department put on an incident number?
OFFICER 1: Yes.
PROSECUTOR: And what is an incident number?
OFFICER 1: Basically, we have to have that to write a report. When we
    figure out a crime actually happened, we get an incident number.
    Everything gets put under that.

The officer could not proceed with an investigation without an incident number, and an assigned incident number occurred only when an officer had made a discretionary professional assessment that "a crime actually happened." He did not explain to the jury that he was professionally obligated to judge a crime by standards of probable cause. Thus, as he testified, the practice of policing was transposed into a subject of law.

State v. Morrison involved domestic violence and more paperwork to come:

PROSECUTOR: And when you respond to a scene and it involves
    intimate partners, people have children together, or people who live
    together, something of that nature, is there additional paperwork that
    you fill out?
OFFICER 1: Yes.
PROSECUTOR: And what is that?
OFFICER 1: That's the form you're holding is a—we just call it a "DV
    yellow."

> PROSECUTOR: And this is a form specific to intimate partners, domes-
> tic violence–type situations?
> OFFICER 1: Yes.

The DV yellow form reappeared in subsequent police witness testimony. Each officer reviewed the conventions of writing reports, explaining how he marked word-for-word utterances made by the complainant in direct quotes:

> PROSECUTOR: And was any part of that form filled out by Ms.
> Morrison?
> OFFICER 2: Yes, the injuries where the victim was struck and she's
> given a questionnaire where she's to answer one through eight and
> circle yes or no, and a signature and date.
> PROSECUTOR: And that was all done in front of you?
> OFFICER 2: Yes.
> PROSECUTOR: And is that a clear and accurate copy of the form that
> was filled out on [that date]?
> OFFICER 2: Yes.

The prosecutor established that the victim-witness was required to complete and sign the DV yellow herself, including a body map to mark her injuries, a series of yes or no questions regarding the domestic violence incident, a signature, and a date. Could the DV yellow form stand in for the victim-witness? The state—not the victim—was the driver of prosecution, and it was certainly not rare for partners in domestic violence situations to recant. Dawn Moore and Rashmi Singh (2018) have referenced such documentary practices as the production of a victim-witness's "data double." A data double is a legal subject, not the victim herself, that is able to attest to the veracity of violence through time, long after the victim has decided whether or not she desires to participate in criminal justice processes (Moore and Singh 2018). The second officer had also taken photographs of Ms. Morrison's injuries, and the prosecutor moved the photos into evidence. The paperwork and the photos comprised the evidentiary artifacts that served as Ms. Morrison's data double, and the police witnesses corroborated the practiced collection of those artifacts.

Drifting from fact witness to expert witness, the third uniformed officer was called to the stand to recount his interactions with Ms. Morrison when he had responded to a "battery" incident in her home. Here, the officer introduced statutory language—that of "battery"—in a way that made it indistinguishable from the complainant's own language.

PROSECUTOR: And who, if anybody, did you talk to at that address?
OFFICER 3: I believe it was Ayanna Morrison.
PROSECUTOR: And what did she tell you?
OFFICER 3: Basically that she got into an argument with the father of her two children and that he battered her.

Establishing a chronic pattern of domestic violence seemed to be an effective prosecutorial strategy to counter the victim's recantation, but by the fourth officer, the jury appeared uninterested and annoyed by the repetition of the witnesses. There were faint groans from the jury panel as the fifth officer was called to the stand. As it turned out, however, Officer Joe Larson commanded the jurors' attention with his erudite demeanor and debonair tone. In the hallway before the trial, Officer Larson told us that he was no longer assigned to patrol but was teaching at the police academy. He also had a military background and had the precisely groomed hair and freshly scrubbed face that might be associated with military comportment. He was tanned and muscled in a way that the other officers had not been, and his uniform was crisply starched. Perhaps it was his pedagogical experience as an instructor at the police academy that captured the courtroom's renewed attention. Instead of speaking to the prosecutor, Officer Larson locked eyes with the jurors throughout most of his testimony. In this way, he approximated more of a detective's demeanor or that of the forensic scientists we describe in chapter 5. He sat up a little straighter, spoke with more animation, and relied on a wider repertoire of hand gestures and facial expressions compared to the other officers. The jury responded in kind, listening to the fifth description of a DV yellow. In the gallery, too, the shift in energy was palpable. "He's like a caricature of the perfect officer," we mused. In our field notes we wrote he was "like G.I. Joe or Captain America."

All six police officers offered testimony about the repetitive work of policing. They described the routine responses to domestic violence incidence calls, the types of paperwork, incident numbers, and conventions of recording speech and injuries. Such details offered by multiple, perhaps interchangeable, uniformed officers corroborated the state's narrative. The police were subjects of both policing and law. The bureaucratic practices of the DV yellow form demonstrated what police scholar Jean-Paul Brodeur (2010) would call the "low policing" of daily routines. "High-policing"—the political work of policing, as Brodeur describes it—included the aggregating function of administrative forms and depictions of intimate partner violence and sexual assault. Police testimony, in this case, was made out to be a more reliable witness to Ms. Morrison's suffering than she herself could be. Police testimony often emerged as highly credible—if not more credible—than the victim-witness in the sexual assault trial. In this case, Ayanna Morrison was deemed unreliable given her recantations on the stand, as well as the jury's finding of guilt. Yet, this hierarchy of credibility attached to police testimony even in cases where it contradicted reliable witnesses. While each police witness had walked the jury through the low policing work of routine report-taking and bureaucratic practice, their collective performance as a consistent and authoritative force aligned with the political practices of high policing that entrenched the political power of police, in this case in the adjudication of sexual violence.

Police and Civilian: Contradicting Witnesses

The taken-for-granted nature of police authority and reliability was performed tediously in State v. Morrison and marks an important entry point from which to approach the juxtaposition of testimony by lay witnesses and that of police officers and detectives. In the two selected cases that follow—State v. Alejandro Lopez and State v. Kelvin Lee—we present detailed illustrations of how police witnesses contradicted the testimony of lay witnesses. Both Crystal Ortega and her mother, Isabel, both of whom testified in the Lopez trial, were key examples of witnesses who offered reliable testimony with conviction and clarity on the stand. In State v. Kelvin Lee, contradictory police testimony discredited the victim-witness, Tamee North. These cases show how errors in police investigation do not necessarily diminish the reliability of police testimony.

Powers of Observation: State v. Lopez

Alejandro Lopez was charged with second-degree sexual assault against his 13-year-old daughter, Karina, who was being seen at Children's Hospital on the day in question. Other families, including Crystal and Isabel Ortega, were sitting in the same waiting room as the Lopez family. During opening statements, the prosecutor told the jury that the two witnesses would testify that they saw the defendant "grab his daughter's breasts, pinch her nipple between his finger, his thumb and his index finger of her left breast. . . . The defendant then ran his hand down her stomach and rubbed her vaginal area over her clothing." Karina, the victim, was unable to testify at court due to her autism. A doctor had explained that Karina was nonverbal. Nevertheless, the prosecution summoned Karina to the courtroom to perform, in front of the jury, her inability to verbally respond to direct examination. Karina was exploited—made a spectacle of suffering—in order for the state to demonstrate it had no choice but to rely on other witnesses and police reports to communicate what had happened to Karina on that day. The prosecutor first called the lead investigating detective, Raymond Liu, followed by Crystal and Isabel Ortega, the two witnesses who had first reported Alejandro Lopez to an office receptionist. The witnesses described seeing Lopez "caress" Karina's breasts and also saw him place a hand on her "vagina" over her clothing. With righteous fury, Lopez's attorney painted a picture of the caring and harrowed father (a masculinized image we address in chapter 6) who was simply calming his daughter by tickling her chest. At age 13, Karina wore a diaper, and the defense argued that the defendant was worried that Karina might need a change and was simply in the habit of checking for wetness over her clothing. In their testimony, Detective Liu and Crystal Ortega contradicted one another. Given their conflicting narratives, the jury had to decide which account was more or less credible.

Calling Detective Liu to the stand, the prosecutor meticulously reviewed his credentials, not unlike the police officers in the previous section. Detective Liu had been employed by the Milwaukee County

Sheriff's Department for 19 years, including working as a detective for eight while assigned to the Criminal Investigation Bureau. His responsibilities in the case included interviewing witnesses and determining "what occurred . . . and if there's any physical evidence to collect" such as security camera videos, body fluids, or photographs. During cross-examination, defense counsel produced a photograph of an image of a diaper bag for the jury, taken by Detective Liu, and remarked that he had failed to notice that Karina wore a diaper. After sarcastically questioning Detective Liu's power of observation, defense counsel then questioned the way he had interviewed the witnesses that day. Wearing a tie and jacket, Detective Liu sat straight and sturdy on the stand and kept his answers short and to the point. He maintained steady eye contact with the defense attorney during questioning.

> DEFENSE ATTORNEY: And, so when you first interviewed Crystal
>   Ortega—and now is that—how is she related to the Isabel Ortega?
> DET. LIU: She's the daughter.
> DEFENSE ATTORNEY: Okay. So, when you spoke to the daughter,
>   Crystal Ortega, that's by telephone, correct?
> DET. LIU: Correct.
> DEFENSE ATTORNEY: It wasn't at the scene?
> DET. LIU: Correct.
> DEFENSE ATTORNEY: And you didn't speak to Isabel Ortega at the
>   scene either?
> DET. LIU: Correct.
> DEFENSE ATTORNEY: Now, there came a time where you met with
>   Crystal and Isabel Ortega then at a residence, correct?
> DET. LIU: Correct.
> DEFENSE ATTORNEY: That would have been Crystal Ortega's home?
> DET. LIU: They both reside there.
> DEFENSE ATTORNEY: Okay.

With a few short questions, defense counsel ascertained that Detective Liu did not speak with Crystal Ortega at the scene of the reported assault but instead had interviewed Crystal in her home. However, this was not how Crystal Ortega remembered things. A young mother of two children herself, she responded to the defense attorney's questions:

DEFENSE ATTORNEY: Now, you recall speaking to a Detective Liu?

CRYSTAL ORTEGA: Yes, I do.

DEFENSE ATTORNEY: Okay. And you spoke to Detective Liu by telephone, correct?

CRYSTAL ORTEGA: In person.

DEFENSE ATTORNEY: So, you only spoke to him in person?

CRYSTAL ORTEGA: And one time he came to my house again after that. I talked to him twice in person.

DEFENSE ATTORNEY: So, you never talked to Detective Liu by phone?

CRYSTAL ORTEGA: I have had a conversation with him by phone to make an appointment to see him in person.

DEFENSE ATTORNEY: You don't recall Detective Liu calling you when this event occurred?

CRYSTAL ORTEGA: I waited for him at the hospital so he [could] take my statement.

DEFENSE ATTORNEY: And then he took your statement at the hospital?

CRYSTAL ORTEGA: Yes.

Playing up the discrepancies in testimony, defense counsel questioned both witnesses, Detective Liu and Crystal Ortega, in a suspicious tone. The jury heard Liu state that he had interviewed Crystal once, by telephone. Crystal, by contrast, claimed steadfastly that she had been interviewed by him twice and in person. The small details of low policing made for high-policing effects, potentially undermining or affirming the authority of the police witness.

Crystal Ortega's mother, Isabel Ortega, was also called to the stand to testify because she was in the waiting room that day and observed the interaction between Karina and her father. On cross-examination, defense counsel asked Isabel if she recalled being interviewed by Detective Liu while Crystal was in the room. Concerned that the witnesses had influenced each other and contaminated the testimonial evidence, defense counsel drew attention to the lack of witness sequestration, a hallmark of police investigation. Liu had claimed that the unusual practice of interviewing two witnesses together was required because Isabel did not speak fluent English and Crystal was needed to provide Spanish-language interpretation assistance.

DEFENSE ATTORNEY: And when Detective Liu spoke to you, your daughter was in the same room, correct?

ISABEL ORTEGA: Yes.

DEFENSE ATTORNEY: And your daughter then acted as the interpreter?

ISABEL ORTEGA: Yes.

DEFENSE ATTORNEY: And so Detective Liu interviewed both of you at the same time in the same room?

ISABEL ORTEGA: First one and then the second one, even if we were in the same room.

DEFENSE ATTORNEY: But all this happened at the same time, the interview?

ISABEL ORTEGA: Yes.

Even though Isabel and Crystal Ortega described observing the same thing at Children's Hospital, defense counsel suggested that the women may have influenced each other. The use of a noncertified Spanish interpreter, suggested the defense counsel, was also unorthodox and a departure from the routines of police investigation.

In his closing, defense counsel did not return to Detective Liu's errors in police investigative practices. He did not amplify what many might call "rookie mistakes": missing the diaper bag, simultaneously interviewing witnesses, and using a noncertified interpreter. Rather, defense counsel told the jury that Crystal's and Isabel's perceptions and memories of the events were unreliable. Detective Liu's testimony, however, was more credible because, as the defense put it, he was "under oath with the penalty of perjury hanging over his head":

> Do I call these witnesses liars? No. What I call them are individuals that decide that their belief is that perception of what they thought they saw. And then what they thought they saw they made it sinister. They made it evil, and they made it diabolical. . . . Now, I submit to you that in this case Crystal Ortega has a lack as it relates to her powers of recollection. Under oath with the penalty of perjury hanging over his head, Detective Liu testified to you that when he interviewed Crystal Ortega he interviewed her on the phone. He testified under oath that that's how it was done. And then when Crystal Ortega takes the witness stand, that never happened.

She took an oath, too, but apparently there's a problem with her powers of recollection in that respect. But let's look at maybe even the powers of observation. Because the powers of observation are very important in this case.

By diminishing Crystal Ortega's "powers of recollection" and connecting these to a deficit in her "powers of observation," the defense attorney attributed greater skill, authority, and reliability to Detective Liu. Like many other cases we observed, several central issues were implicated: as a professional police officer and detective, Liu had a symbolic edge in terms of his presumed powers of recollection and observation. These powers were culturally assumed and also actively implied by defense counsel. Detective Liu also had a technical edge. Prior to the case, Liu was able to review his written reports and tailor his testimony accordingly. Prosecutors often referred to this as "refreshing one's recollection" for the record. Lay witnesses were not allowed to review their reports or other accounts prior to testifying, lest they be accused of manufacturing testimony. As discussed in chapter 2, they were expected to recount events from memory in the theater of the court. Furthermore, the state's case relied heavily on Liu's investigative work and testimony. The prosecutor in the case could not undermine that work by arguing Detective Liu was wrong. It is in these small details and matters of routine—both symbolic and technical—that we see the application of high and low police work in the sexual assault trial. Low police work consisted of the routinization of policing bureaucracy, while high policing unfolded in consolidating the authority of the police witness in the sexual assault trial.

A Version of the Events: State v. Lee

The defense's strategy in *State v. Kelvin Lee* was mainly to discredit the victim-witness, Tamee North, accusing her of lying that Kelvin Lee had threatened her at gunpoint and attempted to sexually assault her. The defense argued that the former couple merely had an antagonistic relationship and Tamee North's accusations were another instance of her vindictive and angry disposition. When questioned directly on the stand about the hundreds of aggressive and demeaning texts messages he had sent to Ms. North, Mr. Lee argued that they were jokes and that Ms. North had a crass sense of humor. Thus, he argued he was simply speaking to her in the way she liked to be addressed and that the prosecution had mistakenly identified his texts as threatening. In a previous article, we analyzed the lawyers' use of the text-messaging transcripts of the conversations between Tamee North and Kelvin Lee at length (Hlavka and Mulla 2018). In this case, police expertise was used to recover the texts from the phones and to interpret the meanings of the text messages:

> The detective methodically read the texts into the record with little variance in tone or inflection, including jarring descriptions of sexualized threats and profanity. He also explained his, "experience in dealing with text messages and phone calls and conversations that deal with street language," which he thought assisted the investigation, "given [my] insight into what things mean." (Hlavka and Mulla 2018, 424)

In our analysis of this sequence of events at trial, we concluded that the detective's tone sanitized the messages sent by Mr. Lee to Ms. North while also marking urban and Black colloquial forms of speech as non-normative and requiring translation (Hlavka and Mulla 2018, 425). The prosecutor, again, reinforced the detective's expertise by asking him: "Could you translate that for us into more normal parlance, please?" By designating the police as the authority to translate witness speech into "more normal parlance," the prosecution continued to imbue the police with credibility not simply as fact witnesses but as cultural connoisseurs.

As with *State v. Lopez*, the authority of the police narrative was reinforced by the gatekeeping mechanism of report writing and functioned in several ways. Police training and protocol created an official artifact charged with symbolic status that often superseded the testimony of other witnesses. However, the report also functioned as a possible critical limitation in trial, dependent on whose narrative and whose voice attorneys decided should predominate. In *State v. Lee* for example, Tamee North testified on direct examination that, after reporting the attempted sexual assault to the police, they "sent [her] to the hospital."

PROSECUTOR: When did you go to the hospital?
MS. NORTH: Um, they sent me to the hospital.

PROSECUTOR: Who?

Ms. NORTH: The police did.

PROSECUTOR: Did they take you to the hospital?

Ms. NORTH: No.

PROSECUTOR: They just sent you to the hospital?

Ms. NORTH: Yes.

PROSECUTOR: Okay. Which hospital did you go to?

Ms. NORTH: St. Ann's.

PROSECUTOR: And how come you went to St. Ann's Hospital?

Ms. NORTH: Because I had scratches, scratches on me. I don't know.
They sent me. They told me to go in.

PROSECUTOR: And where were the scratches?

Ms. NORTH: On my neck, on the back part of my neck, on my chest.

PROSECUTOR: And how did you get those?

Ms. NORTH: Mr. Lee aggressively handling me.

PROSECUTOR: How long do you think you were at the hospital?

Ms. NORTH: Not that long. I'm not sure. It was late. Not that long.

PROSECUTOR: What did they do at the hospital?

Ms. NORTH: They didn't do anything. They just checked me just to see
if I was okay.

PROSECUTOR: Did you go to any other hospitals?

Ms. NORTH: No, ma'am.

PROSECUTOR: Did they take any sort of swabs or anything of your
body?

Ms. NORTH: No. I told them they didn't need to. The police sent
me to the hospital, and I wasn't sure why. I guess it was part of the
procedure. But when I got there, I didn't need any type of help. They
offered me Advil or Ibuprofen.

During this period of testimony, Ms. North appeared slightly uncertain
as the prosecutor inquired about her experience at the hospital: Which
hospital? Who sent her? How did she get there? What procedures took
place? Tamee North explained what happened to the best of her ability,
even when defense cross-examined her on the same subject:

DEFENSE: Now, you said you were then—you drove yourself to the
hospital?

Ms. North: No, I didn't.

Defense: Okay, you were asked did the police take you to the hospital and you said no.

Ms. North: They didn't take me, but I didn't drive myself either.

Defense: In fact, one of the officers took you to the hospital, correct?

Ms. North: No.

Defense: That would be inaccurate?

Ms. North: No. They never took me to the hospital. They drove there behind me but they never took me.

Both the prosecution and defense had the police reports in hand, knowing that Ms. North's account about being taken to the hospital was in direct conflict with the detective's written report. The detective subsequently testified to a different version of events.

Defense: Now, you actually drove her over to the Sexual Assault Treatment Center?

Detective: Yes, I did.

Defense: And where is the Sexual Assault Treatment Center?

Detective: It's located at 945 North 12th Street.

Defense: Mt. Sinai?

Detective: Correct.

Defense: Not St. Ann's, correct?

Detective: Correct. It's Mt. Sinai.

Defense: You didn't follow her or anything? You actually drove her there?

Detective: Yes, I did.

Defense: Part of that is to protect possible evidence and stuff, correct?

Detective: Correct.

In his testimony, the detective explained that he had driven Ms. North himself and that they had gone to Mt. Sinai Hospital, not to St. Ann's. The victim-witnesses testimony, albeit repetitively consistent and clear, was in direct conflict with that of the responding detective. Who's account was more credible? Did the detective make a mistake in his report? Did he fail to follow police procedure and thus intentionally misrepresent the events, or did he really drive Ms. North to Mt. Sinai that night? No matter, the defense attorney returned to this inconsistency in his closing argument, dismissively voicing Tamee North's testimony himself:

> And then when she testified here, too: "The officer never took me. They took me to St. Ann's. I didn't go to St. Ann's with the officers." No? Well, she didn't go to St. Ann's. She went to Mt. Sinai.

These sorts of juxtapositions between lay and police witnesses during sexual assault trials uniquely situated the victim-witness's "powers of recollection" and "powers of observation" as deficient. The defense drew further attention to some potential errors in policing protocol. As with *State v. Lopez*, defense raised the specter of contamination of witness accounts because Ms. North was not isolated from others prior to the detective's arrival at the scene. Both of Ms. North's siblings were witnesses in the trial, and the defense was particularly suspicious that Tamee had time to coach her brother and sister of her version of events, contrary to their testimony that they were consoling their sobbing, fearful sister:

> DETECTIVE: When I got there, she was in her residence.
> DEFENSE: Okay. And who else was in the residence?
> DETECTIVE: I believe it was her brother and her sister.
> DEFENSE: So, they were not kept separate? They were all in the residence together?
> DETECTIVE: I believe so.

The defense attorney returned to this in his closing arguments, saying:

> They left them out together for an hour, almost two hours, left her sister and her up in the house and then they interviewed her, you know. So, I'm not sure how good the police practice is but again, it goes to whole credibility and strength of the state's case here and you have to look at that.

While these small details in the case were not independently compelling, we observed that, together, the inconsistent testimony between the victim-witness and the detective, the prosecution's own inquisition of official police reports, and the defense's condemnation of police practices likely contributed to the jury's lingering reasonable doubt and not-guilty verdict in the case.

The Cunning of Detective Work

The impact that police testimony made on sexual assault trials has thus far been tied to how attorneys represented routine police work. Prosecutors tied officer testimony to cultural status and highlighted consistencies between written reports and witness testimony. Distinctions between uniformed officers and plainclothes detectives aligned around axes of gender. As previously mentioned, most uniformed testifying officers were men, while more women occupied the ranks of plainclothes officers and sensitive crimes detectives. Sartorial approaches to plainclothes varied by gender presentation as well. While all the uniformed officers wore duty belts and prominently displayed their holstered sidearm, most of the men in plainclothes similarly wore Kevlar vests over their button-down shirts and ties to court. Even in the summer heat, we observed one officer who testified while wearing his vest. Another casually hung his vest on a vacant chair at the prosecutor's desk as he walked to the witness stand. In this way, the masculine-identified police officers gestured toward familiarity with the proceedings while projecting the militarized masculinity of policing.

Unlike the men, the women plainclothes officers we observed did not sport Kevlar vests. They often wore suit pants and button-down shirts either under blazers or sweater vests. The detectives within the Sensitive Crimes Unit were practiced witnesses, often taking the role of the officer of the court, seated next to the prosecutor, and aiding in the trial. The revelations of detective work, like those of the police officer, were rooted in routine as well as observation of small, but deeply consequential, details. When testifying, sensitive crimes detectives also weighed in as both fact and expert witnesses and performed the dual labors of low and high policing. While popular imagination suggests that detective work leads to the dramatic recovery of material evidence or tear-filled confessions, investigations constituted a dogged and focused approach to details and documentation. The revelations of these consequential minutiae sometimes produced striking responses from the jury and the gallery and became turning points in cases like *State v. Rafferty*.

Now age 23, Jason Rafferty was charged with repeated sexual assault of a child over a period of years. Nicole, the victim in the case, had been between six and eight, while Jason Rafferty had been 13 when the assaults began. Nicole was a young Black girl, and the Rafferty family was white. Throughout the trial, defense counsel tried to portray Nicole as "precocious," though the basis of this characterization seemed thin. The assaults occurred over several summers when Jason and his sister visited their grandparents. Just before starting the eighth grade, Nicole finally disclosed the sexual abuse to her aunt. Now age 16, Nicole testified that Jason Rafferty sexually assaulted her in the grandparents' home and in their backyard playhouse. The state called only three witnesses to the stand, subject to rebuttal witnesses: Nicole, her aunt, and the lead sensitive crimes investigator, Detective Dempsey. Defense counsel called the Rafferty family to testify, including Jason's sister Miley, his mother, and grandparents. During the trial, most of the family was sequestered and sat on the hallway benches just outside the courtroom, occasionally rolling their eyes or staring down the prosecutor when she left the courtroom during breaks. Court staff also observed Jason's mother peering through the small, tinted, rectangle window in the courtroom door during testimony. The judge admonished her on the record: "[I]f you were in fact listening in the crack of the door, that was a violation of the Court's order and really very much not appreciated." The defense requested that Jason Rafferty's family be allowed into the courtroom following their own testimonies, but the prosecutor objected, arguing that she intended to "put on a rebuttal case" and may later call on those witnesses. The judge ordered that the sequestration order remain in place for the duration of the evidentiary phase of the trial.

Following Nicole's testimony, the prosecution called Detective Dempsey to the stand. When asked by the prosecutor, Dempsey told the court that she was a police officer with the city of Milwaukee for more than 22 years, 14 of which had been in the Sensitive Crimes Division. She described her training and experience, noting the seminars she had taken and specialty courses for interviewing children and youth. The prosecutor asked her to explain some of the "special challenges" in the investigation of sensitive crimes cases:

> Some are with sexual assaults. It's extremely hard for some people to talk about things that have happened to them, so getting that information. A lot of the things we deal with are delayed reports. Then, you know, you don't have all the immediate information that comes out when something is disclosed, right away. Collection of evidence. Also, if it's delayed, there's not a lot of physical evidence, so, working around those issues.

Detective Dempsey shifted back and forth between fact and expert witness with ease, revealing not only her experience with investigating sexual assault cases but also her accumulated expertise in the more common characteristics of victim behavior and disclosure that stood contrary to everyday "common sense." She slipped in details about delayed disclosure and lack of forensic and material evidence even though the prosecutor did not directly ask about these details. Detective Dempsey continued to tell the court the facts of her investigation, at times referencing initial reports from her interview with Nicole. Like the police officers in the previous sections, she presented the reports point by point: the days and times she spoke with witnesses, scene investigations, and evidence collected. Detective Dempsey read from her notes her record of witness demeanor. When asked to describe her practice for interviewing people, including Nicole, she said they were always conducted in private because "I don't like outside influences when I interview."

PROSECUTOR: In your training and your experience, are there common threads or reasons why there seems to be, commonly a delay in child sexual abuse cases, in the reporting of them?

DETECTIVE: Absolutely. Depends on the age of the child, and in this case people—some don't know it's wrong. It's common, you know. It's just something they know. Threats that if you tell, something could happen to you, of fear of threats, just in their own mind they think that something will help if they tell. Some people don't believe they'll be believed. Some people think if they didn't tell right away, that no one will believe them now because so much time has gone by. Some people don't want to make waves in their family, or they don't want the attention on them, or they just don't want to have to deal with it.

. . .

PROSECUTOR: Can you explain why it is a challenge in child sexual abuse investigations to identify when something happened?

DETECTIVE: It's very difficult to get exact times and location because young children don't have a concept of dates and times. They— [pause.] That's why we try narrowing that down—age or certain holidays, things that will stand out to them like first grade. What were you doing during that time frame? Or when did something happen to you? What grade were you in? How old are you? Where were you living at the time?

Tasked with presenting trauma from the past, Nicole's testimony on the stand preceded Detective Dempsey's; it was tender and complicated and filled with precarity. Her mother had been addicted to drugs, so Nicole was sent to live with her aunt. She had to share her memories in front of a room filled with strangers. She detailed three separate sexual assault incidents, painfully struggling to explain why she did not tell someone when she was six or eight. The Rafferty grandparents testified later in the trial that she was a sweet but precocious child who often longed for attention. This was the first use of the term by a witness during the trial. The description of a "precocious" child caught our ear given that, at the time of the abuse, Nicole was no more than eight years old. The term recalled the adultification trends we discuss in the introduction, in which white adults often ascribe more adult-like characteristics to Black girls (Epstein, Blake, and González 2014). In this case, Detective Dempsey was able to do for Nicole what the prosecutor tried to do for Maya in chapter 2—explain the difficulties of children's memories, especially crucial legal storytelling elements like days, times, and locations. Detective Dempsey not only provided the mundane "facts" of police reports and proceduralism but also spoke of the dedication and expertise of sensitive crimes work. The smooth shift from fact witness to expert witness followed from objective accounts of reports filed and evidence collected to a matter-of-fact telling of professional opinions marked by the officer's inherent reliability and cultural capital.

After the prosecution had called all its witnesses, defense counsel called Miley Rafferty, Jason's sister, to testify. Miley began by stating that the sexual assault accusations against her brother were untrue. During cross-examination, the prosecutor asked Miley a series of questions about how Detective Dempsey made more than several attempts to interview her. Taking the stand directly after Miley, Detective Dempsey explained that she left a business card for Miley at her home with a note instructing her to call the police at her earliest convenience. The business card carried Detective Dempsey's credentials: DETECTIVE, SENSITIVE CRIMES UNIT, MILWAUKEE POLICE DEPARTMENT. On the stand, Miley testified that she had received a note from Detective Dempsey instructing her to call about the incident involving "Jason and the neighbor girl, Nicole." When the prosecutor returned to her seat, Detective Dempsey immediately leaned over and whispered something in her ear.

Testimony continued in the case, including that of the defendant. Later in the day, the prosecutor recalled Detective Dempsey to the stand as a rebuttal witness. In a kind of "gotcha moment" rarely seen during trials, the detective described the process by which she contacted Miley Rafferty for an interview:

PROSECUTOR: Your report indicated that you then asked Miley if she knew why you needed to talk to her that day?

DETECTIVE: That is correct.

PROSECUTOR: And is that an accurate verbatim way that you asked her or initiated the next part of the conversation?

DETECTIVE: I'm not sure if it was verbatim, but I usually ask if they know why I'm talking to them.

PROSECUTOR: And what did she say to you at the at time?

DETECTIVE: I believe she said, asked if it was regarding her brother "messing" with the girl who lived next door when she was at her grandparents.

PROSECUTOR: Up to that point in time, had you spoken to any member of Miley Rafferty's family and said that it related to Jason?

DETECTIVE: Not at all.

PROSECUTOR: At any point in time up to that day, had you spoken to any member of the Rafferty family and told them that it had something to do with Jason "messing" with somebody?

DETECTIVE: No. . . .

PROSECUTOR: Did you inquire about how she came up with that as
  what she thought you were there about?

DETECTIVE: Yes. I asked her where she heard that.

PROSECUTOR: And what did she say?

DETECTIVE: Someone in her family told her that. . . . She doesn't
  remember [who].

The jury's demeanor immediately shifted during Detective Dempsey's rebuttal testimony. Eyes darted from the defendant to the detective and back again. The gallery was silent, and the Rafferty family members who were present stopped whispering to each other. As she continued, Detective Dempsey explained that, according to police protocol, she never revealed details of an investigation on her cards or in phone messages. At the time she contacted her, Detective Dempsey had not yet spoken with any of the family members, so there was no way for Miley to have known the purpose behind Dempsey's contact.

At the end of the evidentiary phase of the trial, the judge allowed the Rafferty family to be seated in the gallery for closing arguments. The defendant's mother, her partner, and sister Miley huddled together on the courtroom benches. Jason's grandfather sat directly behind us in court as we were taking notes. During her closing arguments, the prosecutor emphasized that Detective Dempsey's testimony clearly impeached Miley Rafferty, revealing the lies and inconsistencies in her story and cementing the fact of Jason Rafferty's guilt:

[Miley's story] is a complete fabrication because Detective Dempsey did not and would not ever give that kind of information out. But Mr. Rafferty himself said that. . . . So how would Miley know why the police might be interested in talking to them? It's because just like Nicole said, she saw what happened. She knows that Jason was messing with Nicole in the playhouse, and that's why she said it. It's the only possible explanation for coming up on her own with that constellation of facts, and it is also the only reason why Miley went so far with us yesterday to try to get us to believe something else. And, ladies and gentlemen, that gives you more than just the word of Miley. That gives you corroboration.

Following the prosecutor's revelation, Grandfather Rafferty involuntarily drew in a sharp breath and exclaimed in shock, "Oh my God!" He did not return for the guilty verdict later that day or for sentencing several months later. In the final moments of the trial, he, too, seemed convinced by the detective's testimony.

Routinized investigation work could be the backbone to sexual assault cases, but many of the consequential details also rested in meticulous observations and reporting practices. In the case of *State v. Cook* for example, Detective Tracy testified to a vital piece of information that would have otherwise disappeared from evidence. The victim-witness in the case, L'umoya Smith, had escaped from two assailants at a crime scene and fled to a local motel late at night. Screaming to be let into the motel for safety, she was turned away by the motel clerk. Detective Tracy had visited the motel, viewed the surveillance footage of L'umoya Smith seeking assistance outside the motel doors, and noted her disheveled appearance, including details about her unbuttoned pants and how her belt hung freely unbuckled from the loops. Detective Tracy requested a copy of the surveillance video that night, but when she returned to retrieve the videotape a few days later, the motel workers claimed to have mistakenly taped over the footage. Detective Tracy had astutely documented her initial viewing of the video, which, along with her courtroom testimony, substituted for the original technological surveillance. The videotaped evidence that provided corroboration of L'umoya Smith's whereabouts and assault that night no longer existed, but through testimony, the police detective herself functioned as the victim-witness's data double, narrating what she had seen on the now-erased video surveillance.

When Police Are on Trial

Even in the face of erroneous investigation and routine reporting mistakes, the cultural and social status of policing and police work depended on a priori credibility. Police credibility was predicated on the notion that police were following the rules, that is to say, adhering to policies, training, and routines. What happened when police were at the center of sexual assault investigations? Milwaukee police were no strangers to scrutiny and criminal charges, and these cases were explained to us during interviews and through our examination of media archives. We also tracked domestic and sexual assault charges against correctional offi-cers, community volunteer firefighters, and police officers and witnessed a handful of such cases in court during our fieldwork. The specter of police criminality compromised the integrity of sexual assault adjudica-tion. In one case, we watched an officer testify during a sexual assault trial even though he had been recently mired in a complicated internal affairs investigation following his girlfriend's report of domestic violence. Though Internal Affairs ended the investigation without taking disciplin-ary action, the story received significant coverage in the local newspaper. In another example, two other cases we followed involved the testimony of Officer Cruz. Those cases were delayed, and Cruz was eventually removed from both after he was charged with criminal stalking. Another officer had to testify in his place, and the proceedings were delayed for all parties involved in the case. The specter of the criminal police officer created many complications for sexual assault prosecutions.

We offer *State v. Michael Vagnini* as an example of police misconduct and as a critical juxtaposition to the narrative of police officers detailed at the beginning of this chapter. These descriptions are presented as bookends to a very complicated chronicle of policing that is historically and locally rich. Police are a powerful appendage of the state in their everyday presence and functioning. Legal subjectivity emerges from local history, cultural norms, and shared frameworks of understanding (Balkin 1993, 107). The state can also be understood as a "duplicitous artifice built atop prior forms of moral order" (J. Martin 2018, 135). Sex-ual assault adjudication exists squarely within such questions of moral order through the regulation of sexuality and violence. While Martin (2018, 136) is careful to separate the law and police as "radically different ways of conceptualizing state order," the police officer *at* trial and *on* trial presents an opportunity to observe how the subject of policing might also be the subject of law, as we have marked throughout this chapter.

The case against Officer Michael Vagnini[3] and several other officers in the Milwaukee Police Department drew national media attention[4] and public scrutiny. Officer Vagnini was initially brought to court with 25 charges, including multiple charges of 2nd, 3rd, and 4th degree sexual as-sault, misconduct while in office, and illegal cavity searches. Vagnini's victims were dozens of Black men in Milwaukee, violated during routine arrests and stop-and-frisk procedures on multiple occasions. The *Mil-*

waukee Journal Sentinel reported on the prosecutor assigned to the case: "She also did not believe Vagnini targeted suspects by race, but that their degradation was exacerbated by the fact that they were Black and he was white" (Vielmetti, *Milwaukee Journal Sentinel*, June 21, 2013). Vagnini pled guilty and no contest to four counts of misconduct in office and four counts of illegal cavity searches and was sentenced to 26 months in prison. The City of Milwaukee reached a $5 million civil settlement with 74 victims in 2015 (Milwaukee Journal Sentinel, January 19, 2016). A federal jury also awarded $1.99 million in damages to one of his victims in a 2016 trial (*Milwaukee Journal Sentinel*, December 6, 2016). As of December 2020, the case was still not fully resolved, and more victims had come forward over time.

On the day of the defendant's sentencing, dozens of uniformed police filled the courtroom gallery to support their fellow officer. On the other side of the courtroom were dozens of victims and their supporters, court victim-witness advocates, and community members. In accordance with the plea agreement, all charges of sexual assault were dismissed. The prosecutor, an assistant district attorney, was joined by the district attorney, and together they argued for the state during sentencing. The ADA bemoaned Officer Vagnini's criminal behavior and the use of sexual humiliation to degrade and violate his victims. She highlighted the many times that Vagnini had used past police reports in order to manipulate his victims. She argued that he used his power and privileged status as an officer of the law to circumvent the law. Her voice was loud and forceful as it filled the courtroom:

> He used what I believe, based on everything that we have seen, a sort of ends-justifies-the-means analysis. And what is particularly tragic in this case is that Mr. Vagnini, in so many ways, is exactly the person that we would want to be the guy protecting and serving this community. I read every single one of those letters from his colleagues and to a person they describe Mr. Vagnini as exceptionally intelligent, as dedicated, as confident, as knowledgeable and as a leader. That is—those are the qualities that we want in a police officer. But those qualities have to be tempered by the clear understanding that when one is a servant, one can't move from confidence into arrogance. One cannot put oneself above the law. And when one is working hard and creatively to solve crime, to stop crime,

to prevent crime, one must still follow those rules. To use the tool of the power of his office to humiliate, to degrade, is wrong. Because when one does not, when one decides that there are some people in our community who don't deserve their constitutional rights to be protected, then we lose credibility. And that's exactly what happened here.

It was standing-room-only. Every single row of the court's gallery behind the defense table was filled with police officers and their partners in support of Vagnini. Other officers crowded near media cameras against the wood-paneled walls of the back courtroom, something the judge would not have allowed under other circumstances. They toed the line of remaining silent during the ADA's statements, the opposition to her arguments audible through deep sighs and tongue clicks, and visible through their emphatic head shakes and numerous eyerolls.

The DA, likely aware of the cameras trained on him, began his portion of the sentencing argument by explaining there was "simply no way to justify what happened here. It's not a case of walking a fine line on some ambiguous Fourth Amendment motion." He said that Vagnini's actions had brought up "images of Abu Ghraib in the City of Milwaukee Police District Station." This powerful rhetorical slight was met with indignant facial expressions from the gallery and more heads shaking back and forth. The DA reflected on race in Milwaukee, arguing that Officer Vagnini targeted vulnerable Black men, and whether he did so intentionally or not, he used the "power that white has over Black, historically."

When he asserted that Vagnini had not only engaged in misconduct in public office, "but as this court knows from having listened to these men, he sexually abused these men," a communal hiss permeated the gallery. Neither the judge nor the sheriff's deputies commented on the behavior of the officers in the gallery, again allowing behavior that had earned contempt charges in the past for other courtroom visitors. In this way, the courtroom was again demarcated as the territory of law enforcement. When the DA made a record of how a fellow police officer corroborated the victim's allegations, we observed several officers smirking at each other. The DA revealed that this officer was "called a snitch motherfucker by Michael Vagnini in a text that was sent to him. He also had a bullet placed in his locker at his district station by some . . . unknown hero." Such demonstrations of loyalty are characteristic of a "blue wall of silence" (Skolnick 2002).

In retort, defense counsel argued that Vagnini was only acting as he, and his fellow District 5 officers, were trained to act. We recorded his statements in our field notes during sentencing:

> I don't think Michael Vagnini got up and said I'm gonna break the law. He was told to be aggressive, as aggressive as you can be. We gotta pound down these crime numbers, be proactive. Yes, he violated the Constitution, but we all bear the responsibility for letting this happen and go on for so long, for two years. Nobody did anything about it! How come the system didn't pull him aside and say, "You can't be doing that?" No, the supervisor said you're gonna be the head of the train. You're number one. You're doing such a fantastic job, you're at the head of the train. I can see what he did was wrong, but he's not the only one. He's left holding the bag. Shame on other people, those watching over his conduct and reviewing his reports. Why isn't someone saying, "You can't do this, it's illegal?"

Two different accounts of policing emerged from the arguments made by the state and by the defense. The state argued that Vagnini's actions undermined the foundational institution of policing. Drawing on images of Abu Ghraib, the prosecutors referenced racialized torture, invoking the narrative of "one bad apple" that endangered the department's respect and the community's trust. The one-bad-apple refrain was a familiar one. It condemned individual officers while maintaining the collective integrity of the police force.[5] According to the state, Vagnini's misconduct constituted an assault on the integrity of the very foundation of policing. The defense, by contrast, vehemently argued that Vagnini was only one officer amid a culture of corruption. Vagnini, in his attorney's words, was "left holding the bag" for all the other officers doing the same illegal searches, and the police command had let him get away with his behavior because it was effective.

Vagnini's sentencing took place early on during our fieldwork in the courts. As mentioned, civil cases against District 5 officers continued long after Vagnini's sentencing, and attorneys often referenced previous cases of Milwaukee police being sued decades earlier for illegal cavity searches. Meanwhile, we continued to observe officers in court—not as witnesses but as defendants charged with sexual assault, stalking and harassment, and domestic violence. Three sexual assault trials were delayed because suspended police officers could no longer participate. Perhaps this accounts for why, even in the most egregious cases of police misconduct, prosecutors highlighted only the officer's individual faults rather than indicting a system upon which they also heavily relied.

Conclusion: The Role of Police in Sexual Assault Adjudication

We began this chapter with a description of law enforcement officers as they traversed the corridors, courtrooms, and offices of the Courthouse Complex. They managed the gallery, chatted with prosecutors before they testified, and moved in-custody defendants through the hallways, marching them past civilians. The chapter continued with descriptions of police officer testimony in sexual assault trials, themselves subject to scrutiny before juries. These distinct modes of spectacle deepen the contrast between civilians and police: on one side, the forced exposure of men and women in custody as compared to the technocratic performance of police expertise before the courts. The chapter ended by presenting the officer as defendant, charged with dozens of sexual assaults and illegal body cavity searches. A "blue wall" was discursively active through the testimony, but a literal wall was formed in the courtroom the day of Vagnini's sentencing when dozens of mostly white, male police officers filed into court in a mass display of solidarity and bravado. With local media cameras trained on the spectacle, one of the victims sitting in the gallery next to us exclaimed, "Oh boy, look at this now."

These bookends illustrate how the cultural imaginary of the police is variably experienced, reproduced, and reconfigured both in Milwaukee and across the country, depending on one's race, class, and gender (Bell 2017; Desmond, Papachristos, and Kirk 2016; Kirk and Matsueda 2011; Rios 2011; Soss and Weaver 2017). These scenes of violation, spectacle, and conflicting testimony also provide additional context to chapter 1 on jury selection. There are many reasons why attorneys and judges routinely ask Milwaukee County jurors whether they are related to, personally know, or have formed opinions about police officers and other criminal justice agents. Experiences of police harassment, humiliation, and disbelief are certainly not out of the ordinary for sexual assault victims, and as this chapter has shown, the testimony of officers and victims can conflict. The trauma of police reporting and interviewing, however, is rarely revealed in court, because those cases seldom make it to trial. In the introduction to this book, we wrote about *State v. Below*, the highly publicized 2011 case in which uniformed police officers refused to take seriously the sexual assault allegations of nine different women of color (*Milwaukee Journal Sentinel*, March 9, 2011). Many of the victims accused the police of grave misconduct in their cases, and while one officer was suspended for failing to investigate, none of the others were found responsible. Such histories of impunity, gatekeeping, and professional failure circulate through local media and gossip, but the picture of professional virtue presented at trial is one that subordinated these contexts for the sake of the trial's efficacies.

Police testimony often emphasized the routine nature of everyday police work such as interviewing, report writing, and the use of various forms. The repetition of these procedures gave police testimony its consistency. The report was not simply a "factual" exhibit. Rather, it epitomized the officer's discretionary decision-making as he controlled what details were credible enough to make it into the official report. As officers testified, they not only revealed the routine measures taken in a case but also mediated the data double of the victim-witness. Detectives did not startle juries and observers with dramatic discoveries or confessions but instead offered subtle revelations of details that undermined one narrative while reinforcing another. A hanging belt, unbuttoned trousers, or a slip of the tongue were opportunities for reporting and testimony. These subtle observations magnified perceptions of police officers and detectives as embodying enhanced "powers of recollection" and "powers of observation." At times, these dual powers conflicted with the testimony of other witnesses—not because theirs was the truth but because of the cultural and social capital attached to them despite long histories of abuses. Indeed, as the prosecutor who opened this chapter stated, the police "have the case in their hands." The next two chapters focus on additional corroborating witnesses: the sexual assault nurse examiner and the forensic scientist. Such witnesses spend a great deal of their testimony explaining the absence and the fragility of material evidence to juries, albeit in very distinct ways.

4

Nursing Sexual Violence from the Stand

Victimized and Victimizing Bodies

I think most of my [patients] are frustrated if I don't see any trauma. And, I try to explain to them that's normal. That's typically what we see. That doesn't mean something didn't happen to you. There's just nothing here right now. And I think that's hard to deal with when you feel like you've been violated. Especially if they're having pain of any kind. It's like, "Wait a minute. I'm hurting. There's got to be something there. Please tell me there's something to justify my story." And unfortunately, most of the time there's not.
—Katia, a sexual assault nurse examiner

This chapter traces the labor performed by sexual assault nurse examiners, or SANEs, specifically how their clinical expertise is drawn into the courtroom. In the courtroom, the nurse emerged as a complicated central witness called to corroborate victims' narratives. In many of our conversations with nurses, they described various points of conflation of the medical exam with evidence collection, and of evidence collection with courtroom testimony. Some sexual assault nurses focused on their roles as "objective evidence collectors," many assumed that testifying in court was commonplace, and their patients often associated forensic evidence with the increased likelihood of courtroom conviction. As Katia explains to us in the epigraph above, it is common not to find any evidence of specific injury or to locate DNA during a sexual assault forensic examination. The use of technocratic accounts to corroborate the truthfulness of victims' bodies and minds, however, persisted in both the sexual assault trial and the medical examination (Das 2007). One of the primary functions of the exam was to evidence sexual assault in allegedly technical and scientific criteria (Feldberg 1997). Most often called as a witness for the prosecution, the nurse was interpellated into the trial to produce the dialectical tension between narrativized experience and material objectivity—even when no such evidence materialized. Like the police officer before her, the SANE, too, was charged with performing credibility and objectivity. She was asked to focus on protocols and procedures, evidence collection, and verification of the victim report. In contrast with the hyper-masculinized uniformed officers or the conspicuously armed plainclothes detectives discussed in chapter 3, the forensic nurse was part of a historically feminized field of work (E. Martin 1991). Whereas police often appeared in uniform, nurses never testified in scrubs. Instead, they wore civilian clothes in the business-casual style, often opting for neat cardigans and blouses rather than business suits. The forensic nurse appeared in trial as the expert witness most closely allied with the victim-witness, and defense attorneys accused nurses of being biased based on their demeanor and caregiver roles.

Scholars such as Patricia Yancey Martin (2005), Rose Corrigan (2013a), Sameena Mulla (2014), and others have documented the growth of SANE programs and protocols across the United States. In response to identified gaps in patient care, SANE nurses receive specialized training in trauma and rape, evidence collection techniques, and court testimony preparation. Nurses often portrayed the forensic examination as an intimate encounter requiring sensitivity and discretion. In our interviews with 22 nurses, they collectively described how they met the medical, psychological, and forensic needs of their patients while maintaining their commitments to what the criminal justice system required. Such needs often included emotional support and advocacy, diagnostic testing, vaccinations, blood and urine testing, and STD screenings along with forensic examinations, including body maps, documentation, evidence collection, and forensic photography. From the stand, nurses spoke about their interactions with the victim as documented in reports explaining the evidence collected, documented injuries, care protocols, and victim statements and demeanor. SANEs downplayed or omitted the invasiveness, the time commitment, and the pain that might accompany the exam. Rather, testimony tended to focus solely on genital anatomy lessons and the presence or absence of forensic evidence and injury. As fact witness, the SANE could be asked to read what she had written in her medical report, including the victim's emotional state and reported details of the assault. Prosecutors had to tread lightly when eliciting information about the patients' affective states during medical examinations. Yet, much like the role police witnesses played in chapter 3, there was considerable slippage between the nurse as fact and expert witness.

While research shows that the SANE's involvement in adjudication is important, it is unclear how her testimony functions in front of judges and juries. In fact, the impact of medicolegal evidence on case outcomes is the subject of much ongoing research (Sommers and Baskin 2011; Campbell et al. 2009). Some scholars find that it is a significant predictor of case progression through the criminal justice system (Campbell et al. 2009), while others find that medicolegal evidence is a weak predictor of trial outcomes (Nugent-Borakove et al. 2006; Sommers and Baskin 2011; Du Mont and White 2007). While outcomes are one way of understanding the impact of forensic evidence and expert testimony in trials, our ethnographic research treated the court as a site that produced and solidified much more than verdicts alone. Observing SANE nurses testify invited us to analyze how the process and reproduction of cultural norms of sexual violence were disciplined through the "scientific."

When forms of evidence are both imagined and foundational, as we analyze in chapter 1, juries come to expect them at trial. Prosecutors can use the increasing expectation for forensic evidence as one of many justifications for avoiding rape trials. As Rose Corrigan (2013b) shows, the forensic exam can operate as a "trial by ordeal," acting as a "proxy" for a victim's truthfulness and commitment to the criminal justice system. When the forensic examination itself is cast as trial by ordeal, even exams that yield no conclusive evidence serve an essential purpose. Indeed, prosecutors in our study often persuasively suggested victims' resolve by asking jurors during closing statements, "Why would she go through such a harrowing ordeal if she were lying?" Such demonstratable commitment simultaneously casts suspicion on those rape victims who decide not to seek medical care or to participate in a forensic examination. Sociologist Andrea Quinlan's (2017, 12) historical study shows that the sexual assault examination is "not a neutral object" and "reflects and maintains the histories and politics of the worlds of which it is part." Together, Corrigan's and Quinlan's works help to explain why forensic nurses are called to the stand to testify about the absence of evidence more often than its presence.

Among the 34 trials we observed, forensic nurses were called as witnesses in only nine cases. Injuries and DNA were present in only a handful. Recall the incidence data laid out in the introduction of this book: while approximately 1,000 patients undergo a sexual assault forensic examination at the Sexual Assault Treatment Center in Milwaukee Country every year, most of these cases do not advance to trial. For most nurses, then, the courtroom and what occurs there is largely experienced as anticipatory. Testifying is an exercise that is imagined during the clinical encounter but rarely comes to fruition (Mulla 2014). One nurse we interviewed explained:

> When people are interviewed [for this job], they absolutely think like we go to court every month or something like that. And, then when they hear you can work this job for five years and never go to court, that seems a little shocking to most people.

Prosecutors generally found nurses to be credible witnesses at trial due to their extensive experience, expertise, and ability to educate the jury about issues related to anatomy and sexual violence. Defense attorneys, by contrast, often cross-examined nurses based on their qualifications, competence, quality of evidence, and assumed bias toward victims of sexual assault. One defense attorney we spoke with explicitly stated that "they [nurses] are too pro-victim and not pro–getting to the truth of the matter." This style of defense cross-examination was largely unobserved with police, detectives, or crime lab witnesses. As a highly gendered form of labor, the professional standing of nurses is itself culturally specific (Mulla 2014). Thus, we assert that the feminization of the field and cultural assumptions about sexual assault nursing motivated defense attorneys to portray nurses as overly subjective and attached to the victim. When SANEs testified on the stand, prosecutors often employed a tactic of erasing the nurse's care for her patient, whereas defense counsel frequently challenged nurse's reports of the victim-witness's emotional state as biased or as hearsay.

To evacuate their testimony of emotionally charged content, SANEs often sanitized sexual assault, portraying a standardized and sterilized victimized body. This modality may be considered an extension of the ways in which nurses undertake "dirty work" (Hughes 1958), in which nurses are considered abject figures because of their intimacy with pathologized and contaminated bodies, as well as their subordinated place in the hierarchy of medicine. Prosecutors required nurses to demonstrate their desensitization to blood, semen, and other fluids, as well as their ease with discussing sex and anatomy—all ways in which nurses could perform detachment and impartiality. Nurses achieved sanitization of bodies and sexual violence through the routinization of the sexual assault exam itself. These sterile courtroom descriptions stood in contrast with the way nurses described the personalized nature of their nursing care work in our interviews with them. On the stand, SANEs often spoke in terms that erased the specificity of a patient's body and discussed anatomy and reproductive health using language that reproduced a universalized heteronormative reproductive history. It is significant that the victim-witnesses' bodies required this expert interpretation while the victimizing body was neither medicalized nor explained on the stand outside of a few enterprising defense attorneys (as discussed below in this chapter). This finding is attributable to the symbolic representation of the sexed body, in particular the anatomy of the vagina, as challenging and "taboo"—a topic of such conceptual absence and difficulty such that it leads to public ignorance and misunderstanding (Braun and Wilkinson 2001). In contrast, masculinized genital anatomy was portrayed as self-evident and knowable, its specificities introduced to the court through lay witnesses who lacked medical training or expertise.

In this chapter, we trace how the sexual assault nurse deployed medicolegal imaginaries and knowledge to construct the raped body by relying on clinical practices informed by and transported into the legal realm. We contrast this with the ways in which knowledge about the victimizing body was drawn into the adjudicative process. In both cases, heteronormative frameworks infused cultural norms as nurses testified to the resilience of the female body while signaling the fragility of forensic evidence. There are a number of cases in this chapter involving very young Black victim-witnesses. The reliance on SANE nurses in these particular cases can perhaps be accounted for by the inscrutability of Black girlhood and the young bodies of Black girls. The authority of whiteness as embodied by forensic nurses rendering Black girls' suffering bodies legible to the court suggests the racial regimes of producing knowledge of sexual violence.

Documenting Harm: Between Care and Law

In the United States, the *nomos* of sexual violence anticipates many professional roles and medicolegal interventions converging to respond to sexual assault (Hlavka and Mulla 2020; Mulla 2014; Quinlan 2017). The role of SANE nurses in producing evidence and participating in the legal process is an emergent field of study (Du Mont and Parnis 2003; Maier 2012), and as Rees (2015, 141) explains, "medical practitioners who are involved in the post-rape assault intervention . . . find themselves in the peculiar position of being required to meet the normative standards of both medicine and law." It is always worth remembering that, in the United States, nurses are prohibited from making diagnoses or prescribing medication (with the exception of nurse practitioners). Nursing care intervention, then, is not technically therapeutic in the sense that medical intervention is deemed therapeutic (Dougherty and Tripp-Reimer 1985). Nurses are often dubbed adjuncts to medical professionals, and whereas doctors participate in therapeutic intervention, nurses carry out standing orders, assessing and advocating for patient health and well-being (Dougherty and Tripp-Reimer 1985). All medications that were dispensed by SANE nurses, for example, were issued based on orders from a physician who took a supervisory role in absentia even as nurses undertook the daily labors of responding to sexual assault patients (Mulla 2014). A sense of this peculiar position was exposed in our ethnographic work as well. Most of the 22 sexual assault nurse examiners interviewed for this project defined their role as one that straddled healing work and trauma response and of being a "neutral medical professional and collector of forensic evidence." More experienced forensic nurses said that newly trained SANEs had similar expectations to victim-patients about the role of DNA in sexual assault cases. They were often shocked to learn both about the infrequency of documentable injury and that testifying in court often focused on explaining the absence of evidence. The primary utility of DNA lay in identifying a suspect. This was generally not at issue in sexual assaults, because most occurred at the hands of a perpetrator known to the victim.

Many forensic nurses we interviewed began their careers in emergency care work or obstetrics, moving into SANE practice following certification. With advanced degrees and extensive training in health care, physical anatomy, physiology of the body, and trauma and sexual assault, nurses utilized the scientific knowledge central to their fields. In the clinical setting, forensic nurses relied on a range of skills to identify, locate, and describe the evidence they recorded. They often focused on the appearance of the evidence with and without visual aids, describing appearance, size, contours, smells, and the presence of pain as an indicator of injury (Larrson and Melinder 2007; Mulla 2014). These techniques relied heavily on expert sensory attunement to locating, recovering, and describing forensic evidence (Mulla 2016). The clinical treatment and investigation of the raped body was also the site of cultural production. The statutory structures that privileged visual forms of evidence also prioritized the SANE's approach to collecting and documenting evidence that transformed the patient's voice and pain into written record (Mulla 2016). Charts, forms, and standards of care are routinized and adapted across the United States. As one SANE reported to us, statewide coordinators trained nurses "with tips . . . and the best ways to put on paper, truths, facts, hearsays, all that kind of stuff. You always have to write everything as if you may be going to court." Legally, of course, sexual assault statutes emphasized the use of force and the presence of injury, so while the law did not explicitly require visual evidence, it compelled the use of images, body diagrams, and mappable pelvises in clinical practice. Rarely did these documents and forms capture the burden of sexual violence. Instead, they sanitized, constricted, and codified embodied evidence in the process of institutional subjectification. Joyce, a forensic nurse we spoke with, underscored this peculiar position of meeting clinical and legal standards:

We train on how to ask [patients] questions because obviously, they're really personal . . . and very invasive when we're talking about sex. And . . . if someone does find an injury on the body, it's important to document them early as far as making sure you have a size, a color, if there's a shape to it, what is the shape, and then asking the patient if they know how they got that. Because sometimes, those are the most powerful things in quotations as far as saying, "That's where he punched me. I thought I was going to die." That statement is better versus just having a circle on a chart. Making sure your documentation is thorough, making sure your assessment is good, making sure that everything is documented that possibly can be as far as not leaving any blanks on the chart, not leaving things undone, if you will.

Leaving "things undone," in fact, was not out of the ordinary. Another experienced SANE revealed that she found errors in every chart she reviewed, including her own: "I wish I would have, or I wish I hadn't put that, or I forgot to answer that question, or it looks like I forgot to answer it because I left something blank. So, I hate those. I mean, I can find an error with all of my charts." In the case of *State v. Logan*, the forensic nurse testified that she did not use a colposcope on her patient, seven-year-old Janelle, during her forensic examination. (A colposcope is a special instrument for visualizing and magnifying speculum examinations.) On cross-examination, however, the defense attorney pointed out to her that she had marked the use of a colposcope in her written report. The nurse responded,

> NURSE: Then that, that must have been my error. I apologize. I should
>   have reviewed and referred to my documentation.
> DEFENSE: But, as far as you know today, that was never used?
> NURSE: No. Now that I look at this, it probably was used. Because if I
>   checked it, then yes, then I probably did use it. I shouldn't say prob-
>   ably. I did.

Only that which is written in the report becomes available as evidence in court, and how it is written is shaped by medical-legal conventions (Trinch 2003; Mulla 2014). In cases where charts and records differed from the forensic nurse's memory, the record was deemed more credible, standing in as a "data double" not only for the victim but also for the forensic nurse (Moore and Singh 2018). Victims might have come to emergency rooms drugged or intoxicated, telling forensic nurses that they could not recall the attack in detail, in which case their narrative was often limited. Nurses described conventions of documentation to justify the clinical transformation of patients' words such as "It hurts. I don't want to" into "Patient declined due to discomfort" or "unable to do speculum exam because of patient's level of discomfort." While these reports might be less easily challenged in court, the changes made to victims' narratives introduced the possibility of challenging victims' testimony on the stand. The reports "neutralized" the client's emotions and her evaluation of her own body, rendering her voice less credible than the nurse's assessment and, at times, less credible than the documents themselves.

Another nurse deliberated on the unpredictability of photography in forensic examinations:

> When there are injuries, I think its huge to see a photograph of it versus a drawing. Then again, I think it's hard for jurors to understand there were no injuries, and you're showing a picture of a perfectly normal, healthy area that doesn't look traumatized, and yet you have a victim saying a lot of stuff happened and they might question why are there no injuries, you know—even though [the nurse said] this is normal, I think there would have been something.

While evidence collection plays a large role in the professional responsibility of forensic nurses, researchers have also demonstrated that the desire to establish oneself as a professional may result in forensic nurses documenting evidence that undermines victims' credibility even as it enhances the nurses' own professional reputation (Corrigan 2013b; Mulla 2014; Rees 2012). In the next section, we explore the authorizing domain of the courtroom and delineate socialization practices, processes of evaluation, and institutionalized ways of seeing and speaking that are transformed into specialized knowledge (Carr 2010, 18).

Anatomy Lessons from the Stand

We open this section with a composite portrait of the sexual assault nurse examiner at trial to demonstrate the routine processes of credentializing nurses on the stand. Just as victim-witnesses were required to convey affects such as sadness and shame, as shown in chapter 2, nurses—much like police officers—had to perform a range of qualities such as expertise, authority, objectivity, and impartiality. Prosecutors first established her education, degrees obtained, training, certifications, and years in clinical practice. "How many sexual assault examinations have you performed?" "What is the peer-review process?" "Are you up to date on your literature and continued training opportunities?"

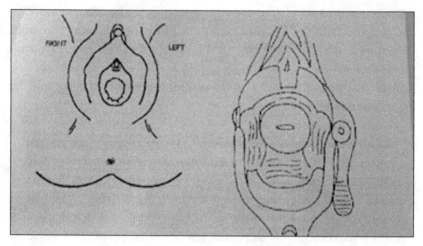

Figure 4.1. Body Map Used as Evidentiary Exhibit. Photograph credit: Sameena Mulla

Gynecology and obstetrics represented one of the most common sets of expertise among nurses. Prosecutors shifted seamlessly from credentializing nurses to anatomy lessons, routinely asking: "What are some explanations for the lack of injury in most examinations?" This question prompted SANEs to perform their expertise by explaining administrative standards, the logics of documents, and customary descriptions of sexed bodies. These explanations often included reproductive narratives about birthing bodies that suggested the deeply held heteronormative values of the *nomos* of sexual violence (Hlavka and Mulla 2020; Mulla 2014). From their self-presentation, to their professional experience, to their modes of describing the body, nursing unfolded as feminized labor on the stand.

In the sexual assault proceedings we sat in on over many months, the most common medical records introduced at trial included examination reports and body maps. Unmarked body maps were often entered into evidence early in the SANE nurses' testimony as a visual aid during the nurses' anatomy lessons (see figure 4.1). Science and technology studies scholar Sheila Jasanoff (1995) has argued that courts are taught to interpret scientific evidence through practices of visualization. The use of body maps during sexual assault adjudication served a pedagogical purpose. In the trials we observed, prosecutors often provided a body map depicting two views of a vulva—referred to as a "vagina" in the shorthand of the court—more or less from the perspective of someone standing or sitting between a patient's legs as they are held in stirrups in the traditional lithotomy position, or alternately without stirrups in what gynecologists often call the "frog position." One of the views on the map included a detailed rendering of the cervix. The view of the cervix can be achieved only during examination using the speculum to traction the pelvic canal and reveal the cervix to the nurse, but the speculum itself was erased. This representational modality normalized the spectacle of the victimized body, rendering it open to the forensic gaze. The body-map images were neat and simple, with black line drawings that belied the visceral fleshiness of human bodies. The absence of the victim-witness during the forensic nurses' testimony, due to sequestration, further alienated the corporeality of the body from its sanitized renderings. The sequestration order can be said to reproduce the work of the drape in gynecological examinations, separating persons and pelvises (Henslin and Biggs 1971; Kapsalis 1997; Mulla 2014).

During these trials, the nurses appeared to offer similar responses to the prosecutors' questions, explaining what we were seeing, how we were seeing it, and the way those body parts functioned. When describing the tissue of the "vagina," forensic nurses variously testified that vaginas were "made to have sexual intercourse often"; "lubricated"; "very stretchy"; "similar to the membrane of the mouth—a mucus membrane"; "like a scrunchy" in reference to a tool for holding back the hair; "able to accommodate something the size of a watermelon"; and "a self-cleaning vessel." These descriptions of a lubricated, stretchy, self-cleaning membrane that was likened to the mouth ("think how quickly your mouth heals when you bite it or have a sore?" a nurse once asked the jury) were designed to explain the minimal or total absence of injury following sexual assault. These anatomy lessons were simplified, generalized, and steeped in heteronormative archetypes. The vagina was always also a symbol of reproduction. For example, in *State v. Moore*, the forensic nurse was asked by the prosecutor to explain lack of injury.

NURSE SANCHEZ: Lack of injury can occur from just the makeup— the general makeup of a woman. There's lubrication to the genital area. If someone is fearful, they may not necessarily put up a fight during the assault because they're afraid for their life, depending if there was a weapon. And generally, the body is kind of made to have sexual intercourse, I guess for lack of a better word. So, often you will not have injury.

PROSECUTOR: And would you describe the makeup of the vagina to be a stretchy or a rigid part of the body?

NURSE SANCHEZ: Very stretchy.

Stretchiness was sometimes demonstrated beyond being simply explained. One forensic nurse told us that during testimony she once removed her scrunchy from her ponytail, performed its elasticity by pulling both sides, and replaced it in her hair as a demonstration of vaginal capacity to stretch. Later, the prosecutor asked Nurse Sanchez to address the vagina's "self-healing" properties:

PROSECUTOR: I wanted to talk a little bit about the properties of the vagina as it relates to healing. Is that okay?

NURSE SANCHEZ: Yes.

PROSECUTOR: How would you characterize the vagina's ability to heal itself?

NURSE SANCHEZ: The inner portion of the genitalia has a high vascular component. There's a lot of blood vessels, so there's high blood flow[,] which allows it to heal fairly quickly.

PROSECUTOR: And when you say, "fairly quickly," are we talking days, weeks, months?

NURSE SANCHEZ: You know, it can vary from person to person depending on their nutrition, if they have chronic illness. Typically depending on the severity of the injury, a very minor injury can take several days. A more severe injury could take a week. It just varies per person.

Women's bodies were sites of struggle for depiction and control. Scholars have routinely identified persistent negative and false stereotypes of the vagina, including the vagina as inferior, secret, or absent in its relation to the penis; the vagina as (passive) receptacle for the penis; the vagina as shameful, unclean, and disgusting; the vagina as vulnerable and abused; and the vagina as dangerous (Braun and Wilkinson 2001; Braun and Kitzinger 2001; Laws 1987; Irigaray 1996). While Nurse Sanchez allowed for variation in times of healing, her examples of different nutrition or chronic disease still limited the typical healing times to a single notion of a healthy patient by attributing variation to pathology. The vagina was distinctly gendered as feminine and described in narrow parameters of normal/healthy or abnormal/unhealthy. Unhealthiness could stem from lack of nutrition, another subtle connection between poverty and, in Milwaukee, its inevitable association with race.

Voiced through the white feminized labor of the SANE nurse (E. Martin 1991), the normalization of sexed bodies reproduced the cultural scaffolding of sexual violence as heterosexual and heteronormative (Gavey 2005). It also generated a dynamic in which white expertise narrated Black women's bodies. As ethnographers in the court, we questioned the purpose of the nurses' demonstratives in our field notes: Why use a scrunchy to illustrate the tensile nature of vascular tissues? Why not a timing belt, or a rubber band, or some object with a less (or differently) gendered provenance? The nurses' testimony largely explained why there was "nothing to see." In U.S. legal practices, vaginas have been objectified and deemed "searchable," for example, when search warrants have been issued to invade a suspect's "apartment and vagina" (Hyde 1997). Discerning the extent to which a body has been injured, however, required a different medicolegal exercise. The injured vagina, in these cases, was cast as inscrutable—perhaps even dangerous—in its secrecy and inability to reveal trauma. The vagina was (perhaps curiously) resilient, reproductive, capacious, yielding, heteronormative, and a slew of other things. The nurses' accounts cast the vagina within a set of institutional categories that were objectifying, even as they qualified the vagina as a worthy legal subject. In her work in Ahmedabad's courts, Pratiksha Baxi has critiqued the longstanding reliance on the medical category of the sexual habitué in India's courts. Baxi argued that there is no medical knowledge outside the law. It is the law that determines the status of disciplinary expertise, exemplified for Baxi in the enduring use of the two-finger test only recently outlawed. This holds true in the context of U.S. sexual assault courts wherein forensic nurses' descriptions of the vagina contextualize a body that does not give up its secrets through physical evidence.

On occasion (but rarely), SANEs would sometimes locate microinjuries observable only through techniques of photographic magnification. Microinjuries were sometimes cast as "nonconclusive" evidence by the prosecutor in opening statements, another nod toward consideration of the forensic examination as a form of corroborative evidence. In opening arguments for *State v. Logan*, for example, the prosecutor told the jury what was anticipated from the forensic nurse's testimony to come:

> In addition to hearing from the detective and the officer, you'll hear from the nurse that performed that examination. And the medical record of that examination will be introduced through that nurse. . . . [L]ikely the nurse will say that the examination didn't include something that they refer to as a conclusive finding. And she'll describe to you likely in her testimony, that conclusive findings of sexual abuse are extraordinarily rare in her practice. And that it's not seen that often. The conclusive finding would be a pregnancy in the juvenile, for example, or possibly a sexual transmitted disease, or a complete tear or transection of the hymen. But even that can be caused by other things. But she will note in the medical record notes here that she did note generalized redness to this six-year-old child's hymen.

These forms of illness, redness, small tears or cuts, and other microinjuries were commonly marked onto a body map and proffered as another evidentiary exhibit (see figure 4.2). This visual representation of the wound, much like the unwounded body map pictured before it, remained devoid of its contours and fleshiness. Literally unencumbered by a body, the map focused in on the vulva—a convention of gynecological research and medical textbooks (Jordanova 1989; Matthews and Wexler 2000). Photographs of the genital examination, which are often a part of the medical charts, were rarely entered as evidentiary exhibits. Many prosecutors found that body maps, when narrated by forensic nurses, were more effective and did not invite the same visceral responses of shame from the jury, a phenomenon that many prosecutors sought to avoid (Mulla 2014). In interviews, SANEs, too, deliberated on the use of photographic evidence in court. Recall the quote in the previous section about how jurors might interpret "a picture of a perfectly normal, healthy area that doesn't look traumatized." The use of body maps over photographs was one more "data double," a technique for generalizing the anatomy of assault and erasing the individual victim-patient from the proceedings.

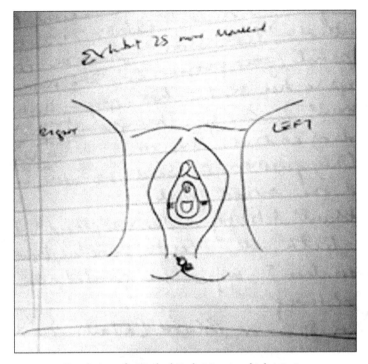

Figure 4.2. Rendering of a Marked Body Map, in which injuries are marked in black (*State v. Peeples*). Photo credit: Sameena Mulla

Figures 4.1 and 4.2 reference an unmarked and marked body map. Red marks depicted injuries found by the SANE nurse during her examination. Figure 4.2 is our version of the body map evidenced in *State v. Peeples*. The map referenced the medical examination of 10-year-old Maya, whose case we discussed in chapter 2. There was no representational differentiation between an adult or child patient. The body maps signified the victim's body as the "scene of the crime" (Mulla 2014). Genitals were pictured as visible to the eye, again adding to the perception of the vagina as a penetrable space (by a penis or, in this case, by the gaze). The flattening of the genital anatomy further contributed to the objectification of the vagina, indexed through the spatialization practices of presenting the area as a clockface. Much more can be said of these mapping practices, but one final point marks the erasure of differently abled bodies, intersexed bodies, culturally marked or modified bodies, and racialized bodies. While most of these cases included Black women and girls, each visual rendering defaulted to a "neutral" or normalized subject.

Along with courtroom observations and extensive in-depth interviews with sexual assault nurse examiners, we also attended several local conferences and training seminars sponsored by the International Association of Forensic Nurses to gain a broad view of changing practices in forensic nursing. During one such conference held in a hotel ballroom, Wanda, an experienced SANE, addressed an audience of engrossed forensic nurses:

> We are being attacked in the courtroom for being CSIs, right? The newest tactic in defense is if I can make her just an evidence tech and an evidence collector, I can limit her testimony to only what she saw. She can't give an opinion, can't talk about patient demeanor, can't talk about any of those things that might be considered hearsay, because hearsay is only allowed to health care providers. So, they want to diminish you into being just an evidence collector. You need to be able to articulate that everything I do here is part of my job as a nurse. As a health care provider. . . . And that you want to be able to speak to that patient's needs. Because, I'm going to basically show you that genital injury means nothing. It really means nothing. And so, what are we doing here if genital injury means nothing? We can assist the prosecutors by telling them what we saw and how this patient reacted. And that's important. In many ways, it's more important than that two-millimeter laceration if we can articulate this is how she was behaving. She was having that post trauma reaction that I see so commonly with patients. And describe that for the jury and educate the jury. Because when it comes down to, he said/she said, that two-millimeter laceration doesn't really mean anything scientifically.

Wanda, a nurse for more than 25 years, informed the audience about the dangers of presenting SANE programs and practitioners as akin to crime scene investigations. Doubling down on the meaninglessness of genital injury and marking the difference between patient care and "an evidence tech," Wanda amplified the narrative role of the nurse, able to "assist prosecutors by telling them what we saw and how this patient reacted." SANEs could provide testimony of her visual encounter with the vagina as well as a clinical account of her patient's expressions of physical pain and trauma. While these expressions were invisible to the jury, they were palpable to the nurse when the patient was in front of her. In the example of *State v. Moore*, the prosecutor asked Nurse Sanchez about the victim-witness's injuries:

> PROSECUTOR: And you noted [the injury] was healing. You saw Miss C. approximately four days after the assault, is that correct?
>
> NURSE SANCHEZ: Correct.
>
> PROSECUTOR: And so, when you say "healing," were they in the process of healing when you saw them?
>
> NURSE SANCHEZ: Yes. They were not fresh. Normally, if we saw what we would call "fresh injury," that would show that there was active bleeding. And generally, you can tell by—if we touch it with a swab—if there's active bleeding, so indicating it was not—it was healing. It was not a fresh wound.
>
> PROSECUTOR: And the abrasion on her left labia minor, would that hurt?
>
> NURSE SANCHEZ: Yes.
>
> PROSECUTOR: And the abrasion on her right labia minora, would that hurt?
>
> NURSE SANCHEZ: Yes. She did report that she was having pain to both of those areas.

In this exchange, the forensic nurse testified to the presence of pain in clinical terms, demonstrating how pain is etched into the medical record she created. In this way, the forensic nurse could report on something a victim-witness told her, whereas reported speech would typically be objected to as a violation of hearsay rules. The creation of a medical record and its admission as an evidentiary exhibit allowed the SANE to circumvent such evidentiary obstacles. For example, in *State v. Lee*, the prosecutor asked the forensic nurse to review her medical chart:

> PROSECUTOR: And talking about pain, did [the victim-witness] tell you she was in pain?
>
> NURSE: Yes.
>
> PROSECUTOR: And what did she tell you?

NURSE: Her neck and her mouth hurt. She was rating that, we always ask patients to rate pain on a scale of zero to 10, so 10 being the worse pain you ever felt, zero being no pain at all. She rated her pain an eight out of 10, and she was given ibuprofen by the Sexual Assault Treatment Center.

. . .

PROSECUTOR: And looking at the eyes, did you examine her eyes?

NURSE: Yes.

PROSECUTOR: And what, if anything, did you note in the medical record?

NURSE: No injury was noted, but "patient reports her eyes feel so dry from crying."

PROSECUTOR: And the oral cavity?

NURSE: I noted no injury that I could see, but she reported pain to her lips and her mouth from oral assault.

PROSECUTOR: And her head and face?

NURSE: No injury was noted to her head or her face.

PROSECUTOR: And to the neck?

NURSE: The back of the neck is shaded on the picture, so [on the form there is a] shaded area to posterior head and neck, [and I wrote] "patient reported pain eight out of 10 from having gun 'shoved' to the back of the head as well as being grabbed and held by assailant. Patient cringing in pain and light touch or palpation during exam."

PROSECUTORS: And are any of those words in quotations?

NURSE: "Shoved" is what she described, the gun being shoved to the back of her head.

Pain itself, a symptom that was deemed significant in the clinical encounter, stood in for a discussion of the victim-witness's emotional demeanor at the time of the examination. Prosecutors were careful to emphasize words in quotations, indicating verbatim statements from patients. As noted earlier in this chapter, forensic nurses rarely commented on the emotional state of the victim-witness, limiting herself to clinical frameworks that evaded the stereotype of feminized caregiver and emotional laborer. Finally, the nurse's testimony in this case situated the victim-witness in time, reminding jurors that her body had changed even in the four short days between the assault and the examination.

In the case of the sexual assault trial, the notion of "vaginal durability" or resilience was demonstrated by supplementing jurors' common sense: their mouths or a stretchy scrunchy or a reminder that women who bear children most often recover from laboring and birthing. The example of a fast healing inner cheek might transcend gender, whereas the capacity to labor might require a wider realm of social experience to resonate with all the jurors. The ways in which nurses demonstrated how a patient's body might endure the violence of rape was nested within how juries also perceived victim-witnesses' bodies within a broader context of racialized womanhood. The nurses' explanations of the body's rapid recovery from injury, and the anatomical capacity to endure the stress of childbirth, are evocative of the ways that Black women's bodies are excluded as vulnerable or fragile in U.S. popular imaginaries in the afterlife of slavery (D. Davis 2019). In the Indian colonial context, Baxi has also documented the British juridical practices that deemed working Indian women's bodies as unlikely to be injured, with colonial courts going so far as to argue that women laborers were indubitably so strong that they were unlikely to be raped in the first place (Baxi 2014). The ostensible physical resiliency of the victim-witness's body stands in stark contrast to the emotional fragility many prosecutors hoped would comprise her testimony as we discussed in chapter 2.

In the courts, we took note of the ceremony of repetition, the formulas proffered when adjudicants were on the record, and the care and thought that attorneys gave to managing the testimony of SANEs. Our fieldwork frequently circled back to the ways in which forms of knowledge-making normalized the absence of injury by scaffolding the findings of a pelvic examination and reinscribing a gendered understanding of the "vagina." It is the persistence of the normative approaches to sex and sexuality, as well as the language used by expert witnesses, that reproduced problematic descriptions and understandings of the sexual assault victim. These modes mirror Emily Martin's (1991) analysis of the romantic language used by scientists when they described the mechanism of fertilization of human sex cells. The conventions of the gynecological examination, such as draping the patient's lower body, were conveyed through the court's practice of witness sequestration and its use of expert testimony to speak on the victim-witness's experience. Just as the patient could not see what the nurse saw during the examination, due to witness sequestration during the trial the victim-witness could not hear how the nurse interpreted the examination and relayed it to the jury. In the circumscribed space of a criminal trial, the justice system became one more arena in which the singular experiences of victim-witnesses were shaped into familiar and normative narratives of gendered violence. Regardless of the outcome of a legal case, nursing expertise served to impart and normalize medicalizing the "vagina" itself through a universalized rendering. If medical charts and body maps, DNA analyses, and explanation of the "taboo" mechanics of the vagina were necessary to understand sexual violence, the penis and other male anatomy were exempt from such incursions. It is worth noting that the nurses' narrative of vaginal durability, resilience, and capacity for healing were perhaps counterintuitive to a jury accustomed to associating femininity with fragility. Nurses' testimony challenged such notions while leaving other normative assumptions in place. In contrast, the victimizing body needed little explanation; it was often left unmarked and unattended.

Exhibiting the Victimizing Body

Although defendants remained silent through most sexual assault trials, their bodies were consistently on display. Due to the Constitution's due process and confrontation language, defendants have the right to hear all the evidence against them, to face their accuser, and to remain silent for the duration of the case. Indeed, defendants rarely opted to testify in court (which is the subject of chapter 6). In most sexual assault trials we observed, the defendant was remanded prior to trial and currently in custody. The courts took great care to hide this fact from the jurors, considering it to be prejudicial. Appearing in orange jumpsuits and shackles straight from jail during preliminary hearings, defendants changed into plain civilian clothes for trial. They wore button-down shirts, sportscoats, or suits brought to the jail or to court by family members during visiting hours. When no such formal clothing was provided, defense attorneys could acquire second-hand clothing supplied by attorneys or judges, sometimes at a moment's notice. Beyond indications such as the clothing being loose-fitting or neckties slack, the jury would not necessarily know that the defendant was in custody. Upon entering the courtroom, wrist ties were removed or cut off by the bailiffs, and defendants were instead restrained with ankle shackles hidden under the defense table and cemented into the floor. Both the prosecutor and defense tables were draped with black floor-length table skirts to hide the shackles from the jurors. Lest the chain jangle when the defendant moved, the judge instructed all present, including the gallery, not to rise when court was called to order, leaving the defendant's status vis-à-vis imprisonment unknown to the jury. It is worth considering the symbolism of the drape as it traverses gynecological and criminal justice procedures, given what jurors can see and know.

It was common to observe jury members sizing up defendants, sometimes taking quick glances and other times lingering when they thought no one was looking. On occasion, even witnesses would watch defendants closely for reactions to their testimony. Jurors could only imagine whether the victim-witness's description of the defendant's actions matched the silent presence sitting before them. Was the defendant capable of carrying out the acts described? Did the defendant now, physically and affectively, resemble the person described by the victim-witness many months, and sometimes years, earlier? In the case of *State v. Mays, Sr.*, the defendant was charged with multiple counts of sexual assault of a child. During his trial, Mays decided to testify in his own defense—a rare occurrence and a decision many defense attorneys often advised against. After the guilty verdict was delivered, we had the opportunity to interview one of the jurors. During our discussion, the juror commented on how the defendant's appearance informed part of her perspective on the case:

JUROR: And the defendant! Whoa!
INTERVIEWER: Mays?
JUROR: Huge, yes! Mr. Mays, Sr. Huge! And I have to tell you that one
  of the things—I didn't look at [the victim] a lot when she was testifying. I looked past her, and I was looking at the trees out the window
  because it was fairly, well, obvious. It was very uncomfortable as she's
  talking about very, very specific things. And I wanted to try to say,
  you know, just listening and taking in the information as I could.
  And even before he stood up and I realized how big he was, what I
  thought when she was describing how when they were having sex

and she was on top and he was holding her by the hips, or she was in front and he was holding her by the hips, it's like, oh my God, he's using her like a sex doll. That's what it is. She was a living, breathing sex doll for him. And it was disgusting. So, he looked presentable. He wore his best clothes, such as they were.

The juror described Mr. Mayes as a good-looking, well-dressed, "huge" man. According to the juror, in comparison to the 13-year-old victim-witness who testified at length in court, his hulking presence solidified for her that he was "using her like a sex doll . . . a living, breathing sex doll for him."

State v. Mays, Sr. did not include a testifying SANE, medical personnel, or a forensic scientist. Although nurses did tell us they were also trained to complete suspect collections and occasionally took photographs of genitalia and other body parts, such orders from police officers were rare. Suspect evidence collection was often focused on recovering suspect DNA to compare with DNA recovered from the victim-patient. Visual inspection was part of all suspect evidence collections, but suspect body maps did not make it to the courts in a single case during our field research. While the defendant's body remained largely unmarked and unattended to by forensic nurses, it was occasionally narrated by lay witnesses and addressed by attorneys. Descriptions of the defendant's comportment, actions, body appearance, size, and strength were primarily narrated in relation to the victim-witness's body. For example, in the case of *State v. Chandler*, the adult victim-witness, Sheila Roman, provided the court with an account of the defendant's actions and behavior and the way he used his body to attack and sexually assault her:

PROSECUTOR: What happened then?
Ms. ROMAN: After that, he grabbed my arm. I didn't expect it. I went to get my purse, which was on the floor, and he—he knocked me out. He punched me. I didn't expect it.
PROSECUTOR: Punched you where?
Ms. ROMAN: On this side of my face. I heard my bones crack.
PROSECUTOR: That would be the left side of your face?
Ms. ROMAN: Yeah, yeah. It's still swollen.

PROSECUTOR: How many punches?

MS. ROMAN: It was a massive punch like I was in a car accident.

Pointing to her face in order to specify where she was punched, Ms. Roman referenced her own body as evidence of the defendant's violence:

PROSECUTOR: You're also pointing to your biceps. Is this the area you were grabbed?

MS. ROMAN: Yeah. This is where the fingerprints were. It was right on this arm.

PROSECUTOR: What happened then when you were on the floor?

MS. ROMAN: I was like froze. It looked like my body had come out of my body. I was just so froze. And he inserted his penis into my vagina.

Through her testimony, Ms. Roman remained the center of the forensic gaze. The blood from a cut on her face from the defendant's punch, the bruises on her arm, and the insertion of his penis into her vagina were not visualized through the defendant's body. Medical explanations of erections or the process of inserting a penis into a vagina were unnecessary. The defendant was not deemed worthy of forensic examination, despite the possibility of bruises to himself and the transfer of blood and other bodily fluids. Rather, it was only through the victim's cooperation with the police investigation and her testimony at trial that the defendant's body was discussed and recorded in court records. Accounts such as Ms. Roman's were common in the courts, describing the act of rape in clinical terms and mimicking the ways in which assaultive behavior was described during forensic examinations. There was no visual representation of the defendant's body or further detail solicited about his body from the victim-witness. Ms. Roman explained how strong the defendant was, however, and how his punch had broken her tooth. She also explained that he had forced her to wash the evidence off her own body:

When he got through with me, he told me to get up and take a shower. I said, "I'm not taking a shower." He said, "Bitch, get up and wash your ass." I thought, if you say get up and wash my vagina area, this must be a rape because I'm going to die.

Victim-witnesses frequently narrate these instances of perpetrators' awareness of forensic science (Mulla 2014). Perpetrators are also impacted by the imagined technologies and potential of forensics, evidenced through their efforts to destroy evidence following sexual assaults.

In cases involving child victims, language was less clinical and reflected the witness's developmental and linguistic capacity to describe sexual violence and anatomy. Attorneys often adopted similar language in their opening and closing statements, mirroring the words and ways in which the child witness spoke. For example, in the case of State v. Logan, the defendant was charged with four counts of first-degree child sexual assault of the victim-witness, Janelle. She was a seven years old at the time of trial and six years old at the time she reported the assaults. During testimony at trial, the nurse read her report indicating that she had observed some redness on the victim-witness's hymen and labia minora. The nurse also spoke of DNA swabs she had taken from Janelle's body when Janelle told her that the defendant had licked her face and other parts of her body. During cross-examination, the defense attorney tried to discredit the exam findings, swiftly suggesting other potential ways to account for the redness in the hymen and labia minora. Questioning the nurse's expertise, he remarked that no medical doctor had been present for the examination and that the nurse had only six months of experience. In response, the nurse explained that she had conducted more than 60 forensic examinations in those six months and that findings such as those reported in this case were outliers, as more than half of the exams she had conducted yielded no findings of injury.

DEFENSE ATTORNEY: And you, you identified some generalized light redness to the hymen, is that correct?

NURSE: Yes.

DEFENSE ATTORNEY: In regard to the light redness in the labia minor and the hymen in that regards, can that redness be caused by some sort of infection or poor hygiene, a bubble bath of sorts?

NURSE: Yes.

DEFENSE ATTORNEY: I suppose it also could be . . . that light redness could occur as a result of maybe toilet paper that is too rough?

NURSE: Yes.

DEFENSE ATTORNEY: Or some sort of wiping that's too much after the child has used the bathroom?

NURSE: Yes.

Here, the defense attorney challenged the finding that redness indicated injury by suggesting that other causes such as "infection or poor hygiene, a bubble bath" or rough toilet paper were the cause. Defense counsel shifted the focus back to the victim-witness's actions toward her own body and away from the harm the defendant was alleged to have caused. Once again, the defendant's victimizing body receded as scrutiny of the child victim's body was the focus of defense counsel's cross-examination of the forensic nurse. References to poor hygiene, infection, and self-abuse, of course, reinforced cultural representations of the vagina as pathological, unclean, or unhealthy and in need of maintenance (Braun and Wilkinson 2001). Defense continued:

DEFENSE: Is it—one of the other things that may be a high probably of, specific to the genitalia in regards to an assault [does] one, look for a torn or missing hymen?

NURSE: The hymen is never technically missing. The hymen is a piece of tissue that can expand and tear like any other tissue of the body.

DEFENSE: But if you see, like if that's absent or if it's missing, and that is an indication of assault?

NURSE: No.

DEFENSE: Not in your opinion?

NURSE: No.

DEFENSE: Okay. How about if it's . . . if the hymen is torn?

NURSE: If it was appearing to be a fresh tear, yes. That would be an indication of an assault.

DEFENSE: You didn't find anything in this regard, correct?

NURSE: No.

DEFENSE: You didn't find any vaginal injury or scarring, did you?

NURSE: No.

Because the prosecutor submitted evidence of "redness" to the hymen, the defense attorney was able to discuss the nurse's finding at length, not only questioning the source but also underscoring cultural notions of the meaning of the hymen itself (Baxi 2014; Carpenter 2005). Women's and girls' bodies were interpreted through the myth of the hymen. The myth was amplified by the common belief that the hymen or the vagina will be altered after first sexual intercourse. So powerful was the myth of virginity that community health professionals and nurses often had to be taught that the hymen did not evaporate or disappear following sexual intercourse (Girardin et al. 1997; Mulla 2016). During the forensic examination, "[I]t was not the level of force required to injure the hymen that [made] hymenal photos such well-touted evidence, but rather the mythology and cultural mystique that accompanies the fleshy membrane" (Mulla 2016).

It was not uncommon for defense attorneys to cautiously hint toward such cultural notions in court, especially in cases of child sexual assault. Whether these myths made it into court before jurors was largely at the discretion of judges. For example, in *State v. King*, the state called a pediatrician from Children's Hospital who had completed a medical examination of the victim-witness in the case. The child-victim was under 12, and the defendant was charged with assaulting her multiple times. During her testimony, the pediatrician told the jury that the child's examination was "normal;" her "hymen was redundant," or plump from puberty, and there was some skin irritation. That is "very typical for sexually assaulted children," she continued; "about 95% of all kids' exams are normal." The prosecutor inquired "How could that be?" to which the pediatrician responded "if there had been an injury, it could have healed quickly due to blood supply."

As defense counsel cross-examined the pediatrician, he continually returned to one thing the pediatrician had written in her report: that there was "no disruption or tears noted on the hymen." At some point, the judge stopped the cross-examination and released the jury for a break. With the jury out of the room, the judge proceeded to reprimand the defense attorney's style and theme of questioning:

[The witness] seems totally lost and I suspect that the hymen is perceived to be some sort of magical seal and it's broken when a woman has sex— and it's not true or a medical fact. From the look on [the pediatrician's] face, I think the witness knows this, too. Medical experts would tell you it breaks for all sorts of reasons, lord knows. I've heard this from dozens of nurses and doctors as a lawyer and judge. Could a hymen be ripped by exercise, medical exam, consensual sex? All are possible, so we're getting a little far afield.

The defense attorney accepted the judge's reprimand, but the reinforcement of the myth of virginity was not retracted and had already been floated in front of the jury. The reprimand and redirection took place outside of the jury's hearing.

Returning to the case of *State v. Logan*, following cross-examination of the forensic nurse, the victim-witness, Janelle, took the stand. During Janelle's testimony, the prosecutor introduced two anatomical dolls so that Janelle could point to anatomical features for which she did not have language. The prosecutor asked Janelle to imagine the first doll was her, even though it lacked her "cute braids and cute barrettes." When asked to describe her own body, Janelle used the term "vagina" and accurately pointed to the location on the first doll. When asked what parts of the defendant's body had touched her body, she said he used his "front part." The prosecutor then handed Janelle a second doll:

> PROSECUTOR: Okay. I'm going to show you another doll. And this one
> is a man doll. And I want you to tell me where on this guy—point out
> where on this guy that—I think you said bottom front part is located.
> Okay. I see you pointing your finger toward—in between the legs of
> the doll, is that correct?
>
> JANELLE: Yes.
>
> PROSECUTOR: Okay. And can you describe for me everything you,
> well, did you see that part on [the defendant]?
>
> JANELLE: Yes.
>
> PROSECUTOR: What did it look like?
>
> JANELLE: A microphone.

During her testimony, Janelle used various words to describe the defendant's penis, including "his thing," and described it as shaped like "a microphone." She did not use the word "penis." The defendant decided to testify in the case, and during cross-examination the prosecutor repeated Janelle's descriptions of his body parts and sexual acts to her, asking him if those details were true. The defendant challenged Janelle's description of his penis:

> PROSECUTOR: So when Janelle, now a seven-year-old little girl, says that you were taking her clothing off of her, that you were putting your body on top of her, removing your penis that was about so big, as she demonstrated in the video—I'm holding my hands about, you know, maybe six inches apart, that was round on top, and that you put that in her private part, and then you put that in her mouth, and that clear stuff came out, that is all just a lie for no apparent reason? You didn't do any of that?
>
> DEFENDANT: No, ma'am. I didn't.
>
> . . .
>
> PROSECUTOR: So, when she describes the appearance of your erect penis in detail and how ejaculate came out of it, that's not a fact?
>
> DEFENDANT: No. She also said that it shaped like a microphone. Now, this microphone is shaped pretty much like a penis. But you said, "kind of like the microphone in front of you," and she said "no, nothing like that." So[,] then, where are these facts?

The defendant did not testify about his own body but rather referred to the courtroom microphone as shaped like a penis. He then noted that Janelle disagreed when asked if the defendant's penis looked like the microphone before her, challenging the prosecutor's use of the word "facts."

Attorneys also elicited testimony about defendants' bodies from various witnesses. In the case of *State v. Young*, the defendant was charged with three counts of first-degree child sexual contact with a person under the age of 13 and one count of incest with a child. Tasha, the victim-witness, testified first, followed by a police officer, a school friend, and a social worker. Tasha's mother then took the stand to testify. After corroborating Tasha's testimony that she and her mother disclosed the sexual assault to the police, the prosecutor abruptly asked:

> PROSECUTOR: Is it fair to say you've been intimate [with the defendant]?
>
> DEFENSE: Objection!

The judge immediately called a sidebar and directed the bailiffs to remove the jury for a short recess. The discussion occurred in open court so that the court reporter could put it on the record; during this exchange, Tasha's mother remained on the stand in the witness box. She looked confused from time to time, shifting nervously in her chair and turning her body away from the defendant (her former husband), who also remained in the courtroom. The prosecutor explained that, because the victim-witness gave a brief description of the defendant's erect penis (noting it was "curved"), Tasha's mother could corroborate her statement. Field notes from the trial indicated that the attorneys and the judge continued their discussion for some time, defense counsel arguing that if testimony about the "curved" penis was allowed into court that he would have to call witnesses who could testify to the fact that penises are curved in general. At this point, Tasha's mother interjected: "Not the ones I've seen." Her voice seemed to catch her by surprise as she pulled back her slight grin, perhaps recalling that she was in court that day to discuss her daughter's disclosure of sexual assault. The attorneys persisted, arguing over what a "curved penis" meant. Finally, the judge decided to allow Tasha's mother to testify about the appearance of the defendant's penis because the victim-witness testified to it and the mother had "firsthand knowledge of his penis." Defense counsel disagreed, arguing that all penises are curved up or down, as Tasha's mother again interjected: "No, not like this." Once more she became teary, and the court clerk handed her a tissue from the box on her desk. Following the brief recess, the jury was allowed back into the courtroom, and direct examination continued:

PROSECUTOR: Have you been intimate with [the defendant]?
MOTHER: Yes.
PROSECUTOR: Have you seen [him] with an erection?
MOTHER: Yes. His penis is curved.

No further questions were asked by the prosecutor, and defense counsel crossed:

DEFENSE: When you say curved, what do you mean exactly? Can you draw a picture of it?

Tasha's mother looked upset and breathed deeply into the microphone.

> MOTHER: I hate to be vulgar, but . . . [she drew a quick picture from
> the stand].

Defense counsel approached the witness stand and took the picture
from Tasha's mother. He stared at it for a few moments and then turned
back to the defense table. As he was walking, the judge asked if he intended to mark the picture as an exhibit, and defense answered: "I may."
He never did, and during closing arguments the prosecutor reminded
the jury: "[The victim] described his penis as curved when erect! Now,
remember what her mother said—who has sexual knowledge of him—
she said that the noticeable feature was the curved erect penis, and
showed defense counsel a picture."

This was not the only case that included testimony regarding a defendant's penis. Recall the earlier discussion about hymens in *State v. King*.
Defense counsel, while questioning the victim-witness's mother (who
testified that she did not believe her daughter was sexually assaulted by
her husband), established that she and the defendant had been sexually active together. Defense then asked: "Can you describe for me his
penis?" Judge Van asked the witness to step down out of the witness box
and the bailiffs to remove the jurors from the room. Another protracted
discussion ensued between the attorneys and the judge about the imagined size of the defendant's penis. In his argument to the judge, defense
counsel indicated that he intended to "elicit that he has a large penis."
Judge Van responded:

> Not a chance. That's beyond the pale. I don't care if he's 12 inches, no foun-
> dation. It's preposterous. I don't care if he's hung like a horse or a light
> switch. I have been in this assignment for over three years and never!

Defense complained to the judge over three different times that he had
"to put on a defense for my client!" intending to argue that Mr. King's
penis was so large that it would have undoubtedly caused damage to the
victim's hymen.

In addition to witnesses who narrated the defendant's body into the
trial, defense attorneys also commented on their client's physical stature

and capacities. Recall the attorney in *State v. Jordan* in chapter 2 who took to the floor during closing arguments to demonstrate the plank position that he thought his client was incapable of holding due to his arthritis. In another case, *State v. Jackson*, defense counsel argued at great length in closing arguments that his client was slim in stature and the victim-witness "weighs 206 pounds. So, she's not a small person for this guy supposedly pulling her backwards. He can't use his body weight against her anymore when that supposedly happened." Defense questioned how his slimly built client could possibly abduct an unsuspecting woman off the street by running up behind her and pulling her into the back seat of a car. In all these instances, no expert knowledge was required to make the defendant's body legible to the court of law. Often, an ableist orientation toward masculine violence, and the self-evident nature of masculine virility and strength, brought the victimizing body into the courts almost wholly through the voices of others.

The *Nomos* of Sexual Violence and SANE Nursing

This chapter has examined nurses' testimony elicited by prosecutors and defense attorneys in criminal sexual assault trials. We argue that the raped body is constructed through medicolegal imaginaries, heteronormative commitments, and expert knowledges largely used to explain the absence of evidence. This same expert knowledge, however, was silent when it came to narratives of the assaulting body. The self-evident nature of male anatomy reflected a deep genealogy of standards for medical knowledge and education that depict male specimens as "normal" while female anatomy is treated as variant of the species (Jordanova 1989; McGrath 2002). Forensic nurses' testimony explained the inscrutability of the vagina, the reasons why injuries to vaginas are uncommon in sexual assault, and the resilience of female genital anatomy. They also constructed the female body as a heteronormative reproductive body always already penetrable, regardless of whether the victim testifying was a child, an adult, heterosexual or nonheterosexual, maternal or nonmaternal.

In contrast, it is only through lay witnesses that details or commentary about the physical appearance, capability, or anatomy of the defendant were entered into evidence. We further argue that, in the absence of DNA evidence and legible physical injury, experts testified to the resilience of the female body, objectifying its function using heterosexual reproductive norms and capabilities. Thus, we reflected on how the feminine body is mapped during trial, whereas the masculine body seemingly required no such diagramming outside of a mother's drawing of her former husband's "curved penis." This examination invites us to think about how men's bodies fit into the heteronormative narratives produced through expert testimony about women's bodies. In the few cases where genital injury was discovered during a sexual assault forensic examination, nurses amplified the significance of what appeared to be minimal injury by emphasizing the rareness of physical injury and testifying to the pain experienced by victims. This pain was most often recorded on medical charts via victim self-reporting according to a subjective pain scale. In an interview, a forensic nurse discussed the possible pitfalls of emphasizing genital injury in court:

> I think that the more that forensic nurses can create a fuller clinical picture of what happens during that encounter and spend less time really focused on the genital injury, the better juries understand the context of the medical evidence. The problem is that when prosecutors put forensic nurses up there and try to highlight the genital injury as being overly indicative of force or sexual assault, they run into trouble there because a good defense attorney will cross on that pretty quickly and often very effectively and make it very clear that those injuries are pretty nonspecific.

For nurses on the stand, it was important to move away from a focus on genital injury, but because of the jury's expectations and defense counsel practices, such injuries were inevitably interpellated into the defense's strategy.

Finally, we noted the affective qualities that characterized the testimony about victim and defendant bodies. Both the defense and the prosecution drove home the importance of corroboration: the defense through a concerted effort to focus on inconsistencies within and between narratives, and the prosecution in their work to draw out such consistencies. The corroborative practice relied, in part, on the testimony of the nurse, who as a clinician lent authority to a version of events that was neither consistent nor inconsistent with the complaining witness's testimony. The clinical authority of the forensic nurse was demonstrated through her recording practices, her knowledge and practice with anatomy, and her expertise plotting injuries onto body maps. As a clinician, she was also allowed to voice the victim-patient's pain at the time of the forensic examination, documenting patient utterances and testifying to the victim's quoted words in ways that may or may not have reflected the patient's meaning.

The language SANE nurses used to describe the vagina's resilience also objectified the vagina—it was "like a scrunchy" or "a self-cleaning vessel." This resilience was grounded within a heteronormative scaffolding in which all sexual practices were penetrative and vaginas were durable, stretchy, maternal, and robust organs. The racialization of bodies and body parts was subtle but potent. Of course, the rendering of the body maps defaulted to a racially "neutral" subject. However, most of the cases described here included Black women and girl victims and Black adult men as defendants. Returning to the work of Davis (2019) and Baxi (2014), we find it important to again note how the reproductive imaginaries collide with the racialized, gendered body described as strong and durable, able to be penetrated without injury and able to birth. In chapter 6, we discuss how these reproductive and sexualized imaginaries mapped onto Black defendants as well. Attorneys described Black men's bodies as unique, identifiable, and assaultive and often invoked the racial stereotype of the large penis. And it was always the white—or white-presenting—forensic nurse who, as the expert, narrated the raped Black woman's body. Overall, we suggest that the nurse's medicolegal expertise was used not to introduce undisputable evidence but instead to make legible the body and voice of the victim-witness precisely because U.S. legal culture casts doubt on her body and her testimony.

The next chapter focuses on the forensic scientist and her role as legal storyteller in the courts. Although microinjuries (or what Wanda earlier called "millimeter lacerations") were sometimes present during forensic examinations, more often than not the symptoms of sexual assault could not be visualized or localized, making it difficult to formulate the pathology of sexual assault as Georges Canguilhem (1991) might in *The Normal and the Pathological*. Between the nurses and the other witnesses, a variety of absences were explained away: lack of injuries, lack of fingerprints, imperfect DNA matches (or absence of DNA altogether), and delays in disclosure. Whether compelling and insistent or repetitive and tedious, the parade of witnesses who testified to the absence of evidence established that all of these were securely "normal." As the SANE nurses in this chapter discussed the absence of visible injuries—even microinjuries—the forensic scientists in chapter 6 introduced the low likelihood of DNA transfer. In all these instances, the body of evidence was marked by size, stature, strength, or resilience. The next chapter demonstrates how attorneys paradoxically marked the court's science as both authoritative and ephemeral. The forensic scientist was charged with making the links between expert knowledge and "common sense," and we will show that one of the ways this was achieved was in reproducing the erroneous premise of race as genetic.

5

The Evidence Does Not Speak for Itself

Performing Forensic Expertise

Forensic science has long enjoyed a mythic status, especially in popular culture but in law as well, as an almost magical means for solving crimes. Forensics is the "silent witness," it "never lies," and it cannot misremember or be biased or bribed.
—Cole and Lynch 2006, 41

Forensic evidence is often regarded as independent, dispassionate, and objective. It can shed light on criminal proceedings charged with emotion and sullied by limits of human recollection. In the wake of public scrutiny of evidence-testing backlogs and the popularity of forensic analysis among the public, stakeholders hotly debate these resources (Innocence Project 2017). In the world of sexual assault adjudication, however, very few cases that reach trial include forensic evidence. In interviews, prosecutors shared that the existence of DNA was rare in rape cases, and when it was present, it functioned primarily as corroborating evidence rather than serving as the "slam dunk" case evidence romanticized by media and fictional crime dramas and reality series on television. "The probative value of DNA evidence rests on practices, circumstantial knowledge, and administrative assurances," wrote Michael Lynch, Simon Cole, Ruth McNally, and Kathleen Jordan in their ground-breaking opus *Truth Machine: The Contentious History of DNA Fingerprinting* (2008, xiii). They further asked: "How are the credibility and scientific status of evidence presented and undermined in adversarial discourse?" In Milwaukee's sexual assault trials, forensic scientists present and interpret DNA results from evidence collected, most often from the SANEs we discussed in chapter 4.

As described throughout our book, material and forensic evidence becomes meaningful only in light of the testimony already presented to the court. Therefore, when forensic evidence is available, the forensic scientist's testimony comes last in a sequence of witnesses, typically following the SANE nurse. Juxtaposed with each other, these witnesses often presented differently in court. As seen in chapter 4, the SANE subtly conveyed some of the emotional and social components of her interaction, evidence collection, and examination of the victim, whereas the forensic scientist, removed from the context of evidence collection, created a sanitized, scientific narrative about the nature and meaning of its recovery. Nurses were both fact and expert witnesses, striving to establish themselves as credible and objective because of the nature of their care work. In contrast, the forensic scientist remained distanced from the crime scene and clinical setting and was afforded a similar "mythic status" as that given to forensics itself. In short, cultural norms around scientific expertise and authority framed witnesses' participation in the trial.

The context of forensic evidence is fundamentally grounded in the embodied nature of sexual violence and the contact between the bodies of the victim and the defendant. While these are the focus of the victim's testimony, the immediacy and viscerality of sexual violence were mitigated by the witnesses who followed her. In chapter 4 the nurse labored to describe the evidence she did or did not find during her examination. She also offered some detail about the victim's demeanor and emotional state at the time of the examination, describing pain, injury, and the fleshy realities of sexual assault examinations. The forensic scientist's style of testimony was a marked contrast. Working with evidence collected by others, they transformed it into an artifact of law that transcended the emotionally fraught reality of the victim-witness. The forensic scientist's intervention also allowed for the transmutation of corporeal evidence of bodily fluids and tissues, ranging from semen to saliva to skin cells, into the clinical language of proteins and DNA. In short, forensic scientists used sanitizing language that did not dwell on the origins of the examination findings. Using statistical calculations and leaving the inner workings of their analysis hidden from the jury, the forensic scientists offered a frame for the jury to create their own associations between DNA findings and the witness, one that rested on racial identity and probability interpretations. As expert witnesses, forensic scientists restricted their testimony to the strength of their calculations, leaving the decision about the meaning of the calculations up to the court.

The forensic scientist was unique in that she was often the most well-prepared and practiced witness called to testify. Immaculately dressed in sober, dark-colored suits, moving through the courtroom with ease and familiarity, and testifying while making eye contact with the jury were some of the telltale signs of a trained professional. The ease with which numbers and figures rolled off her tongue was another indicator of the witness's experience and preparation. This preparation was a collective effort to which many forensic scientists in Milwaukee County attended with as much care and patience as they took to analyze evidence with precision. The collective nature and undertaking of the scientist's expertise was often erased during testimony however, during which the "we" of forensic science (Kruse 2016) was often supplanted by the witness's "I" in the courtroom. The individualization of expertise emerged as a careful erasure of the work of others and was compounded by the conventions of an adversarial justice system in which one may only speak for oneself. The role of the forensic scientist in sexual assault adjudication, then, served as the embodiment of a reified, imagined, and wholly self-contained scientific expert. This expertise was not simply deployed as technical and clinical; it was also performed in ways that sanitized the visceral traces of a defendant's violent body.

Quantification and Authority

In an interview with a former prosecutor turned felony court judge, she shared with us some of the troubles of explaining "negative evidence" in criminal cases when truth lies in numbers rather than human experience:

> JUDGE COLIN: I'll tell you this, my last couple of trials as a prosecutor, I've spent an equal amount, if not more time on negative evidence, explaining to the jury why I did not have certain forensic evidence. I literally counted how many people, including the paramedics, the firefighters, everybody who had been on the porch to disturb evidence and corrupt it, and had to spend a lot of time with the jury explaining why none of the bad guy's DNA was found on the

porch. Because they do come, I think they do come to expect it. It's shocking! It's like, you're not willing to take another human being's word that they say this happens anymore.

Science, technology, and society (STS) scholars have pointed out that ideals of objectivity and quantification are expressions of "dangerous subjectivity" (Daston 1992; Daston and Galison 1992; Porter 1995). The phrase "mechanical objectivity" is used to denote the authority given to "impersonal numbers" rather than judgment and experience. Judge Colin's quote points out the "mechanical objectivity" attributed to forensic DNA and the public trust placed on so-called scientific accuracy over and above eyewitness testimony. Historian Theodore Porter (1995) identified how objectivity and quantification became most important where trust was low and suspicion was high, a dynamic that characterizes the rape myth of the lying victim. In Judge Colin's striking quote, the image of DNA evidence and impersonal numbers is attributed to a "truth machine" (Lynch et al. 2008) and convinces jurors who are unwilling "to take another human being's word." A recent turn (or re-turn) in anthropological scholarship addresses this very issue, asking us to question the lure of quantification and measurement in responding to the wages of human suffering. Diane Nelson's *Who Counts?* (2015), Vincanne Adam's edited collection *Metrics* (2016), and Sally Engle Merry's *The Seductions of Quantification* (2016a) are among the many works that parse the swirl of numbers, enumeration, counting, metrics, statistical prognostication, ghosts of past events, or augurs of the future in contexts surrounding human rights, public health, human trafficking, gendered violence, and genocide. Nelson writes that

> numbers, of various kinds, are part and parcel of those selfsame world-making projects. . . . Numbers transverse and transect all terrains of life. They offer powerful tools of generalization and equivalence, but they are also deployed in particular instances, through situated and singular practices, and create complex relations between one and many, past and future. (Nelson 2015, 4)

Enumeration was one of the techniques that forensic scientists deployed when testifying in sexual assault trials, introducing them to numbers in the form of statistical probabilities that framed genetic evidence.

As this chapter will demonstrate, these statistical probabilities were gleaned from FBI reference data and rattled off with a breeziness that belied the labors that attended the calculations. The confidence with which DNA evidence is presented often contrasts with the reality of its prosecutorial effectiveness. In interviews, prosecutors shared with us that DNA evidence in rape cases was both rare and often unhelpful in arguing one's case. Most of the trials we observed did not involve any DNA evidence or testimony by forensic scientists. When DNA was discovered on the body of a sexual assault victim during medicolegal investigation, it often served simply to shift the defense narrative, wherein the defense would argue contrarily that sex between the defendant and the victim was consensual. This might account for some of the broader analyses by colleagues in criminal justice fields who note that increasing availability of scientific and medicolegal evidence in U.S. criminal prosecution of violent crime does not correlate with any particular outcome. That is, in many studies of prosecution at the state level, juries are not more or less likely to convict based on the inclusion of such evidence (Baskin and Sommers 2010).

In Milwaukee, prosecutors linked the emphasis on DNA evidence to a historical moment. One defense attorney we observed on many occasions put it this way:

> When I started [with the public defender's office] there was a case. . . . It was pronounced because it was one of the first DNA cases. That was like in '89 or '90. And since DNA has been accepted, it's really changed the dynamics of cold hits. You get cold hits from samples of guys who are caught years later and they find out that this is their man. That's changed a lot of things. It's made it a more scientific approach. . . . [This resulted in] a lot more involvement of the state crime lab.

Milwaukee's use of DNA evidence tracks with the history recounted by Lynch, Cole, McNally, and Jordan, who describe the early challenges to DNA evidence when it entered the U.S. and U.K. courts in the 1980s (Lynch et al. 2008, xiii). They subsequently wrote that DNA became a kind of gold standard of evidence in the 1990s, even establishing new norms of admissibility for other forms of evidence in the late 1990s. A published interview with one of the assistant district attorneys involved in the introduction of DNA evidence in Milwaukee prosecutions mirrors this timeline:

> I did the first DNA case in Milwaukee County—a serial murder case from the late 1980s and early 1990s when DNA was in its infancy. DNA evidence became the lynchpin for the case, which was a big one, and we secured a conviction.

That case involved an unknown suspect and relied on matching evidence from various crime scenes to those in a DNA database. Such matches are deemed "cold hits." The defense attorney quoted above recounted the rise of the cold hit, or the idea that a DNA database might be used to compare DNA recovered from crime scenes where no suspect had been identified. In sexual assault cases, the cold hit is premised on the myth of the stranger rapist, which may account for the lack of efficacy of contemporary DNA evidence in U.S. sexual assault adjudication. If most sexual assaults do not involve strangers, the primary purpose of relying on DNA evidence to identify a suspect does not exist. As already noted, most sexual assault victims were able to identify the suspect because they were often friends, relatives, or otherwise known to the victim. The legal questions of consent and use of force could not be resolved by DNA evidence. Rather, it simply corroborated the fact of sexual contact. An experienced prosecutor in the district attorney's office told us:

> DNA doesn't solve cases really, but I mean, sometimes it's helpful. I'm not going to say it's not helpful. But with adult cases, there's nothing on a sperm that says, "I came here consensually."

Confirming sexual contact may, in fact, be a useful legal tactic when the defense argues that no sexual contact occurred whatsoever or where the legal statutes do not require proof of use of force, for example, when a sexual assault victim is incapacitated or legally does not have the capacity to consent. Thus, DNA could theoretically play a very significant role in cases with child and adolescent sexual assault victims. The defense attorney quoted at the outset of the chapter confirmed the role delayed reporting could play in evidence recovery, saying "you talk about DNA, but a lot of times there's such a delay that there is no DNA." Another prosecutor recounted, with both sarcasm and disgust, a particularly "creative defense about floating DNA"—or the argument that, when people shared living spaces, DNA might end up on a variety of household items including a young child's undergarments just from using a shared laundry hamper. In another case we observed, the defense attorney said that his client had merely spit on the victim-witness and that was why his DNA was on her body.

In *The Social Life of Forensic Medicine*, Corrine Kruse (2016) also casts Swedish prosecutors as "legal storytellers." In her study, the legal storyteller stages the narrative of the trial, weaving together the evidence into the broader theory of the case. Beginning with the trial, she moves backward through the process of building a case, ending in the laboratory, where she locates the forensic scientists who analyze the evidence introduced at trial. She argues that each site of criminal justice investigation and prosecution relies on different modes of knowledge production. Her Swedish prosecutors manage the evidence produced by forensic scientists as a compelling storytelling element. In a context such as the United States, in which the forensic scientist is called to testify about the report they generated, this chapter asks: What kind of legal storyteller is the forensic scientist when they take the stand? Through interviews and observations of forensic scientists' testimony in court, we also discuss the ways in which they are prepared to perform testimony. If, per Sally Merry, quantification has seductive power, what techniques does the forensic scientist deploy to draw in her audience?

Setting the Scene: How to Be a Forensic Scientist

In this section, readers might note a shift in tone and style as we present an ethnographic description of a prototypical forensic scientist. The descriptions here draw on six distinctive jury trials involving five different forensic scientists, plus an interview conducted with one of these forensic scientists with her supervisor present. We do not distinguish among the various trials because of the small population of forensic scientists and our effort to maintain their anonymity. Because they worked so closely with one another and developed very similar styles of testimony, the forensic scientist emerges as a composite figure within this chapter. This shift parallels the marked difference between the forensic scientist as a witness and other witnesses that we have discussed in preceding chapters.

The testifying forensic scientist might easily answer casting calls to play criminalists on TV shows, one of the many CSI effects identified by Simon Cole and Rachel Diosa-Villa (2007), in which courtroom practices seek to emulate expectations jurors may have gleaned from media exposure, as described in chapter 1. As a storyteller, the forensic scientist took great pains with her appearance. As such, the forensic scientist always wore a suit to testify. The suit, as we observed, was always dark: black, navy, perhaps a deep gray. All but one of the forensic scientists we saw were women. Hair was simple and away from the face, and glasses were a frequent accessory. In the cases we observed, the testifying forensic scientist was always white, although we met racially diverse crime lab staff over the course of our research. As we have emphasized in earlier chapters, the scene of the white forensic expert testifying in court unfolded in a city that was roughly 40 percent African American, where adjudicants are overwhelmingly Black and Latino/a, and court staff, including judges, prosecutors, defense attorneys, and clerks, were white. The forensic scientist was comfortable in the courtroom; her comportment, style, and rote responses to questions constituted a living performance of "mechanical objectivity." Never the first witness to take the stand, she navigated the courtroom with foreknowledge, moving purposively through the courtroom entrance, then passing through the door of the bulletproof barrier separating the gallery from the space of the trial. She did not have to be led to the witness stand, and she did not flinch when the heavy door slammed shut behind her. The slam of the door took getting used to—we once saw the door smash a prosecutor's hand, breaking the bones of her finger. The forensic scientist easefully approached the witness stand, her familiarity with it glaringly contrastive to the victim-witness or the forensic nurses who may have testified before her. Only police officers and detectives, as described in chapter 3, appeared as familiar with the courtroom. In bodily demeanor, too, detectives and forensic scientists' postures and self-presentation communicated that "I am at home in this court." Without being instructed, the forensic scientist immediately raised her right hand and faced the clerk of the court after climbing the witness stand. As if memorized, she repeated the oath without hesitation and took her seat, acknowledging the jury with a brief glance before steadily meeting the prosecutor's gaze.

The legal storytelling proceeded in systematic fashion. First, the prosecutor had to establish the forensic scientist's expert status so that she could testify both to the facts of the case and offer an opinion. Where was she educated? What were her degrees? How long had she worked at the crime lab? What was she trained in as a forensic scientist? Could she explain what accreditation standards applied to the crime lab? What were the protocols for working with evidence? What was peer review? The questions were never unexpected, and the forensic scientist sometimes nodded subtly before proceeding to answer each anticipated question. She further turned her gaze and her body slightly toward the jury, addressing her responses to them and not the prosecutor.

Before entering the court to testify, the forensic scientist was sitting on a bench in the courthouse hallway reviewing her report, but she did not mention this, and the prosecutor did not ask her about it during testimony. Her responses flowed. They seemed neither stilted nor rehearsed in any obvious fashion. Sitting in on as many trials as we did, however, the scripted nature of the responses was undeniable. In these courts, every forensic scientist we observed responded to these questions in strikingly similar ways. This excerpt is reproduced verbatim from a court transcript:

PROSECUTOR: Ms. NAME, by who are you employed?

FORENSIC SCIENTIST: I'm employed by the Wisconsin State Crime Laboratory in Milwaukee.

PROSECUTOR: And what are your duties there?

FORENSIC SCIENTIST: I'm a forensic scientist in the DNA analysis unit. I perform forensic examination on evidence that comes into the laboratory. I perform DNA testing and statistics, writing reports, and testifying in court.

PROSECUTOR: And could you describe your educational background that qualifies you to hold that position?

FORENSIC SCIENTIST: I have a bachelor of science degree from [major state university] in biology. I've also taken a number of biochemistry classes from the University of Wisconsin–Milwaukee, and I also underwent the DNA training program at the Wisconsin State Crime Laboratory in Milwaukee.

PROSECUTOR: And what does the training program consist of?

FORENSIC SCIENTIST: The training consists of a series of lab practicals, lectures, examinations, and shadowing other analysts, and all of that is done in the different categories of evidence handling, screening, DNA analysis, statistics, report writing, and testifying in court.

As a legal storyteller, the forensic scientist relied on a scripted speech that she had mastered and was able to deliver in a seemingly spontaneous fashion. The precision of each answer demanded the jury's attention, and her comportment established her scientific expertise. There was no uptalk and no dangling question at the end of her statements as other witnesses commonly exhibited, unsure if they had answered a question completely or to the attorney's satisfaction. There was no rambling, hesitation, or pauses in her speech.

Whereas other witnesses simply offered broad responses to unclear questions posed by attorneys, the forensic scientist confidently asked the attorney to clarify. If she did not remember the details of the case, she told the attorney that she could not remember. Like clockwork, the prosecutor then introduced an exhibit: a copy of the forensic scientist's report. Flipping through each page, the forensic scientist verified that this was an exact copy of her report. The prosecutor then asked if having the report before her would serve to "refresh her recollection." The forensic scientist affirmed this, consulted the report as needed, and proceeded to answer the original question. Whether citing from the report or speaking from memory, the forensic scientist was confident and direct in her manner of speaking. In contrast, on a few occasions we observed defense attorneys vehemently cross-examining victim-witnesses for allegedly reviewing police reports prior to testifying or receiving assistance from prosecutors in preparation for trial. Defense attorneys habitually chided the victim-witness over memory and recall, contrary to the fact and expert witnesses who followed.

In her scientific performance of authority, the forensic scientist incorporated just the right amount of jargon, selectively introducing technical terms she precisely defined. She explained the concept of "chain of custody" and her careful adherence to its protocols; she identified the different types of DNA identification tests, including the conventional standard, Y-STR (Short Tandem Repeats) testing, and touch DNA. She tacked back and forth between her technical terminology and colloquialized descriptions of the techniques she employed to compare DNA samples to one another. A masterful translator in an ethnographic sense, she explained how she clipped a small piece from a buccal swab used to collect cells from the interior of a cheek, pausing to tell the jury that it is "like a giant Q-tip" before continuing to explain her process. Tacking back to technical terminology, she explained that her forensic analysis was "blinded." She did not know who the parties were in the case and identified samples only by number. Providing the jury with administrative assurances, she told them that in order to prevent contamination of evidence she was very careful to work with only a single piece of evidence at a time.

Her next task was then to compare the DNA profiles she developed with standards provided by the police or SANE nurses. The forensic scientist explained that a "standard" is a DNA profile from a known individual. To the ethnographers, the term "standard" sounded more authoritative than the thought of using more giant Q-tips to swab the cheeks of the witnesses and the defendant. The jury often appeared attentive and interested in the testimony, and a few jurors nodded their heads as the forensic scientist continued with her technical explanations and went on to deliver her expert opinion on the DNA comparisons. The probabilities of her analysis involved numbers that were difficult to imagine. The first level of analysis required the scientist to state whether she could rule out a match between the DNA profile retrieved from the sample and the DNA profile of the suspect. Is it possible that the DNA from the buccal swab belonged to the defendant? Yes, the forensic scientist testified—the suspect could not be excluded. It is impossible to be absolutely certain about the source of a trace, but the forensic scientist's role in court was to "produce a figure that allows conclusions about the relationship of a trace and its suspected source and that makes the results' value knowable, management, and communicable" (Kruse 2016, 89). The prosecutor then asked the forensic scientist to describe the reasons why DNA might not be transferred from contact between two people or why, once transferred, it may degrade or wash away:

PROSECUTOR: And when you're dealing in a case that has—where you're looking for DNA that may have been put on someone else's body are there any factors that would affect your ability to find DNA from someone else's body?

FORENSIC SCIENTIST: The presence, the lack or not—or absence, I guess, of a body fluid from another person would prevent us from seeing a very strong DNA profile. And the manner in which it was collected, the time that it was collected, whether somebody washed or bathed, depending on the body parts or the piece of item would affect any chances of us seeing DNA.

PROSECUTOR: Are there any conditions on the human body that would cause DNA to possibly degrade?

FORENSIC SCIENTIST: There—it depends on the body parts. They're—inside of a person's body cavity there are obviously lots of DNA cells from that individual's body, so if there is not a lot of foreign, what we consider foreign DNA or DNA that's not belonging to that person, we would not necessarily be able to see it. Your body naturally flushes out other—other profiles pretty easily, and so I think that's—I think that answers the question.

PROSECUTOR: And specifically when looking at someone's mouth, are there any natural conditions in the mouth that affect the ability of foreign DNA to remain in the mouth?

FORENSIC SCIENTIST: Yes. In your mouth you have amylase, which is something. It's an enzyme that helps you break down your food you're eating, so it's naturally going to start breaking down anything that's inside of your mouth pretty quickly when you are—when something's in your mouth.

DNA, the jury learned, was vulnerable to the elements. Following her testimony, the likelihood that DNA had been recovered at all began to seem improbable, unlikely, and perhaps even miraculous given potential degradation. Under these circumstances, its very existence asserted its definitive and probative value as evidence.

The prosecutor then asked the forensic scientist whether the profile she developed matched the DNA profile of the suspect. The forensic scientist explained that she conducted a statistical analysis. We imagined her with pen and paper, laboriously calculating probability scores, but in an interview she told us that, at the crime lab, of course, she used software (although she also mentioned that they could do the calculations by hand if needed). During the interview, she was less confident and looked at her supervisor frequently, sometimes asking her if she was allowed to answer our questions. Though we provided questions ahead of time, her answers were not scripted. We had seen her supervisor at court on several occasions, observing the forensic scientists from the gallery as they testified. Although she shared her reliance on statistical software with us during the interview, she did not tell the jury about how she derived the calculations. Therefore, the labor of "statistics" was one of the scientific metrics she did not expose for scrutiny by the jury. Asked about one piece of evidence tested, she phrased her conclusions as probabilities:

> [T]he probability of randomly selecting an individual in the U.S. population that would have this same major profile would [be] 1 in 1,009 individuals in the Caucasian population, 1 in 337 individuals in the Asian population, 1 in 1,005 individuals in the Hispanic population, 1 in 1,150 individual in the African American population[,] and 1 in 320 individuals in the Native American population.

The statistical probabilities were attached to racial categories, which the forensic scientist did not unpack for the jury. At the end of this chapter, we will return to the use of these racial categories and how they reinforce the problematic discourse of a simplistic genetic basis for race. The prosecutor asked the forensic scientist another question about her opinion about the DNA found on a hand swab:

PROSECUTOR: And did you run a statistical measurement?
FORENSIC SCIENTIST: Yes, I did.
PROSECUTOR: And what was that?
FORENSIC SCIENTIST: May I refer to my notes?
PROSECUTOR: Yes.
FORENSIC SCIENTIST: Probability of swabbing an individual in the population that would have this same autosomal STR profile as on the foreign male DNA from the finger swabs would be rarer than 1 in 16 trillion individuals.

PROSECUTOR: And 16 trillion is kind of a hard number to imagine. In relationship to the world's population, how much is that?

FORENSIC SCIENTIST: The world's population is estimated to be seven billion people and this profile was rarer than 1 in 16 trillion people.

PROSECUTOR: So just so I understand, it's your opinion to a reasonable degree of scientific certainty that the DNA on the pre-void gauze is [the defendant's]?

. . .

FORENSIC SCIENTIST: Yes, it is consistent with his.

These numbers are enormous and rarely encountered in day-to-day life, resembling what Lynch and colleagues (2008) described as certainty produced through an implied "vanishing point." In this excerpt, with assistance from the prosecutor, the forensic scientist offered a helpful comparison by citing the "world's population" in order to make the probabilities more meaningful. The numbers themselves are a show of "high science" and "mechanical objectivity"—requiring computational techniques, machines, and digitized databases lest the jurors attempt to comprehend the underpinning scientific principles and practices. "High science" symbolizes an ideology where machines are more reliable and more accurate than human action and expertise.

During one trial, the forensic scientist was called to testify by the prosecutor, beginning with the customary questions. The defense attorney began cross-examination by asking the forensic scientist to repeat her training. The forensic scientist, again, confidently and mechanically repeated the list of skills with which we had become familiar (note that this response is excerpted from a different trial than the one printed earlier in this chapter).

I'm a forensic scientist in the DNA analysis unit. I perform forensic examination on evidence that comes into the laboratory. I perform DNA testing and statistics, writing reports, and testifying in court. . . . The training consists of a series of lab practicals, lectures, examinations, and shadowing other analysts, and all of that is done in the different categories of evidence handling, screening, DNA analysis, statistics, report writing, and testifying in court.

The defense attorney's ears perked up when she heard that the forensic scientist was trained to testify before the jury. "What do you mean," she asked, "that you have been trained to testify in court?" It was the only time we saw the forensic scientist stumble. She hesitated before responding that she was trained in how to present information to the jury in a way that they could understand it. In a rare moment, the proverbial curtain revealed the workings behind the scenes, and the forensic scientist's responses were potentially perceived as scripted, practiced, and canned. The defense attorney continued to push forward the point, questioning the forensic scientist's impartiality by suggesting partisanship on the part of the crime lab. Why should she be prepared to testify? Shouldn't she answer honestly and without a commitment to being persuasive? The defense attorney dismissed the forensic scientist as an impartial authority; she was not simply an applied scientist. She had been called out as a legal storyteller.

Developing Scripts Behind the Scenes

The poise and conciseness of the forensic scientist suggested organizational support for cultivating a mode of testimony. As a legal storyteller, the forensic scientist practiced her expert mode of telling, evident in the routinized listing of professional training and skills. Only one defense attorney was enterprising enough to ask follow-up questions about the level to which such preparations indicated a deeply orchestrated approach to testimony, making the argument that the forensic scientist was biased in favor of the prosecution. In fact, forensic scientists' narrative of independence was challenged in a recent Needs Assessment Report prepared by the National Forensic Science Technology Center. The report concluded the Wisconsin State Crime Laboratory and other crime labs in the United States appeared as an "operating arm of law enforcement rather than deriving scientifically-supported conclusions from the evidence submitted" (NFSTC 2018, 2). The report further noted that decisions impacting scientific operations, influenced by law enforcement, "can be perceived as impacting the impartiality of the laboratory, with potential for creating bias and conflicts of interest," and provided recommendations for improvement. This criticism was not confined to crime labs in Wisconsin and reflected an international conversation occurring about the state of forensic science.

The similar responses and turns of phrase and the mode and style of self-presentation of the five forensic scientists that we observed during our field research suggest a deeply collective practice for approaching testimony. Preparing to testify then, was one of the major topics we discussed when we had the opportunity to interview one of the forensic scientists. As noted earlier, in contrast to her sharp composure during testimony, in an interview she was much less formal, more relaxed, and generally spoke with less confidence, as one might expect, than when she was on the witness stand. She also arrived with her supervisor and, as previously noted, at several points during the interview asked her supervisor's permission to answer our questions. It was clear that testimony was treated as a serious part of professional development and was an expertise achieved through collective cultivation. The forensic scientist explained to us:

> We sit down with people and we say, okay, here are questions you are typically going to be asked. "What is this? What is DNA? What are STRs?" And you need to be able to explain it, you need to be able to explain it in a way that people can understand it.

The training focused on the framing of direct examination by prosecutors, the questions likely to be asked, anticipation of possible courtroom scenarios, and collective sharing of testimonial experiences with other scientists. The collective endeavor of preparation and performance was extended to those forensic scientists with more courtroom experience as well, as they instructed those less-experienced scientists who did not understand courtroom etiquette. The forensic scientist also discussed creating and sharing effective language or descriptions. When we asked how they explained probabilities involving numbers so large they required unpacking for the jury, our interviewee responded that this was "part of our canned statement."

Together, the forensic scientists cultivated a collective investment in a structure of anticipation. As defined here, a "structure of anticipation" references the shared investment in a likely trajectory of a set of events that shapes the comportment and behavior of a cohort of experts as they contribute to their professional duties. For example, forensic nurses are often enmeshed within anticipatory structures that foresee the courtroom as the eventual arrival point for all sexual assault interventions, even when they are familiar with empirical analysis that document the high levels of attrition in investigation and adjudication (Mulla 2014, 59). It bears considering that structures of anticipation are formed through collective information gathering, and actual outcomes have very little impact on shaping expectations. "You know, this could happen, that could happen," the forensic scientist shared as she explained to us how she might present potential scenarios to her fellow scientists so that they, too, might participate in cultivating a similar structure of anticipation.

During training, this anticipation culminated in a mock trial. In the forensic scientist's own words, she described the extensive preparation process and performance assessments that included video recording and peer review:

> And there's a mock trial at the end of everyone's training where they sit down, and I've been the prosecutor before, and I run them through what would be a typical prosecution, and then depending on who's doing the defense, we've had some attorneys come in and be the defense attorneys. . . . And, after that's over they sit down with the technical leader, and I think their supervisors, they're videotaped, and they go through the videotape. So, it's a long process, and then eventually they just go to court and somebody goes with them.

The interviewee added that every forensic scientist was "required to be evaluated once a year for court," so a supervisor or senior colleague would accompany them and observe their testimony annually. According to a "DNA Discovery Checklist" prepared by the Wisconsin State Public Defender's Office, attorneys were also able to request proficiency testing results and testimony evaluations for each individual forensic scientist. In contrast with the forensic scientist, most witnesses do not have access to preparation for testimony and often testify with very little support from either the prosecution or defense attorneys.

Mediating the Defendant's Body

This chapter began by contrasting the work of forensic nurses with that of forensic scientists. Another key difference between them was how the forensic scientist mediated the evidence in the trial regarding the defendant's body. Scripted testimony was again made effective through the adoption of sanitizing language and almost always focused on forms of evidence connected to the defendant's body, often minimizing the DNA contributions of the victim-witness. The discovery of DNA evidence also cemented an impression of the defendant as a secreting body. DNA analysis itself materialized the collisions and intersections between an offender and a victim, as well as the effluvia and bodily secretions that left signs of violent contact.

The affective labor that the forensic scientist performed was key: with cool detachment, she generated a clinical portrait of the defendant's body and the trace secretions that were likely found on the victim's body. Forensic scientists commonly screened for traces of blood, semen, and saliva. Skin cells were another source of DNA, but it was impossible for forensic scientists to identify the origin of autosomal material. Unlike other witnesses, the forensic scientist typically and carefully discussed these forms of material and forensic evidence for the jury without disgust, repulsion, or shock. In short, their courtroom performance modeled for juries how to respond to potentially upsetting or unsettling evidence.

> First, I would like to mention that semen was not identified on several of these items. The next test that we would have performed was a test to look for possible presence of saliva. Amylase was detected on a few of these items.

In this testimony, the forensic scientist directly referenced the presence of saliva, a bodily fluid that indicated unwanted oral contact. To manage this potentially disturbing phenomenon, the forensic scientist pivoted toward her analytical strategy, focusing on one particular enzyme—amylase—that did not trigger the culturally conditioned aversion that the term "saliva" often elicited. She then outlined which items were found to carry amylase.

This linguistic sanitation was a common tactic in the forensic scientist's arsenal and projected a clinical demeanor. Like various moments during jury selection, it also signaled to the jury how encounters with disgust were to be met with an analytical orientation. This signaling parallels Sameena Mulla's ethnography of sexual assault intervention, in which she described the way SANEs were trained. In one particularly jarring episode, a police trainer played a deeply traumatic 911 recording in which a sexual assault victim was attacked while connected to the operator. In this instance, the trainer did not provide nurses time to process the call or to express their distress. Rather, they were polled about how the 911 recording shaped their understanding of possible sexual assault timelines (Mulla 2014, 80). While the trial did not have the trappings of an explicitly pedagogical exercise, the forensic scientist's approach to the visceral and disturbing details sanitized the evidence while also leaving its horrific possibilities and implied acts of violence at the edge of jurors' imaginations.

On cross-examination, the defense attorney further sanitized and minimized the presence of DNA evidence on items entered as evidence in the trial. The forensic scientist remained clinical but continued to gesture toward the defendant's assaultive and leaky body as mediated through the evidentiary exhibits brought into the courtroom.

> Amylase was detected on a few of these items. There was a pair of underwear, which amylase was detected [on that]. There was also bite mark swabs, where amylase was also detected. Also from the labial and mons pubis swabs.

This testimony described the presence of saliva, through its component enzyme of amylase, on various evidentiary exhibits, ranging from a swab of a bite mark to samples collected during a genital examination. The scientist adopted the linguistic strategy of using clinical language (for example, for genital anatomy) to sanitize the sex acts alleged in the criminal complaint while also describing the intimate and forceful nature of the events. A second linguistic strategy—that of frequent and repeated use of the passive voice—also appeared in this response, as it was impossible to attribute either the amylase or its discovery to an individual. This strategy also elides the problem, raised in the next section of this chapter, of positing the knowledge-making practices of forensic science through the "I" or the "we." In this example, the forensic scientist was a peer reviewer testifying on behalf of the analyst and report writer who had originally undertaken the work. By using the passive voice, the testifying scientist indicated for the jurors that she, herself, had not undertaken the analysis.

The defense attorney's strategy during cross-examination was two-fold: to limit the jury's interpretation of the evidence by asking the scientist to specify those bodily fluids that had not been found, and to minimize the specter of the leaky assaultive body associated with this client by asking questions regarding the quantity of evidence.

> DEFENSE ATTORNEY: There was no semen detected, correct?
> FORENSIC SCIENTIST: That is correct.
> DEFENSE ATTORNEY: And then there were swabs taken of a complaining witness's right inner thigh and no semen was detected. Isn't that correct?
> FORENSIC SCIENTIST: That is correct.

Here, the defense attorney clarified that no semen had been found on some of the submitted evidence exhibits. Mirroring the forensic scientist's tone, the defense attorney referenced the victim-witness's inner thigh but only as it was related to the lack of forensic evidence found there. By asking the forensic scientist to describe the lack of semen, the defense attorney invited the jury to consider the legal significance of both semen and saliva.

The defense attorney also diminished the notion of the defendant's body as one that shed copious amounts of evidence. It was important for the defense attorney to establish that DNA had been found in very small quantities on only some of the evidence gathered.

> DEFENSE ATTORNEY: So, DNA contained within the nucleus of the cell. It's obviously smaller than a cell in terms of physical stature, right?
> FORENSIC SCIENTIST: That's correct.
> DEFENSE ATTORNEY: How small is it? What size is it? Can you tell us?
> FORENSIC SCIENTIST: The—in one cell of an organism the amount of DNA is about seven picograms. That's a very tiny fraction of a gram.

And you consider a gram the size of about a nickel to a quarter, I
don't recall the exact fraction that a picogram is but it's about—I
think it's about a millionth of a gram. So it's very, very, very tiny fraction of a gram.

DEFENSE ATTORNEY: And it's a microscopic amount, right, we can't
see it?

The defense attorney went on to ask the forensic scientist how much
DNA she needed to carry out a valid DNA analysis, to which she replied
25 picograms. Performing a quiet arithmetic, the defense attorney said:
"You need about four cells?" These general questions by the defense
worked to minimize and limit the DNA analysis during the trial. They
also suggested that the defendant's body was neither assaultive nor
lugubrious, as a modest four cells' worth of material was the minimum
required to develop a full DNA profile.

By sharing their experiences, observing each other in court, and
providing notes and feedback, forensic scientists worked collectively to
achieve effective court testimony. This included preparing each other for
the unexpected by discussing various what-if scenarios. This practice
of preparation and training is succinctly expressed during testimony in
the standard litany of duties and responsibilities as "testifying in court."
During our interview, the forensic scientist emphasized how the collective nature of forensic practice and testimony contributed to her confidence and professionalism on the stand. It is striking to note how during
testimony the "we" of the crime lab was often supplanted by the "I" of
the witness.

The "We" and the "I"

The singularity of the "I" that peppered witness testimony when forensic scientists took the stand was partly produced through the structure
of adjudication itself. Rules of evidence required witnesses to speak only
in their own name, and attorneys sought to avoid hearsay by asking
each witness to describe only what he or she had said rather than what
someone else had said. Witnesses could, however, testify to the acts they
had observed others performing. This line was often drawn between
speech acts and other forms of action. Thus, forensic nurses could

testify that they had seen a victim-witness crying in the emergency room, but they could not tell the court what the victim-witness had said during the examination, as reported speech could fall squarely in the category of hearsay. Drawing attention to this distinction does not, however, fully explain the hesitation of forensic scientists to describe their activities using the plural pronoun "we." A further explanation is likely attributable to the 2009 Supreme Court case *Melendez-Diaz v. Massachusetts*, which represented a turning point in adjudicative practices. The case determined that defendants had a right to cross-examine forensic scientists. This decision closed the door to earlier practices in which reports could be submitted by forensic scientists and consulted without cross-examining the report writer. The introduction of other collaborators and experts at the laboratory could potentially have invited scrutiny from an enterprising defense attorney. Prior to evaluation, forensic evidence had passed through many hands in the chain of custody, including multiple screeners and analysts in the crime lab. Sociological and anthropological analyses of scientific knowledge production have often delineated its exceptionally collaborative qualities, be they evidenced through long lists of citation and attribution, discussion of processes of peer review, or the interdisciplinary expertise required to design and carry out experimentation (Latour and Woolgar 1979; Traweek 1988). Current understandings of the scientific community hinge on its investment in unitary paradigms, scientific practice, and scientific revolutions (Kuhn 1962).

Outside the courtroom, however, forensic scientists emphasized the collective nature of their practice of analyzing evidence. They referenced the "forensic community" when describing how methodological choices were made, describing the rise of STRs in the DNA Analysis Unit. When we asked how they maintained up-to-date scientific knowledge, the forensic scientist we interviewed described the dynamic in the lab as follows:

INTERVIEWER: And how do you guys keep up? I mean, so you're on a daily basis working but then I imagine that there's also a lot of science that's filtering through, so is there a person who's the person in the laboratory whose job it is to sort of keep abreast, or do different individuals take an interest in different areas, or. . . .

FORENSIC SCIENTISTS: It's kind of a collective. You have a technical unit leader, and she's in charge of ensuring that we do literature review every year. We're required to read a certain number of articles per year in our field and record that. If we have an interest in something, we do projects sometimes. We pull that in, or if I see an article that I think is really interesting, I can say, "Hey, can we have this available for literature review?" So we do that.

In this interview excerpt, the forensic scientist described what was a very clear collective endeavor, one that is comparable to how many scholarly specialties function in terms of maintaining familiarity with new research developments. In the interview, we noted that the forensic scientist slipped back and forth between the "I" and the "we." When we compared the use of the "we" and the "I" to pronoun usage during testimony, we observed a pattern of greater discrimination and separation between the plural and singular pronouns during testimony. Forensic scientists were unlikely to use both pronouns in the same response during trials, opting for one or the other and limiting the use of the plural first-person pronoun to early testimony about general practices in the lab. We discuss this in greater detail below. During the interview, the forensic scientist was also clear about her connections to other institutional responders in sexual assault intervention and adjudication. SANEs and scientists frequented some of the same training venues and participated in training one another. Prosecutors sometimes followed through with feedback and shared trial results. In contrast, during trials, the forensic scientist took great care to cast herself as neither for nor against the prosecution. "We're scientists, so we're not for one side or the other. It's just: here's what we found. Here's what it means, and the jury does with it what they will."

On the stand, the forensic scientist maintained a delicate balance between the collective body of knowledge and the scientific community in which she was embedded, speaking primarily in the first person. For example, forensic scientists sometimes used the plural pronoun to discuss generic practices within the state crime lab.

We will perform examinations on the evidence to determine whether stains are present on the item, and we isolate the DNA from cells. We break open the cells using the agents that will allow us to isolate the DNA itself from the rest of the body—or the rest of the organism from the cell itself. We quantify the DNA. We determine how much there is present in the item. We perform an amplification procedure which is—basically we make millions of copies of those sets of DNA we isolated in order to be able to see the actual profile that is present.

This forensic scientist educated jurors generally about the protocols of handling and analyzing DNA in the state crime lab. The discussion was very accessible at this level and remained simple. The examinations and techniques for identifying bodily fluids were left relatively ambiguous, with no discussion of the types of extraction processes used or the exact mode of analysis and identification. Forensic scientists on the stand simply never used phrases such as "solid phase extraction" or "differential extraction," "RFLP," "capillary," or "PCR," leaving juries with only a vague sense of how the process worked.

After the prosecutor had asked the forensic scientist about the general practices of the crime lab, she then began to ask the forensic scientist specific questions about her involvement in analyzing genetic material in a case.

PROSECUTOR: Were you the analyst who reviewed the material sent by the Milwaukee Police Department with regard to this case?
FORENSIC SCIENTIST: Yes, I was.
PROSECUTOR: And when you looked at the evidence, were there any— was there anything of note?
FORENSIC SCIENTIST: Nothing that I noted.
PROSECUTOR: So all of the security measures were still intact?
FORENSIC SCIENTIST: Correct.
PROSECUTOR: And were you the first analyst to work on this case?
FORENSIC SCIENTIST: Yes, I was.

Having established the general practices of the crime lab, the forensic scientist responded specifically about her own involvement analyzing the evidence for the case. The answer that the forensic scientist provided had carefully elided the question of memory. The expert responded as though she did not remember anything out of the ordinary about the case, though in reality her response—"nothing that I noted"—gestured to the recursive nature of her knowledge. Having just reviewed (rather than recalled) the case by reading through the case report, she was able to truthfully respond that she had not noted anything out of the ordinary. Had the evidence appeared to be tampered with, she would have written a note on the report. Because there was no annotation in her chart, she responded in a way that implied she did not recollect anything out of the ordinary.

The expert presentation of the forensic scientist was less predicated on her ability to memorize the pertinent details and more on her ability to blend her current self who was testifying with her past self who prepared the report in anticipation of a trial. As such, the forensic scientist indicated they did not memorize reports by rote:

> I look through the report. I look through all my notes. I see was there—because, you know, sometimes we go to court quite a bit later—was there anything unusual about this? . . . Unless it's a very short report with a very few items, I typically don't memorize because I don't want to rely on my memory and say something incorrectly.

By relying on her report and not her memory, the forensic scientist achieves a consistency in her testimony that lends it greater credibility. Compared to the witnesses that came before her, the report and the analysis constituted a singular perspective during the trial, and the forensic scientist carefully managed her responses so as not to err from the report. Consistent use of the first person throughout the remainder of her testimony reinforced the impression that it was the forensic scientist as witness who held the relevant knowledge pertaining to the case, while the collective "we" established that her mode of knowledge projection was produced within the normative standards of a reliable and respected community of forensic scientists.

While we rarely saw challenges to the forensic scientist's testimony, vigorous cross-examination was more likely to occur when the staffer who had written the report was unable to personally appear before the court. This occurred in two cases. In one case, the prosecutor did not explain to the jury why the report writer did not appear. In a second case, the forensic scientist who had written the report was deployed by the military for a period that precluded her participation in the trial. In both cases, a senior forensic scientist reviewed the case and appeared in the court to testify about its content. Ideally, the individual who testified in the report writer's place was someone who had participated in the crime lab's peer-review process. Prosecutors often asked forensic scientists to explain the peer-review process of forensic science. One forensic scientist responded:

> All of the reports in our cases get analyzed and reviewed by another techni- cal analyst in the—in the section that will go through my entire report, all of my data, and make sure that I followed all the policies and procedures that we have in our laboratory, and also they will come to their own con- clusions based on my data and will only approve or sign off on it as long as their conclusions are the same as the ones that I have in my report.

The peer reviewers are another way that forensic scientists justified their collective scientific endeavor. This description was also relatively ambiguous in the sense that nothing more was said to unpack the type, function, or process of peer review. Was the peer-review process, for example, blinded in any way? Were the results subjected to a variety of procedures or techniques? Though this is not the case in Wisconsin's criminal procedures, some forensic crime labs are privately owned and operated. In a single case we observed, a paternity test was sent to a private lab. When testifying on behalf of a report writer who could not appear, the forensic scientist and prosecutor explained that the stand- in was a suitable witness based on her earlier involvement in the peer review process. In these moments, the forensic scientists were more apt to explain the process of analysis as a collective endeavor. In the case of the deployed report writer, the prosecutor explained:

> The original analyst, Ms. [NAME], she's not here anymore. She's doing forensic analysis in Iraq. So [her substitute] is testifying today because she was one of the original peer reviewers on the case.

In this case, the substitute witness opened the door for an evidence con- tamination argument by the defense attorney seeking to cast doubt on the absent forensic scientist and the peer-review process.

DEFENSE ATTORNEY: And no one would know if any mistakes were made, only Ms. [NAME] would know? Mistakes can be made, right?

FORENSIC SCIENTIST: Yes.

DEFENSE ATTORNEY: Even if trying to do things perfectly?

FORENSIC SCIENTIST: Yes

DEFENSE ATTORNEY: Nothing in her notes about moving things around?

FORENSIC SCIENTIST: Correct. We were taught to only have one piece of evidence open at a time, but there are no notes there, correct.

DEFENSE ATTORNEY: So you wouldn't know if she had multiple items open at the same time?

FORENSIC SCIENTIST: No, but I would certainly hope not.

In her responses, this forensic scientist was measured and confident. She did not take offense at the defense attorney's attempt to cast doubt on the report's results. She maintained a steady volume and even tone and did not break eye contact with the defense attorney at any point. The defense attorney questioned the integrity of the report's findings, suggesting the possibility of cross-contamination among different items of evidence. While the forensic scientists' established lab protocols required accessing a single item of evidence at a time, because someone else had completed the testing of these items, the peer reviewer could not truthfully respond that her colleague had followed the protocols. While the prosecutor argued that "DNA supports what [the victim-witness] said," the defense attorney told the jury that "the prosecutor and I and [the crime lab] will never agree—that is for you to decide."

All of the forensic scientists we observed were able to provide the relevant probabilities of a DNA match to the defendant without consulting their research reports. These utterances were issued in a steady and clear fashion, with varying degrees of reference or explanation of how such calculations were made. The discussion of such large numbers with steady composure and confidence lent the forensic scientist a greater aura of authority. Next, we turn to the production of these probabilities and their unexamined relationship to racial categories.

Race, Population, and Databases

Earlier in this chapter, we introduced the types of probabilities that forensic scientists invoked when they described their results. The forensic scientists did not explain the historic or geographic origins of the racial populations named in the testimony. Neither did forensic scientists explain that there is a strident resistance to biologically reductive notions of race based on genetics (Roberts 2011; Tallbear 2013). Though they used the terms "Caucasian," "Asian," and "Hispanic," they did not explain whether these categories were genetically meaningful. Forensic scientists allowed the unexplained object of "race" to stand in for the complex demographic category they referenced, allowing race to harden and naturalize as genetically determined.

Probabilistic comparisons were the primary mode of meaning-making during the trial, but care had to be taken to do so within the narrow prescriptions of the law. DNA discovered at the crime scene, the victim-witness's body, was compared to the DNA collected from a known source: the defendant. The similarities between the standard taken from the defendant and the DNA collected were understood not as a complete match but as a diminishing set of probabilities that the DNA belonged to anyone else. For example, during a trial the scientist explained how

> [t]he random probability of seeing this Y-STR profile in the general population is one in 2,342 individuals in the Caucasian population, 1 in 337 individuals in the Asian population, 1 in 1,145 individuals in the Hispanic population, 1 in 2,015 individuals in the African American population, and 1 in 329 individuals in the Native American population.

Forensic scientists were careful to explain similarities between DNA samples through such probabilities, avoiding what defense attorneys termed the "prosecutor's fallacy" (Lynch et al. 2008, 156). According to the DNA evidentiary checklist used in preparing prosecutions involving such analysis, defense attorneys had to consider

> [i]f the DNA analyst or the prosecutor confused the meaning of the statistics and instead of saying the probability of this allele existing is 1 in

[whatever number] said that the probability of anyone other than the defendant committing the crime was 1 in [whatever number].

If the prosecutor overstated the meaning of the statistics by conflating the mere existence of a sequence of DNA with the probability of anyone other than the defendant committing the crime, this was termed the "prosecutor's fallacy" and could be challenged by the defense. The case *R. v. Deen* is often cited as the case law that overturned the independence of DNA evidence, limiting what conclusions forensic scientists could make in court. In this case, one forensic scientist stated that "my conclusion is that the semen has originated from Deen" (Lynch et al. 2008, 177). This was successfully challenged, and scientists were no longer given leeway to comment on events that occurred prior to their involvement in the case. As such, forensic scientists were careful to describe probabilities of a DNA sequence occurring. In the Milwaukee County courts, forensic scientists more commonly concluded that the DNA they had analyzed "was consistent with" that of the defendant. To do so, the forensic scientist often turned to DNA reference databases to explain how often the identified profile occurred randomly in the population. They articulated results, as seen in the excerpt above, through frequencies in relation to populations organized as racial groups. Ambiguity arose, however, in how they represented the population under comparison. The mere term "population" implied an exhaustive and broad-reaching set of mapped human genomes. The inclusion of racial attributes also conferred significance to race as having a genetic component. Michael Lynch and colleagues (2006, 160) wrote that "when DNA evidence is presented in court the proponent is asked to estimate how frequently a given profile occurs at random in a relevant population." How a relevant population was defined is open to greater criticism. In England, for example, "the recommended procedure involved calculating allele frequencies for different 'ethnic' populations and using the highest probability for the surveyed population when estimating the RMP [random match possibility] for the combination of alleles in a given profile" (Lynch 2006, 160). Compiling reference databases based on these ethnic or racial categories assumes that

urban neighborhoods and isolated villages often include concentrations of persons of similar ethnic origin with extended family ties, persons who

are more likely to share genetic alleles with one another than with randomly chosen individuals from a more broadly defined population group
or 'racial' subgroup. (Lynch 2006, 161)

As careful as forensic scientists were to define the probabilities of
the mapped genome in relation to four racial categories, they were
equally careful not to make any comments opining on the race of the
defendant, who was always present during the trial. It is clear in these
descriptions—and in the underlying assumptions about crime and who
commits it—that race stands in as a proxy for geographical locality, time,
and in-groups while also promoting a fantasy of multigenerational residential stability. This point was also argued in the case of *R. v. Deen* as
testimony addressed Deen's status as "half-caste" or "mixed race" while
also asserting that a "Negroid pubic hair" had been found at the crime
scene (Lynch et al. 2006, 164). During the appeal, Deen's attorney called
a forensic scientist who challenged the essentialist notion of racialized
pubic hair. These histories and scientific realities were submerged during sexual assault adjudication in Milwaukee County. Forensic scientists
understood that the racial categories they mobilized were not genetically
distinct subcategories but rather were proxy variables. Additionally, our
interviewee made the point of explaining, in relation to any DNA evidence they had discovered, that

> [w]e don't assume the race of the person who left whatever it is. . . . So, it
> might be more common in one population than the other, so we like to
> give all of them just to give you a better idea of how rare or how frequent
> that might be. It has nothing to do with the person who's on trial or who
> left it. It's just, we give all of them.

While the forensic scientist's understanding of probabilities and evidence interpretation eschewed directly implying that race was genetic,
it allowed jurors to make such assessments and did little to challenge
reductive notions of biological race.

In another trial, a forensic scientist mobilized the comparative unit of
"population" in describing the likelihood of DNA evidence being linked
to the defendant. She explained that

the probability of randomly selecting an individual in the U.S. population that would have this same major profile would be 1 in 1,009 individuals in the Caucasian population, 1 in 337 individuals in the Asian population, 1 in 1,005 individuals in the Hispanic population, [and] 1 in 1,150 individuals in the Native American population.

This delivery closely paralleled the deeply scripted performance of all forensic scientists, except for one forensic scientist who offered a greater degree of transparency as to how probabilities of STR were calculated. Her testimony substituted the concept of "population" with that of "database." Asked by the prosecutor whether the forensic scientist had done anything once she had compared the defendant's DNA to crime scene evidence, she responded:

[The DNA profile] is entered into a database that consists of a number of male Y-STR profiles to see if that is present in that database. And they were compared to 5,259 or 5,259 male individual profiles that were in that database. And this particular profile was not observed.

The prosecutor pressed on:

PROSECUTOR: And why is [DNA] entered into that database?
FORENSIC SCIENTIST: To determine if the rarity or how common this profile might be.
PROSECUTOR: Okay. And using that database, are you able to come up with some statistic of the frequency of Mr. [NAME]'s Y-DNA profile?
FORENSIC SCIENTIST: Yes. There is a listing here of the various ethnic populations. And I don't know if you want me to list all of those, but this particular set of numbers was derived because of the fact that his profile was not observed in this particular database.

As the reference database was discussed in court, it became clear that it was not the exhaustive aggregation of every DNA profile ever collected by governing agencies. It was sampled from 5,259 "male individual profiles," but the relationship of these profiles to the general population was a projection.

The slippage between population and database was even more pronounced in a different trial, during which the forensic scientist corrected herself as she testified:

Applying a 95 percent upper confidence interval, the expected frequency of finding this particular Y-STR profile in the population is, excuse me, not in the population, in the database, is approximately one in 8,929 individuals in the entire database. One in every 2,433 individuals in the African American population. One in every 1,212 individuals in the Asian population. One in every 2,899 individuals in the Caucasian population. One in every 1,389 individuals in the Hispanic population. And one in every 990 individuals in the Native American population.

The forensic scientist corrected her use of "population" where she meant "database," but then she went on to summarize the racially specific analyses in relation to populations without explaining, again, that the populations were those aggregated within the database. Once more, those racial categories were left unexplained.

Conclusion: Interpreting Science

The successful presentation of DNA evidence was as tethered to the perception of the fidelity of its scientific rigor as it was to the expert ways in which it is made legible to juries. The forensic scientist could not give away the performative nature of her legal storytelling role for the DNA evidence to be taken as scientific and authoritative. Statistical probability was produced through a series of figures that appeal to laypeople who make up the jury. The science that was explained to the jurors was selective, leaving intact their popular imagining of a genetically simplistic racial marker. The selective invocation of weighty correlations stood in contrast to the decontextualized account of racial genomics within the courts, tapping into and naturalizing taken-for-granted interpretations of racial biology while emphasizing the quality of the DNA identification process. Yet, the testifying forensic scientists put as much care into their scientific technique and quantitative literacy as they did in their self-presentation. Whether by coincidence or by design, the whiteness of the forensic scientist and the taken-for-grantedness of race within the presentation of probabilities contributed to a performance of scientific authority. In one case, a seamless performance of expertise came undone when the preparation for testimony was scrutinized in trial. But without a probing defense attorney, the legal storyteller's performance was compelling, underscoring the careful self-presentation and preparation entailed in the performance of analytical expertise that makes DNA evidence meaningful and corroborative.

Once the forensic scientist had completed her testimony, she practically showed herself out of the courtroom, poised and confident. If she had been effective, her ease was interpreted as expertise. The large numbers with which she had wooed the jury suggested the possibility, probability, and likelihood that the defendant's DNA was found on the victim-witness. Though race was not on trial, the forensic scientist deployed racial groups as shorthand for populations that reinforced a principle of biological race. Because that issue was left unexamined, the jury was likely to retain this popular imagining of simplistic racial markers.

6

The Good Father

Masculinity, Fatherhood, and Scenes of Admonishment

> Ladies and gentlemen of the court. The defendant is a wonderful man. I miss him and love him. I was thinking, not everything is white and black. There is gray, a color no outsider can see. I want my freedom back. I want my daddy back.

These were the words that 12-year-old Ruthie's mother read to the court at the sentencing hearing of her husband, Isaac Miller, who plead guilty to second-degree sexual assault of a child. Ruthie was not present for the sentencing, but her mother requested permission to read from the victim impact statement she said was written by her daughter. Ruthie's statement characterizes the ambivalence of fatherhood when it is the father figure who is the perpetrator of sexual violence. The love the victim feels for her father is the power he uses to gain her trust and sexually coerce her. It is not possible to know whether the words written by Ruthie were her own or resulted from the influence of her family. The father is also, in this case, the husband. The convoluted nature of family relations in sexual assault cases compounded the tensions of adjudication. Ruthie's mother herself begged the court to be lenient with "the love of her life" and pleaded that he was "a good father and husband, not a monstrous criminal." In referencing "outsiders" who could not understand what was truly unfolding in her family, Ruthie pointed to the secrecy and privacy that engenders sexual harm within the family, often perpetrated by a paternal figure who wields violence against both his children and his partner. Silence can be related to love, coercion, and the unbearable weight of keeping the family together and whole. Was Ruthie's mother ventriloquizing her daughter? Or was this Ruthie's authentic statement? Both scenarios were likely to be true. After his wife and his employer had voiced their emphatic support for Isaac Miller, he contritely made a statement on his own behalf. The court's decision was rendered, we will argue, through a calculus that credited the race-class intersections of the Miller family, while it disadvantaged other fathers who are differently marked by race and class.

This chapter focuses on the last testifying witness: the defendant. Unlike other witnesses, defendants were not compelled to testify—they were to be regarded as innocent until proven guilty. In fact, defense attorneys often advised defendants to remain silent, shielding them from self-incrimination. Even still, some defendants chose to give up this right and testified on the record from the stand. Others only spoke during their sentencing hearings, and still it was common that defendants' family, friends, or attorneys spoke on their behalf. This chapter thus probes the cultural narratives attached to the defendant, including that of race and class as it intertwined with the symbolically dense cultural signifier of fatherhood. The court marked its moral typology of the father when it cast his harm as spilling over from the family into society. While scholars have argued that adjudicated incest cases receive relatively short sentences (Corrigan 2006), our research showed that cases involving the sexual assault of children by fathers and father figures received far more variable sentences in the Milwaukee County court system. In fact, the two cases we discuss in this chapter vary in punishment from a four-month sentence in the county jail to a decades-long sentence to be served in the state penitentiary. We demonstrate that these variations are shaped by the ways in which courts interpret the relationship of the father to the child, to the family, and to society. In short, there are multiple pathways for considering the form of sexual harm visited upon the victim, and both judges and prosecutors participated in constructing sexual harm (Small 2019).

As a historical genealogy, fatherhood holds positive ideological privileges within families and communities, and many men enjoy the patriarchal configurations and social privileges of moral authority and provider. Men variably inhabit these privileges depending on the boundaries of race and class, demonstrated through a host of paternalistic lessons and humiliations provided by judges to rape defendants and their families during sentencing hearings (Gonzalez Van Cleve 2016, 62). One judge we observed bemoaned the "problems" he perceived in the "African American community" as he sentenced a defendant who had earlier conveyed his desire to fulfill his social obligations as a father to his own children:

> Is it a problem in Milwaukee, kids growing up without their fathers? Yes. Is that a particular problem in the African American community in Milwaukee? Yes. . . . I see fathers who literally don't care one iota about their child and in some cases don't see them, don't talk to them, don't pay support[,] and couldn't probably identify them, but to say you're concerned about your son growing up without a father . . . this is all your fault.

In this transcript, the marking of fatherhood was racialized and monetized. Recorded for the record, these determinations of fatherhood accrued as a form of legal and social archive. Thus, we argue that this literal marking is a metonymic act that symbolizes the court's racial surveillance of the family through the spectacle of the hearing and the creation of the court record (Browne 2015).

Focusing on the cultural narratives surrounding defendants at trial and during sentencing hearings, we demonstrate how the courts engaged with the contradictions of patriarchy in which men are provided a "license to harm" (Presser 2013). Invoking genealogies such as the Roman *patria potestas*—in which the father had right of life and limb over his wife and children—our analyses are situated within the ideological, symbolic, and material discourses of fatherhood as that which is imbued with power and authority. Whereas *patria potestas* may seem long past, marital rape became illegal in all 50 U.S. states only as of 1993. This is a sobering reminder that the male head of a household is a privileged legal subject within our legal traditions (Yllö and Torres 2016).

Though fathers no longer have the statutory right to discipline the family or sexually assault their wives, defense counsel narratives echoed genealogies of paternal privilege. Over the course of our observations, all but four of the defendants we witnessed in court were men. Therefore, the subject of sentencing is overwhelmingly a masculine-identified figure. The rhetoric of fatherhood was a powerful commonplace from which to argue the relative merits and faults of the defendant. This rhetoric was often employed by attorneys and even defendants themselves during trials, as was the case for the defendant Jerry Johnson in chapter 2. During an interview afterward, Johnson's defense attorney noted that he was impressed when the defendant spoke lovingly about his daughter on the stand because it "humanized him." Judges, too, spoke at length of the merits and deficiencies of defendants as fathers, either crediting them for their successes or admonishing them for their failures.

Ruthie's words "I want my daddy back," read by her mother, doubled as a victim impact statement and a statement pleading for leniency on behalf of her father. The punishment he received contrasted heavily with that of another defendant, Tony Young, who was found guilty of first-degree sexual assault. Whereas Miller plead guilty and adopted a posture of penitence, Young was found guilty by a jury after a trial and maintained his innocence during his sentencing hearing. A second point of contrast—though one that we as researchers interrogated with care—is the difference in racial identity of the two families involved. Miller and his family were white; Young and his family were Black. In the next section, we turn to *State v. Young*, a trial replete with moments in which the defendant was both denigrated and lauded for his role as father, themes that were carried through to his sentencing. The second section returns to the sentencing of Isaac Miller, expanding the ways in which the court, the family, and the defendant himself produced narratives of failed and successful paternity throughout the hearing. The court's acknowledgement of Miller's successes as a father and its conclusion that he was "sincere" in his penitence may have attributed to his mitigated sentence. Both cases also contained moments in which it was not simply the defendants but their families who were also addressed by the court. In the final section, we widen the scope by discussing several cases in which judges directly addressed the defendant and his family during sentencing hearings. These admonishments documented the father's criminality for the court record while simultaneously revealing his "true" nature to his children and partners. These public commentaries and forms of record-making were further examples of racial surveillance practices that distinctly fixed Black and brown fathers and Black and brown families within the everyday routines of the law and the legal archive. Examining these various moments in which fatherhood was invoked in its idealized and caricatured forms shed light on the ways in which the court reproduced white heteropatriarchal notions of appropriate performances of masculinity according to racialized and classed notions of the welfare state.

Negating Paternal Care: *State v. Tony Young*

By the time we observed *State v. Young* in November 2013, we had already observed 22 jury trials—seven of which involved father figures, including biological fathers, stepfathers, mothers' boyfriends, grandfathers, and uncles. In this case, Mr. Young was charged with three counts of first-degree child sexual contact with a person under the age of 13 and one count of incest with a child. The assaults came to the attention of authorities after Young's then–15-year-old daughter, Tasha, wrote a letter to her mother (who retained custody following her parents' divorce) explaining that she had been keeping secret how her father sexually assaulted her on multiple occasions. She disclosed that the assaults occurred between the ages of seven and nine on weekends when she was at her father's house. Only two weeks earlier we observed another case involving a father figure before Judge Williams, the same presiding judge in *State v. Young*. In that case, compelling testimony from the victim and other witnesses had portrayed a fraught family life wherein the defendant displayed sexual entitlement over all the women living in his house, including his stepdaughter, her mother, and several girlfriends. Perhaps because the victim did not tell anyone about the sexual contact for a number of years in order to protect her family, or perhaps because the mother testified that she did not believe her own daughter's accusation, the jury acquitted the defendant of three charges of sexual assault. After that case, we had the chance to talk with the defense attorney, who confided to us: "The biggest threat to your children is mom's boyfriend—I know that to be true." In this confession, the defense attorney shared her experience of representing many men accused of assaulting their children and stepchildren.

In *State v. Young*, the defendant was in custody at the time of trial. He was dressed in a black suit with a crisp white button-down shirt so that the jury would not know he was in custody. The suit fit him well, which was not always the case. Before the jury entered the courtroom, Young's defense attorney handed him a tie to wear. The prosecutor called the victim, Tasha, as the first state's witness. Tasha, African American like her father and mother, was a youthful 16-year-old. She walked slowly into the courtroom and passed through the heavy door separating the gallery from court personnel. She wore a long-sleeved black crew-neck shirt with khaki-colored jeans. A small tan-colored purse was strung across her shoulders for the duration of her testimony. The small purse gave her a less adolescent and more childlike appearance. Her hands were lightly folded in her lap, and she looked directly at the ADA for most of her testimony, speaking clearly into the microphone. Following some opening questions about Tasha's educational background and age, the prosecutor asked Tasha to explain her parents' divorce and custody arrangements. Tasha described how they had been apart since she was two years old. When she visited her father, Tasha testified that she slept in his bedroom because he lived in close quarters with her grandmother and great-grandmother in a duplex on Milwaukee's North Side. The prosecutor then introduced the letter Tasha had written to her mother, labeling it Exhibit 1. The introduction of the first exhibit triggered an objection from the defense attorney, so both attorneys retired to Judge William's chambers to hold a discussion out of the jury's earshot. While they argued before the judge, Tasha was left alone on the witness stand, exposed to the jury, the public seated in the gallery, and her father, the defendant. She hung her head down, concentrated on the letter she had written, which the prosecutor had left in front her. Her soft sighs were audible, as the microphone was left activated during the sidebar. Though Tasha's eyes almost never strayed from the letter, from time to time she glanced quickly at the jury. While some judges would remove the jury during sidebars, Judge Williams's choice to retire to his chambers left Tasha and the defendant exposed to each other and to the silent gaze of the jury. A full seven minutes passed before the judge and attorneys returned and the trial continued:

PROSECUTOR: Why did you write that letter?
TASHA: To tell my mom what Tony did to me. He molested me between the ages of seven and nine.

Though we could hear Tasha's testimony clearly from the gallery, the defense attorney hollered out, "I can't hear her! Please have the witness speak up!" The exclamation startled the jury members, who turned to one another and then back to Tasha, who did not seem visibly ruffled by the outburst. We noted that Tasha referred to her father by his first name, suggesting a fracture in her relationship with him as her father, the prosecutor would later suggest. Judge Williams glared at the defense attorney as the prosecutor continued.

> PROSECUTOR: What is your first memory of this behavior?
> TASHA: When I was in the bathroom with Tony. He was in the bathtub with his clothes off, too, and he started washing me. His hand touched my vagina.
> PROSECUTOR: This happened over a few years?
> TASHA: Yes.
> PROSECUTOR: What is the next memory you have about being molested by Tony?

Tasha said she had no specific memory, but she remembered "excessive touching" every time she saw Tony overnight. In her descriptions, the conflation of care and abuse were palpable. Her recollection of paternal care—the act of being bathed—was sutured to something she could only articulate as "excessive touching." Tasha's dawning awareness of her father's ministrations as abusive was linked to her educational experiences at school. When the prosecutor asked how she knew the touching was "excessive" or "wrong," Tasha responded: "Sex education. I didn't know really what a father should be, what my expectations should be. He'd put his penis in my hand." Because of sex education, Tasha was able to describe the body parts that her father touched and to identify his actions as wrong. The prosecutor continued her examination:

> PROSECUTOR: Would he say anything?
> TASHA: A couple times, when he touched my vagina 'til I was shaking, he whispered "that's called an orgasm."

These statements disabused listeners from any sense that Tasha had somehow misunderstood normal father-daughter relations. The defendant had framed his disturbing utterance in the mode of paternal education, teaching her to name the experience he had imposed on her body. Following this framing, Tasha's descriptions of "[Tony's] head on my chest and his stubble from his beard" could not be mistaken for paternal tenderness but were clearly something sinister and unsettling. As she described the many acts of sexual victimization she had experienced at the hands of her father, the prosecutor commented that she seemed somewhat "emotionless" during her testimony:

PROSECUTOR: You seem so matter of fact, why?
TASHA: 'Cause there [are] some things I can't change.
PROSECUTOR: Why didn't you tell? Why did you keep this a secret?
TASHA: I thought it was normal at first, then I was too scared to tell because it was my dad. My mom raised me to not tell adults what I think they should do.

Tasha's response to the question emphasized the inevitability of her past and revealed the adolescent's liminal state discussed in chapter 2. She could not change what had transpired. She offered three additional reasons for maintaining her silence. First, she said she thought it was "normal." Echoing her earlier sense that she did not know "what a father should be," the mere fact that the sexual assault was carried out by her father gave her the impression that such acts could be quotidian events in father-daughter relations. She followed the first part of this statement with a second reason: that she was "too scared" to tell because her father was the abuser. Her testimony revealed the child's submission to the authority of the parent. Would she be believed? Or would she be punished for her honesty? Finally, she stated that she had been raised by her mother not to tell adults what they should do. In this third part, she marked the submission of children to all adults, not simply to her father.

PROSECUTOR: Were you being obedient?
TASHA: Yes. I was raised to follow directions.
PROSECUTOR: When you realized this wasn't normal, why didn't you tell someone?
TASHA: I was afraid. I didn't think anyone would believe me because people don't think a father would molest their daughter.

In this second section of testimony, the prosecutor emphasized Tasha's subordinate position as an "obedient" child. This obedience was not irrelevant to the conditions of her victimization by her father, a powerful figure who she was raised to obey. In her response, Tasha also reiterated her fear, this time linking her concerns to the terror that she would not be believed because of the very nature of her relationship with the abuser. As Tasha stated, "[People don't think a father would molest their daughter." In this characterization, Tasha indexed social norms and a community resistant to the possibility that fathers sexually assault their daughters.

Despite her fears and concerns that she would not be believed, as she grew to recognize her relationship with her father as sexually abusive, Tasha sought assistance. Looking down toward her hands as she testified, Tasha explained that she wrote the letter to her mother because she "wanted help." Tasha had been able to halt the sexual assaults by insisting on ending her relationship with her father. She stopped going to his house, clarifying: "I was tired of being touched and feeling guilty, 'cause what was happening to me was my fault." Toward the end of direct examination, the prosecutor asked her why she had not demanded that the abuse end. Addressing the jury with resignation, Tasha said she did not tell her dad to stop because "he's my dad."

With the prosecution's direct examination complete, defense counsel used cross-examination to probe Tasha's testimony in order to discredit her. Pacing throughout his questioning, he began by raising issues around parental discipline. Tasha was poised throughout, though she crossed her arms tightly across her chest. Defense counsel asked Tasha whether she ever told her mother about the sexual abuse while the incidents were alleged to be taking place, whether she was truly close to her grandmother, and when exactly her mother had remarried after divorcing her father. He then veered sharply in a new direction, asking Tasha whether her mother had allowed her to start dating in 2010. She responded "yes" just as the prosecutor raised an objection based on relevance. Judge Williams elected to allow the line of questioning but warned defense counsel to keep it brief.

Defense counsel established that Tasha was 13 years old when she started dating young men. While he could not offer any editorializing on why this might be relevant to the case, these facts were perhaps introduced to frame Tasha as sexually precocious and to suggest that her dating life presented opportunities for sexual encounters and sexual knowledge. As the defense framed it, Tasha's dating life introduced additional parental (and paternal) discipline in her life. Defense suggested that Tasha was lying about her father sexually abusing her in order to get attention. He argued that she sought more freedom from her familial responsibilities, drawing attention to parts of the letter she wrote to her mother. Defense counsel said, "Tasha, this letter, there are six lines in the letter about the molestation. That's it. The rest of the letter talks about hanging out with friends and responsibilities."

In the letter to her mother, Tasha wrote that she was tired and did not want to do so much work around the house. She explained that her mother was very ill with multiple sclerosis, fibromyalgia, and arthritis, while her brother suffered from cerebral palsy and epilepsy. Because of their various illnesses, Tasha had to shoulder much of the household responsibilities. On the stand, Tasha insisted that she did not mind helping around the house. Rather, she was tired and needed emotional support, noting that she now had a psychologist. Defense counsel ended cross-examination by sowing additional seeds of doubt by asking: "Didn't you call your father when you got in an argument with your stepfather . . . ?" and "Didn't Mr. Young tell you to focus on your grades and not on the boys?" He emphasized that Tasha had not cut off all communication with her father, even calling on him to intervene in a conflict with her stepfather. He also drew attention to Young's paternal instruction while again referencing Tasha's dating life. Mr. Young had told her to focus on her grades, not boys. Was the defense suggesting that Tasha was boy-crazy and resented her father's reprimand?

Upon re-direct, the prosecutor pivoted sharply from the defense's framing of Mr. Young's interactions with Tasha as ones of paternal discipline and care, focusing instead on how the defendant had groomed his own daughter for sexual assault. She asked Tasha to confirm that her father showed her sexual anatomy books and pornography when they were alone in the house together. The prosecutor also returned to the role of sex education in Tasha's decision to come forward. Had the sex education curriculum covered abuse within families? Tasha replied that it had not. Rather, the school curriculum introduced ideas of "good touch/bad touch" and warned her to be suspicious of strangers. She had taken what she learned about "bad touch" and interpreted her own situation. Defense then asked for permission for another round of questioning. His questions were again about the letter Tasha had written. During much of the defense attorney's questioning, the jury varied from appearing dispassionate to actively shifting uncomfortably in their seats.

They attentively observed as he asked Tasha why she had written about wishing she were a prettier girl.

> DEFENSE: How would being prettier have changed this?
> TASHA: There is nothing in fairy princess tales about fathers molesting their daughters.
> DEFENSE: So, it's some sort of fantasy?

In this exchange, defense counsel raised the possibility that Tasha's account of sexual abuse was fantasy. The prosecutor objected to the statement, and Judge Williams overruled it. Tasha became teary for a moment but answered: "I'm not really sure, he brought me low self-esteem." She went on to offer a solemn description of the power her father held, not only to force her to participate in sexual acts against her will but also to hold her emotionally hostage and lower her self-esteem. Tasha's testimony ended here, with no further questions from either the prosecutor or the defense. Judge Williams excused her from the witness stand, and the trial continued.

By the end of trial, we had observed three days of testimony by Tasha, her mother, a school friend, police officers, and a school social worker, with more objections, sidebars, and departures to the judge's chambers than in any other rape trial we previously observed or documented thereafter. Young chose to remain silent at his trial and did not testify. During her closing argument, the prosecutor reminded the jury that Tasha's testimony had been believable, true, and consistent. She argued that there was no plot on Tasha's part to manipulate her father:

> She had no intent to get her father in trouble. She's that devious? That evil and cunning and plotting? No! It doesn't make any sense. What the defense is doing is blaming the victim and it's not true.

While defense counsel introduced the specter of reasonable doubt, he also used his closing argument to connect with the jury. Perhaps reflecting on his own tone and glib demeanor during cross-examination, defense counsel insisted to the jury: "I don't enjoy beating up on a teenager—I have a teenage daughter, but we have to ask questions." Here, the defense attorney—for the first and last time—positioned himself as a father, noting that his treatment of Tasha *only* reflected his imperative to do his job and "ask questions." After all the evidence was presented and arguments made, the jury found the defendant, Tony Young, guilty on all five counts charged, including incest with a child.

About two months later, during Young's sentencing hearing, both prosecution and defense once again raised the trope of fatherhood to alternately argue for harsher and more lenient sentences. This time, Tony Young was in custody and was led into court in his orange jumpsuit. He entered the courtroom with his head hanging down and did not make eye contact with his family members seated in the gallery. Neither Tasha nor her mother were present for the sentencing, although the prosecutor had contacted them in accordance with Wisconsin's victim notification laws. The prosecutor reported to the judge that neither the victim nor her mother had submitted written victim impact statements.

Judge Williams began the sentencing hearing by announcing the charges of four counts of first-degree sexual assault of a child and one count of incest. Defense offered some corrections to the presentencing investigation report submitted by the Department of Corrections, and then the prosecutor began her sentencing argument. Without a jury present, her tone was more pointed and argumentative than it had been during the trial. She informed the judge that she was recommending a 30-year sentence, to be structured with 20 years in custody and 10 years of extended supervision. The victim had been "sexually assaulted in various ways" from the ages of seven to nine years old. She reminded the judge that the assaults had taken place when "the child had placement with her father" during weekends and stated she was Young's "biological daughter." The prosecutor made a note for the record that she had initially offered Tony Young a plea deal of 25 years but had since revised her recommendation because the case had gone to trial, forcing Tasha to testify and to publicly detail the harms she had suffered. Judges and attorneys often acknowledged the victim's spectacle of suffering during sentencing hearings, although the blame was squarely placed on the defendant, never the state.

In explaining the way in which Tasha had come to "pour her heart out" in a note to her mother, the ADA noted that Tasha internalized blame for her suffering, writing that "if she had been prettier or better" it might have changed the outcome as "none of the princesses in the fairy-tales she recalled were sexually assaulted by their fathers." She went on to characterize Tasha as "candid and truthful on the stand," then lamented that Tasha would always associate her first sexual encounter with being a "frightened child with her own father." By including such details, the prosecutor contrasted the ideal of paternal care and the violent reality of paternal harm. In this case, the powers and privileges of patriarchy and fatherhood authorized a "license to harm" through the familial obligations of the obedient child, the precarious custodial arrangements via Tony Young's living conditions, and the cultural fiction of the stranger sexual predator dictated in school sexual education. Tasha's father had used these social and structural conditions and his status to sexually exploit and assault his daughter. The ADA further argued that the defendant had polluted his daughter's earliest experience of "sexual initiation" and had further visited harm upon her by forcing her to testify.

While defendants have the right to maintain their innocence and to be tried before a jury of one's peers, the court often interpreted this as a refusal to take responsibility for the crime in the event that a guilty verdict was rendered. Young's family, including his mother and fiancée, appeared in court to offer their support and make statements that spoke to Young's redeeming characteristics. His brother accompanied them to court but did not speak during the hearing. Defense counsel began his sentencing argument by letting the judge know that Young's family was present. He addressed Young's criminal record, which he said did not include any "assaultive offenses." Then he began to give an account of Tony Young's background: "He grew up in a good home with a good family. He had his mother and his father. His father died when he was young." The court could interpret the information about the death of Young's father early in his life any number of ways: as a sign of his father's presence and involvement in Young's upbringing, or as absence, read against the deeply rooted stereotype in the courts of the pathology of the Black family in relation to the missing father. Continuing, defense repeated that Young's family represented "good people," telling the judge that they were all employed. Young himself was a high-school graduate and a certified nursing assistant and had cared for his grandfather, who had passed away five months after his arrest. Young had also been honorably discharged from the army and was "contributing to society but for his offenses." He emphasized that Young was neither "cold nor calculating . . . and was just a normal guy." He requested a 15-year sentence, just half of the 30-year sentence requested by the state. This noticeably shorter sentence suggested that defense counsel strongly regarded Young's redeemable characteristics even when the offenses carried a longer maximum sentence. Defense offered the defendant's paternal care for his family members, as well as his culturally normative masculine accomplishments, including Young's military service and his successful employment, as mitigating factors to his sentence.

Young's mother began her statement of support by telling the court "Tony as a child never gave me any problem whatsoever." She shared that his teachers had been impressed by him and that he always had an interest in caregiving, amplifying the defense attorney's earlier statements. In addition to the grandfather already mentioned, he had cared for many of his elderly family members, including her own great-grandmother. She marveled that her son had such a good relationship with her father's physician that the doctor had given Tony his personal pager number. She shed light on Tony's caregiving not only for the elders of the family but also for the children, adding that "all of Tony's nieces and nephews were fond of him." One of her grandnieces would cry for her Uncle Tony when she was sick or hurt, taking greater comfort in his caregiving than in the care of her own mother. Finally, she closed by communicating that she understood that "what had transpired" was serious.

Young's fiancée spoke next, expressing that Tony's "open spirit and loving heart" did not fit with what he had done. "I hate how he looks on paper," she said. As the fiancée spoke, the prosecutor locked eyes with the coauthor Sameena, who was seated in the gallery, and raised her brows in a subtle expression of annoyance. Tony's fiancée said she understood that he "has to do prison time" but wept while she pleaded "please don't take my man away from me forever." We return to such pleas for leniency in the book's conclusion. With the fiancée's statement completed, it fell to Judge Williams to describe the conditions he weighed in crafting Tony Young's sentence and to announce his punishment. Young himself did not make a statement during the sentencing hearing—an unusual choice, as most defendants spoke at this time. In addition to the statements of both attorneys and Young's mother and fiancée, Judge Williams had access to a full report from the Department of Corrections as well as other information that had been excluded from the jury trial. Unable to share his perspectives during the trial, the sentencing hearing was a forum for the judge to express his interpretation of the facts. He, too, had formulated his own narrative interpretation around Young's failures and irredeemably as a father.

Addressing Young directly, Judge Williams said to him:

> Here, you sexually assault your own child starting at a very young age. This was horrific conduct. The child should be safe and protected. You violated that. A child should not be exposed to this conduct . . . and you brought that down on her. I watched her testify. She was very credible. First, she thought you wouldn't do it if it was wrong. Then she thought it was her fault. Then she became fearful and couldn't disclose [it] to anyone.

In short, Judge Williams formulated his address as a failure to correctly father. He argued that Tony Young's actions had not only damaged Tasha but also irreparably damaged the father-daughter relationship. "She no longer refers to you as 'father,' but as 'donor.'" Judge Williams lamented: "No matter what I do today, I can't give that back to her." Working systematically through the factors that he could consider in setting a punishment, Judge Williams stated that Young's crimes were deeply aggravated. "You are her father," and he stressed how the social obligations and taboos of fatherhood did not prevent the defendant from victimizing his own daughter.

Judge Williams also considered Young's criminal record, noting his drug charges and possession of illegal weapons. He then stated:

> You have four children and you're not supporting the children and you don't know how much you are in arrears. This reflects on your character. You have strong family support. But you hide from them—you haven't shared with them.

In stating that Young had strong family support yet hid his true nature from them, Judge Williams indirectly addressed his mother's and fiancée's statements. These factors all contributed to the 40-year sentence that Judge Williams announced at the end of the hearing, which was longer than both the recommendation of the prosecutor and the defense attorney. Young would spend the first 25 years of his sentence imprisoned and would then serve the final 15 years under extended supervision. His mother and fiancée wept quietly, and Young nodded to them as he was led out. The two women blew kisses at him as he left the courtroom. Only five minutes later in the hallway just outside, we overheard a masculine voice say: "A guy just got 40 years!" Young's family winced in reaction to this pronouncement and then walked out of the courthouse accompanied by Young's lawyer.

"Your Obvious Sincerity": The Sentencing of Isaac Miller

The sentencing hearing was the ideal forum to observe how the cultural rhetoric of fatherhood comes up against the logics of power and sexual violence within spaces of intimacy. While the prosecutor and defense counsel often offered competing narratives of the defendant as father figure, the judge could craft a sentence that suggested which narrative was more dominant, and that interpretation became part of the case record. The sentencing hearing was the ultimate theatrical performance, in which the courts decided which types of fathers were to be suffered despite their perpetration of injustices and which types of fathers were categorized as irredeemable. As public spectacles that were also a matter of record, the sentencing hearing also served as the site of archival production in which the courts built a corpus of decisions that set standards about fatherhood, family, and the law. In June 2013, we observed the sentencing hearing of Isaac Miller in Judge Darr's courtroom. The defendant did not go to trial but instead opted to plead guilty to second-degree sexual assault of his 12-year-old stepdaughter, Ruthie. Ruthie's words, as read by her mother, opened this chapter.

While interviewing prosecutors and defense counsel, we discovered that many attorneys believed that more and more defendants in sexual assault cases were choosing to go to trial. One prosecutor speculated that such defendants had "a higher incentive to deny the allegations" based on social taboos and their inability to take responsibility for their actions. This was especially apparent in cases in which the accused was a parental figure to the victim. One defense attorney explained that her sex-offender clients are often unable to "come to grips with accepting responsibility . . . and I think that's because they either don't want to believe that they do this, or they've got family members or a wife or a father or mother that they don't want to upset and say, 'Oh, by the way, I touched him.'" If the social sanction of the family played an important role in a defendant's inability to accept responsibility for his actions, a family's support and acceptance figured equally essential to how the defendant might narrate his tale of malfeasance.

Facing a maximum penalty of 40 years in prison, Miller, a white middle-aged man, pled guilty to second degree sexual assault of a child under 12 years of age. Accepting a plea agreement often emerged as a point in the defendant's favor, as the court interpreted it as accepting responsibility for the crime. Judges often viewed sparing the victim the labor of testifying and saving the community taxpayer dollars as a positive. In cases involving fathers and daughters, the plea agreement was also interpreted as paternal care. Isaac Miller's willingness to take the plea agreement and spare his stepdaughter the trauma of taking the stand contrasted markedly with Tony Young's continued denials. Miller maintained that he had sexually assaulted Ruthie only in the haze of sleep. Deeply tired, he said he had not realized that it was Ruthie who lay in the bed next to him. He stated that he thought that Ruthie was her mother and, because of this, had proceeded to engage in sexual touching. He did not deny the harm that had come to Ruthie from his "mistake," but this narrative allowed him to claim both paternal care for his victim as well as his manly desire for his wife—two tropes representing culturally normative masculine markers. While the court would go on to laud Miller for taking responsibility for his crime, his narrative of having sexually assaulted his stepdaughter as a sleep-induced accident could have been interpreted as an excuse rather than as an admission of guilt. His entire defense emphasized the crime as a momentary lapse rather than as suggestive of a pattern of behavior.

Miller's wife limped into court on a pair of crutches while dressed in a suit and accompanied by a victim-witness advocate. Nothing about the Millers was especially remarkable, and they both seemed a bit mussed. Unlike other defendants and family members we observed during many sentencing hearings, their clothes were wrinkled and loose-fitting; his khaki pants were baggy, and her long shapeless skirt hung to the floor. Like her husband, Miller's wife had her hair in a ponytail, and many flyaways framed her face. She gazed lovingly at Isaac Miller as she took her seat. She explained to the court that she would read two prepared statements: the first on behalf of herself, and the second on behalf of Ruthie, her daughter who was the victim in this case.

Beginning with her own statement, Ms. Miller explained that she was convinced that her husband suffered from an undiagnosed mental health problem in addition to insomnia and perhaps Asperger's. Reading from a small sheet of paper shaking in her hand, she called the sexual assault an "accident," repeating the defense argument that her husband mistook her daughter for herself in his sleep. She said that the other children missed their stepfather greatly and that the victim was plagued by guilt for reporting the assault. All of her children looked to him as a stepfather. Like Young's fiancée, Miller's wife began to sob as she read from her statement:

> The children all accept what is happening, [and] this is all too much. . . . I wish it could all go back to the way it was. The love of my life touched my baby and I want to hate him.

She again emphasized that the assault was merely an accident, calling it an "unintentional mistake . . . brought on by sleep deprivation." Her statement ended with her declaration that "I still love him and I find it in my heart to forgive him. . . . [H]e is undeserving of the title of molester or the scarlet letter of felon." Following the mother's own statement, she proceeded to read Ruthie's short statement. Crying again, the mother returned to the courtroom gallery to await Judge Darr's decision. These statements cast the father as having failed his family while simultaneously centering his absence as the cause of great suffering for his wife and her children, including the victim of his violence. Judge Darr thanked Miller's wife and said she was "sorry for everyone's loss." Judge Darr's acknowledgement of the family's difficult position and grief was uttered with compassion. The prosecutor then offered her summary of the defendant's actions:

> Isaac Miller is a person in this 12-year-old girl's life. She trusted him. Her mother trusted him. The facts are undisputed. The defendant puts his hands in her pants and touched her vagina. . . . He doesn't seem to have been asleep, and he has a clear recollection of what happened. I

understand where the family is coming from, but the victim needs to be safe as well.

The prosecutor's description of Miller as "a person in this 12-year-old girl's life" rather than her stepfather or even her mother's husband is peculiar. It evacuated the relationship of its father-daughter dynamic, even as Ruthie's statement pled for the court to give her her "daddy back." The prosecutor also cast doubt on the veracity of the defense's position that Miller was suffering from sleep deprivation. Even as she pointed out the need to hold Miller responsible, the prosecutor stated that she understood where his family was coming from in their pleas for leniency. At no point did the ADA imply that Miller simply hid his true self from his family. By contrast, in *State v. Young*, neither the judge nor the prosecutor made conciliatory statements regarding Young's family. Although the prosecutor in the *Miller* case could recommend up to 40 years' imprisonment for the crime of second-degree sexual assault, she instead recommended that Judge Darr consider a nine- to 12-month conditional sentence with work-release privileges.

After the prosecutor finished, Miller's defense attorney began his argument by stating to the court that Miller was a "homeowner with a mortgage" living with his wife and her children. Upon his arrest, his client had waived his rights and provided a full statement admitting to the incident. The incident occurred because of the "many stresses in [Miller's] life." Defense counsel insisted that Miller had a "good character" and that he had made a "less-than-conscious slip." He offered a letter from Miller's employer describing him as a "valued employee" and pointed out the presence of his supervisor in the gallery that morning. The combination of facts about Miller's status as a mortgage-holder and as a valued employee were other markers of successful masculinity and paternity. As the owner of his home, Miller was also cast as a provider for his wife and "her children," perhaps as a signifier of his chosen devotion rather than as a biological directive. The defense attorney then added:

> Many of his friends are here in the gallery. Lots of offenders have good jobs and make good money. And most people have friends who'll go to bat for them. When an allegation like this surfaces, people, friends, especially employers will pull back. But not in this case.

In other words, the presence of Miller's friends, family, and employer in the gallery demonstrated they were "unstinting and unwavering in their support" and should allay the court's concerns as to whether he was a risk to the community. Miller's supervisor even made a short statement on his behalf, invoking his own status as a father. Before the court, he attested that his confidence in Miller was such that he would trust his own teenage daughter in Miller's care. The defense attorney finished his argument by stating to Judge Darr: "[My] client, in the correct fatherly way, loves Ruthie. He is a good candidate for probation. [The act was] one or two minutes out of 37 years of life."

Judge Darr asked Miller if he planned to make a statement. He indicated he did; he cleared his throat and began to speak slowly and steadily:

> A few months ago, I did something I never thought I was capable of doing. [I became] the kind of person I hated . . . I am to blame. I promise I'll spend the rest of my life making up for it. I need to tell [Ruthie] I love her and I'll never hurt her again.

Finished with his statement, Miller seemed the very embodiment of contrition as he wiped tears from his eyes while his wife's audible sobs filled the court.

Noting Miller's tears, Judge Darr addressed the defendant and the court, stating that "I think the record should reflect your obvious sincerity." Because court transcripts are only written text, such remarks by attorneys and judges were the primary way that demeanor entered the official record. The judge then continued with the rest of the sentencing, noting her disbelief that sleep deprivation could be blamed for the crime: "I've been sleepy, sleep-deprived. I would never touch the genitalia of a 12-year-old boy. I just don't see how it happened. A 12-year-old-girl? She should be playing with Barbies."

There was an obvious tension between Judge Darr's sequenced utterances. In noting the defendant's "obvious sincerity," she generated a record of Miller as a truthful person. With her next breath, however, she stated that she did not find the story of being sleep-deprived to be credible. She did not go so far as to state this plainly, instead noting that, having also been sleep deprived herself, she never committed a sex offense. In short, while the court credited Miller with taking responsibility for his crime, he had in fact stopped short of admitting to having intentionally sexually assaulted his stepdaughter and continued to maintain a narrative that could be characterized as a fabricated excuse. Judge Darr said she was happy that the victim finally disclosed the sexual assault, explaining to Miller that his

> behavior needs to be checked. Once you cross the line, it's easy to keep crossing. Sexualizing young girls at younger and younger ages. [Ruthie] needs to know the guilt flows from [your] actions. No one should feel guilty for being honest. Probation is very generous in this case. I take into account the unwavering support of your friends and employers.

Despite her admonishment and the seriousness of the offense, Judge Darr imposed and stayed a four-year sentence of two years in custody and two years under supervision for a full four years of supervision. (A "stay" is a suspension of the sentence as long as the defendant adheres to all the conditions of supervision.) Judge Darr then ordered the defendant to serve four months in custody as condition time, crediting him for five days he had already served, and also ruled that he would serve the four months with work-release permissions. The judge ordered no contact between the defendant and Ruthie and told Ruthie's mother that she would need to petition the court if she wanted to change these conditions in the future. This statement to Ruthie's mother was the only point at which the judge directly addressed Miller's family.

Fathers and Daughters at Scenes of Admonishment

The contrasting forms of address in State v. Miller and State v. Young illustrated the range of admonishments that judges directed at defendants. In this last section, we briefly describe more cases in which judges addressed the defendant and his family. This form of disciplining, as we have noted, was an admonishment that unfolded during courtroom proceedings as well as one that was permanently preserved in the court record. Our own field notes were replete with scenes of admonishment in which judges dressed down the defendant and his family. These events and their documentation in court repositories reproduced official narratives of the failures of the father, characterized by penal logics at the intersections of race and class. As a racializing practice, Black and Latino/a fathers were faulted for their perpetration of paternal harm, and that paternal harm was interpreted as socially learned and socially transmissible. Sentencing hearings revealed the extent to which the judge cast paternal failure as influencing the family and harming the wider community. When paternal harm was indexed as jeopardizing social welfare beyond the family, it was more harshly punished. In the following sections, we discuss the sentencings of Milton Mays Sr., Alvin Evans, and Travis Trenton.

A Propensity for Crime: State v. Mays Sr.

The sentencing of Milton Mays Sr., an African American man in his late thirties, included a particularly memorable admonishment of both Mays Sr. and his family. Mays Sr., who we wrote about in chapter 4, was found guilty of repeated sexual assault of a child and was facing a possible 40-year sentence. He was tried in Judge William's court some months after we observed the trial of Tony Young. The case centered on the disappearance of a 13-year-old girl who surfaced at Mays Sr.'s home. Though she was not his daughter, it was worth considering the ways in which paternity played a role in the courtroom rhetoric at trial and during his sentencing. During the trial, Mays Sr. said he was merely sheltering the victim and did not want her roaming the streets. Someone had seen the missing-person notice for the child and called the police. In the course of the investigation, police interviewed a witness who described seeing Mays Sr. having sex with the young girl on several occasions. Unlike most of the cases we had observed, the detectives who testified during the trial were from two units: Sensitive Crimes and Human Trafficking. This information was never revealed to the jury, though the judge brought it up during sentencing. During the trial, the prosecutor privately revealed to us that Mays Sr. was under investigation for sex-trafficking but that the sexual assault case was the only charge to go forward. Sentencing Mays Sr. for his conviction, and chiding him and his family for his failure as a father, were tied to the court's knowledge of the sex-trafficking investigation.

Mays Sr.'s children—many young adult sons and daughters—had sat through his entire trial, making passionate statements in support of their father during his sentencing hearing. Even his naming as "Mays Sr." marked the defendant as a paternal figure. While it was not unusual for friends and family to attend jury trials, most families would come dressed formally and sit quietly in the gallery. Mays Sr.'s family did not conform to this norm, bringing a more casual atmosphere to the courtroom. The many young men and women who arrived each morning were dressed appropriately for the summer heat outside, if not for the staid courtroom inside. In denim cutoffs and tank tops, they kept their banter down during the court proceedings, but their chatter filled the courtroom and hallways whenever court was not in session. Few formal rules demanded courtroom decorum, but court personnel seemed irritated by them throughout the trial. One court officer commented to us that the feeling of the trial was "circuslike."

Like Young, Mays Sr. was found guilty at trial but maintained his innocence throughout. When the sentencing hearing began, Judge Williams noted that Mays Sr. refused to take responsibility for his crime and continued to deny his guilt. He also made it a point to disapprovingly state that Mays Sr. owed more than $100,000 in outstanding child-support payments. While it was common practice for judges to weigh information that did not emerge from the trial in crafting their sentences, unpaid child support constituted one way in which the poor and the overly surveilled might find themselves disadvantaged. Child-support payments, which technically are not a criminal matter, could become a strike against the convicted. This lack of payment registered as a paternal failure.

Mays Sr. also had a previous criminal record. The judge described him as having a "propensity for criminal behavior," evidenced by previous battery charges, drug-related offenses, car thefts, as well as an involvement with a homicide case for which he had been arrested but not charged. Of the sex-trafficking investigation, Judge Williams noted that, even though the trafficking case had not been charged, "it is the state's good faith belief that there has been pimping and pandering." Mays Sr.'s facial expression was a composed mask of calm while Judge Williams's tone was deeply paternalistic, aimed at both the family and the convicted. With the specter of the trafficking investigation lurking beyond the sentencing, the court cast the family itself as one under suspicion of belonging to a collective criminal enterprise. Given the judge's detailing of Mays Sr.'s "propensity for criminal behavior," was the defendant therefore responsible for leading his children to follow in his footsteps?

Defense counsel argued that Mays Sr. had the right to maintain his innocence, and he then presented evidence that Mays Sr. was respected and well-regarded. "He has a great deal of support—15 letters, and 15 people in court in support of Mr. Mays." Among Mays Sr.'s supporters were his mother, his daughter, his son, the mother of his children, former coworkers, and friends. Defense argued that "this really revealed Mr. Mays's character as a father" and that his incarceration would damage his family and children. Defense counsel emphasized that Mays Sr. was the primary caregiver for his younger children and a very involved father when it came to his older son and daughter. His daughter would have to take over his responsibilities as head of the household to see her teenage brother successfully through high school. The high school–aged son was struggling when he lived with his mother, but after moving in with Mays Sr., defense counsel claimed, his attendance was better and his attitude toward school had improved. What would happen if he were to lose the influence of his father?

The defense attorney also argued that, "child support not withstanding," Mays Sr. had always worked to support his family except during periods of incarceration. He had a successful business flipping cars with a friend and had a high-school education. He had no mental health problems and was an intelligent man who "presents as a gentle and soft-spoken human being. [He] has never raised his voice, never [been] aggressive—I find him to be very nice. I don't think he's a smooth talker." He continued that, while the trial had ended with a finding of guilt, his "client has always said he is not guilty," further noting that the crime did not seem aggravated. There had been no violence, no force, and no use of weapons. The child had sought out Mays Sr. willingly, and she had lied about her age. He thought she was much older than she said she was and did not know that she had been reported missing by her family. Mays Sr.'s daughter was the next to speak. She wept as she told the judge that the victim was a habitual liar. This daughter described the victim as someone out to destroy the lives of innocent people. She asked for the court to be fair "and reasonable and return my father to his family."

Mays Sr. chose to speak on his own behalf, beginning his address to the court by speaking about seeing a television commercial with his own daughter that asked: "Parents, do you know where your children are?" He stated that he would not be seated before the court if a parent—presumably the victim's—had asked this very question. "I take care of my kids; I'm sympathetic of her situation." He added that, "when [the victim] grows a conscience, maybe she'll think about how many lives she destroyed." He told the court that his only desire was to be with and raise his children. These words reproduced the idea of the home as the site of social reproduction, particularly of the parental labors required for raising and influencing children. Where Mays Sr. faulted the victim's parents, this very logic also gave leeway for the judge to hold Mays Sr. responsible for his failures as a father.

As was customary, the judge had the last word. Judge Williams contradicted the defense attorney's assertion that the circumstances were not aggravated. He found the situation of a 13-year-old runaway to be deeply troubling. Although Mays Sr. had characterized himself as a caring father who would have helped the young girl had he only known her true age, Judge Williams said he was manipulative and had a "pattern of involvement with younger women." He had "violated the naiveté of a young vulnerable girl." He made it a point to list out all of Mays Sr.'s prior convictions, rehearsing a history of criminal cases beginning when Mays Sr. was only 13 years old himself. As the judge spoke, his gaze passed from Mays Sr. to his family in the gallery. Of all of the charges in Mays Sr.'s criminal record, Judge Williams lingered over his abuse of the mother of his children. "Children need financial as well as emotional support," the judge told Mays Sr., and "when you choose to have seven children, you need to support them . . . financially." He sentenced Mays Sr. to a total of 21 years: 13 years to be served in prison, and eight under supervision. His daughter left the sentencing in tears, while the rest of the family trailed after her shaking their heads in disbelief.

Fall from Grace: State v. Evans

Unlike Mays Sr., Evans pled guilty to second-degree sexual assault of his (now former) girlfriend's daughter, Jenny. Where Mays Sr. and his family were Black, Evans, his former girlfriend, and her children were all white. Evans was also a retired firefighter, attracting the local media's attention. Following the assault, Jenny's mother had broken her ties with Evans.

Accompanied by her three daughters and their father, Jenny's mother addressed the court about the gravity of Evans's crime. She worried that he had used the six years of their relationship to groom Jenny as a victim, assaulting her when she was 12 years old. Her daughter's trust had been completely frayed by the experience of having been victimized by a "man she knew, and loved; she referred to him as her dad—she looked up to him and loved him like a father." Jenny's 10-year-old sister wrote a statement, which the mother read to the court: "What [he] did to [my sister] was horrible. [He] is just a horrible memory now. I hope he doesn't hurt another family. He should go to jail." Notably, Jenny's sister presented a point rarely considered in cases of sexual assault in white families: the specter of predatory behavior potentially reaching beyond the boundaries of the immediate members.

News cameras were stationed in the gallery and filmed the proceedings. In the middle of the hearing, the court clerk entered the gallery to quietly instruct the cameramen that they could not record the children. Jenny's mother and father emphasized the harm that Evans had done not only to Jenny but also to their other children. "I have all the kids in therapy," Jenny's mother told the judge. Jenny's father explained that the harm extended even further:

> I want to echo everything their mother said. [He] seemed like a nice guy. I was happy for her; I trusted him, and I feel very betrayed because he hurt one of my kids. I just wanna see justice done. This has impacted all my daughters and my son, even though he's younger. I know it's affected their trust in men. It's also affected their grandparents.

Evan's former wife, a woman he had known for more than 40 years, was the first to testify on his behalf during the defense's sentencing arguments: "Alvin has always helped people. He's a good father. He's involved in the community." She added that he had been a full-time firefighter for 18 years and that over the years he had lived in households with many children. Never before had any child accused him of a sexual offense. Looking directly at Jenny's mother and calling into question her own parenting, she continued: "I pray for [you] and your family. . . . [H]e was always there for your children when you were going through a low point and couldn't take care of your children." Jenny and her sisters crowded close to their mother during this part of the hearing as she draped both her arms around them. Their faces registered disgust, and one of the young girls shook her head in disbelief.

Evans's defense attorney argued that his client was deeply concerned about the victim's well-being. Furthermore, his client recognized that alcohol was a key component in his behavior and that he needed intervention and treatment to manage his alcohol use. He continued:

> This is a good man who has struggled to do good. . . . He will always be a convicted felon. He will always be a convicted sex offender. He will always be on the sex offender registry. He has been publicly shamed and dishonored because of what he did.

The attorney added that Evans had sold his home and moved to a different area of Wisconsin and was clearly taking responsibility for his crime. The defense attorney added: "I don't think jail or prison is necessary to protect the community. He has been publicly shamed and humiliated." During these proceedings, Jenny became tearful and collapsed into her mother's arms. This did not go unnoticed by Judge Van as he glanced toward the victim's family while Jenny began to cry. When Evans spoke during his hearing, Jenny and her father left the courtroom. Evans expressed his remorse and awaited his punishment.

After a break, Judge Van returned to issue his ruling as the news cameras continued taping. He began by stating that the gravity of the case had to be "carefully qualified," as it did not compare to some of "the most sickening sexual assaults one can imagine." The age of the victim, however, did increase the gravity of the crime. The judge raised his voice and addressed Evans directly:

> What you did in this case is reprehensible—there is no excuse for what you did! Nothing! Nothing excuses assaulting children—it's not accepted by society. It's not accepted by this court. And it's not accepted by Milwaukee County.

Judge Van continued to lay out the logic of his sentence. Evans had "brought shame to [his] family" and had "embarrassed firefighters." He noted, as the prosecutor had already argued, that "people who are trusted because of their status need to be held to a higher standard." Staring squarely at Evans, the judge said: "You have put a black mark on your entire life [and] when you pass away, you will pass away as a sex offender." Judge Van's remarks about privilege, status, and public humiliation echoed those offered in cases of sexual assaults perpetrated by police officers in chapter 3.

The judge rejected the idea of drinking as a mitigating factor, arguing that Evans, as a mature adult in his fifties, could not make excuses about alcohol use. Returning to the seriousness of Evans's crime, Judge Van noted that "the girls and their sisters are in this courtroom in tears. Her mother is in tears because of the emotional harm you have caused," adding: "[Y]ou've changed the victim's life forever. . . . I doubt that the victim will ever forget that this occurred." While the news cameras were barred from taping the victim and her sisters, the judge's description was recorded by the news cameras and became part of the court record. As he continued, Judge Van simultaneously interspersed serious admonishments with mitigating factors in order to foreground his sentence. He stated that Evans was a "limited to moderate risk to the community," stating that "I believe Mr. Evans is remorseful, shamed, and embarrassed by this behavior." Pivoting from these mitigating factors, the judge then sharply denounced Evans, telling him directly: "I don't know what was going through your head—I'm not a psychologist or psychiatrist, but something is wrong with adults that are attracted to children, period!" This led him to the conclusion that the defendant clearly had rehabilitation and treatment needs. He added that there had to be some type of punishment because Jenny "will have trust issues with boys, trust issues with men largely, if not solely, because of your selfish actions."

Judge Van then outlined the specifics of sentencing, telling Evans he was required to submit a DNA sample, a condition that is required of all convicted felons. He added that the obligation to give DNA was for the purposes of "punishment, deterrence, and part of rehabilitation." He then seemed to relent, noting that Evans had "many pro-social aspects." He sentenced Evans to a six-year term, split between three years' imprisonment and three years' supervision. The six-year sentence was, however, imposed and stayed, under the condition that he would serve nine months in the House of Corrections and adhere to all the conditions of his probation. The judge also issued a no-contact order, forbidding

Evans from having contact with any children under the age of 16. He could only have supervised contact with children who were related to him and was ordered to stay away from the victim, her family, and her mother. After two months in the House of Corrections, Evans would be granted work release privileges for his final 30 days.

The sentence itself stood in contrast to the yearslong sentences frequently served by other defendants convicted of second-degree sexual assault. According to the court, Evans's harmful actions were limited to his former family members, even though he had moved to another area of the state and Jenny's sister voiced her concern that he might "hurt another family." Much like Officer Vagnini in chapter 3, Evans's fall from grace and public humiliation were deemed significant forms of punishment. His criminality was attributed to his personal psychology, and thus a mental health assessment awaited him in the future. No inquiries were made as to how he had been parented, what community he grew up in, or whether he had been socialized to make poor choices. His crime, therefore, necessitated individual discipline rather than community correction.

"Some Sort of Perversion": State v. Trenton

Travis Trenton was charged with two counts of possession of child pornography. His case was one of the few in which the judge sharply rebuked a white defendant and his white family. Trenton plead guilty and faced a mandatory-minimum five-year sentence for each count, required by Wisconsin state statutes. At the time, no other sex offenses carried a minimum sentence. The images found on Trenton's computer were of children he did not know. His daughter and girlfriend were both in the gallery to lend their support during his sentencing, and his daughter opened the hearing telling the judge:

> He's a good father; he's a hard worker—we always had family time. We were always close. He isn't a danger to children. He's never done anything to me or my friends. I hope you give my dad the minimum sentence.

Trenton's girlfriend was tearful as the daughter spoke, soon thereafter adding her own testimony in his support. She explained that they were in a committed relationship for a year and spoke cryptically about how "similar things happened to both of us in our childhoods." She speculated that "I think there's something wrong with me for being a victim of molestation. I was promiscuous; I had two failed marriages." She insisted that Trenton had changed her life and noted that "he's trying so hard." They had planned to marry, and she was convinced that "he would never harm a child—that's not who he is; please have mercy and give us the chance to heal together." Her statement complete, it was Trenton's turn to make a statement. Looking down slightly, Trenton spoke on his own behalf: "I apologize to family and friends [for] the embarrassment I've caused them." His daughter began to cry as he expressed his commitment to building a relationship with his family. "I want to be remembered as a good person; I apologize to counsel and court staff."

Defense counsel argued that there was no victim in this crime because it involved charges of looking at child pornography. However, Judge Van responded in a very sharp tone, clarifying that, from the court's perspective, "you did harm a child. You harmed not one, but [hundreds] of children. Because if there was not a market for it, you wouldn't harm all these children." Pointing to Trenton's daughter, the judge continued: "You have embarrassed and disgraced her. She needs to know what you were looking at, so I'll read some of these." Judge Van proceeded to read some of the descriptions labeling the images that had been found on Trenton's computer, which detailed the ages, positions, and sex acts from nine of the many photos that the judge was "subjected to view" during the case.

In detailing the content of the images in the presence of Trenton's daughter, the judge himself contributed to the spectacle of suffering, prolonging the experience of embarrassment, disgrace, and disgust for which he had just earlier condemned Trenton. What is more, Judge Van gave vivid descriptions of the images of child pornography in a tone both crass and detailed (here a penis and there a vagina, both positioned just-so). Rather than forego the descriptions altogether or approach their content in a clinical fashion, the judge reproduced the pornographic essence of the archive of images that had led to Trenton's arrest and conviction. In short, to justify the harshness of the mandatory-minimum sentence, the judge subjected those present in the court to pornographic descriptions of children and perpetuated their circulation as text.

Judge Van remarked: "I generally don't like mandatory minimums, but legislation got it right this time." He continued to berate Trenton, stating that, because he was "downloading sick images," the aggregation of child pornography on his computer was "not some mistake." The judge added that "you have some sort of perversion." Then, addressing all those in the court once more, the judge continued: "He is clearly overly-sexualized," noting that the presentencing investigation reported that Trenton had "about a hundred sexual partners" and had attended "swinging parties" and "nudist beaches" and admitted to watching pornographic films. "I hope your daughter and significant other understand you have issues. . . . [H]ow would you feel if this happened to your daughter and not these images that are out there?" Before delivering the full sentence—five years on each count—to be structured with six years in prison and four years under supervision, Judge Van continued to address Trenton's daughter and girlfriend, dragging the entire family into the degradation, humiliation, and punishment of Trenton. By asking the defendant how he would feel if his own daughter were to be a victim of child pornographers, he threatened Trenton and grotesquely objectified the young woman accompanying her father to court.

Conclusion: Who Can Be the Good Father?

All the cases we have discussed in this chapter demonstrated not only the court's logics of sentencing but also the range of discretionary decisions available to felony judges. They also displayed the de facto modes of surveillance and the marking of racialized fatherhood that occurred in concert during sentencing. The charges of second-degree sexual assault, faced by both Miller and Evans, carried a maximum of 40 years' imprisonment. Evans received nine months and Miller even less than that. Both men were granted work-release privileges. Twice, we saw defendants sentenced to 35 years in relation to charges of second-degree sexual assault. Trenton's case required a minimum-mandatory sentence because of the legislation governing child pornography in Wisconsin, tied to arguments about the wider social harms of child pornography. The judge, having little recourse, thus crowed his outrage.[1] Beyond the few crimes that carry mandatory-minimum sentences, judges could exercise a wide range of discretion in sentencing convicted sex offenders.

Prosecutors, too, exercised great discretion when they decided which crimes to charge. And while prosecutors rarely raised the issue during interviews, they did acknowledge how case outcomes might be determined by race and class differences. One prosecutor stated:

> I don't think a Black defendant or a poor Hispanic defendant or a poor white defendant gets sentences worse because of their race or social economic class. But I believe that a middle-class, upper-class white defendant gets so much better of a deal or so much better of a sentence.

She attributed different outcomes to the privileged defendants' abilities to seek private rehabilitation for court-ordered treatments such as interventions for drug addiction and sex-offender therapy:

> [I]f you can take a white male and middle-class, upper-class, or a young kid who's got wealthy parents and say he's been seen by Dr. [NAME] for six months or a year and look at how great they're doing and they're not a threat to society, and the doctor comes in and testifies they're not a threat to society, that's going to give you a better sentence than this guy who can't do any of that.

In addition to not having recourse to private treatment (which Miller made use of), the crimes Mays Sr. and Young committed carried heavier sentences than second-degree sexual assault. The charges themselves are a scaffolding for weighing the gravity of the sexual offense committed by each defendant. All the defendants are then cast as successful or unsuccessful fathers during sentencing.

In the courts, the cultural signifier of fatherhood is narrated through tropes of masculinity, sexual power, virility, and aggression. It is the judge's decision whether to frame these tropes as appropriate and normative versus abnormal and criminal. Mirroring the way in which the state's potential to mount legal action oscillates between threat and guarantee (Poole 2004), fatherhood swings between threat and possibility. This was illustrated during one of the most unusual court cases we observed, in which a father represented himself in a trial for which he was charged with sexually assaulting his five daughters. As his youngest daughter testified tearfully, he called out to her: "I've got you, baby!"

His exclamation seemed a spontaneous response to her obvious anguish. The judge immediately cleared the court and uttered his concern that the statement was a threat, even though the prosecutor and clerk explained that it was a vernacular expression of support, using many racially adjacent terms to explain that the vernacular was part of local Black linguistic repertoires. The court oscillated between the possibilities of interpreting the moment through either frame of threat or support. In Miller's case, the judge stressed the possibilities of his care and responsibility, whereas other fathers—such as Young, Trenton, and Mays Sr.—were cast as irredeemable because their violence had exceeded the boundaries of the family. The court could interpret the role of the father as socially fundamental, as familial obligation, as state compulsion, and as personal failure.

In crafting punishment, the court often took up the rhetoric of fatherhood to justify its severity or leniency. Fatherhood was one of many cultural tropes with which juries are familiar before they even enter the courtroom and are instructed to use their "common sense" as they attempt to evaluate the alleged actions of a defendant. Because sexual violence most often occurred between kin and others known to the victim—rather than strangers—attorneys and witnesses struggled to represent the complicated relationships between defendant and victim. When the defendant was a father, his violence was framed through his ability to exhibit or withhold paternal care. He might have argued, then, that what the court, the jury, and even his own family perceived as harm is actually paternal care or discipline. In weighing a sentence, the court reconfigured the father figure within common heteropatriarchal understandings of the family and of manhood along a spectrum of successful and failed fatherhood. The defendant deemed successful by the court in discharging his fatherly duty was shown leniency in sentencing, whereas the father who had failed was the subject of harsh punishments. The role of the father was, in some cases, understood as intergenerational and rooted in the defendant's own experience as a child. These narratives of intergenerational transmission of pathology almost solely centered on Black families, whereas white families, though admonished, were not subject to similar interpretations. The crimes of Trenton and Evans were cast as a source of shame to their families and communities, but these defendants were not questioned as to the familial origins of their criminal behaviors. Rather, the perception that they were solely responsible for their criminal behavior contributed to the court's recriminations. This marking of Black sex offenders as deficiently fathered themselves and as deficiently fathering their own children, in contrast to the independent white sex offender, demonstrates yet again the racial surveillance we drew attention to at the outset of this chapter.

As we indicated in the introduction to this book, criminal courts are the site of daily ceremonies of "racial degradation" (Gonzalez Van Cleve 2016), and the attendant social commentary that emerges concerning fatherhood is mired in racializing and racist narratives inflected by class. Judges and attorneys engage with problematic artifacts of outdated social policy that pathologize the Black family by citing absent or derelict Black fathers (Moynihan 1965) or by commenting on the disciplinary "machismo" of Catholic Latino patriarchs. White fatherhood did not emerge as a social phenomenon. It was unraced and void of cultural stereotypes. When we witnessed the admonishment of white fathers for their crimes, they were most often chastised as individual "bad actors," with few queries about their ties to community or the origins of their criminality. For men of color, racialized narratives were reproduced by evoking the welfare state, public safety, and normative heteropatriarchal families. The Black father was further suspected of poisoning his own children, either by failing to provide economic support and damning them to a life of poverty or by drawing his own children into an intergenerational criminal enterprise. Such cultural narratives attached squarely and successfully to men of color in an urban courthouse embodied by patterns of segregation, mass incarceration, disproportionate poverty, and joblessness in communities of color. But even as the father figure was capable of the most abhorrent acts seen in the courts, he simultaneously embodied the potential to be cast as the most morally redeemable subject worthy of the court's leniency. In naming fatherhood as one of its central concerns, the criminal justice system both engaged with and reproduced the gendered and racialized conditions that created the vulnerability that resulted in sexual victimization in the first place.

Conclusion

Race, Place, and Subjugation in the Courts

This book has demonstrated that the court is a site of risk not only for defendants but also for participating victims and witnesses. Over the course of our research, we repeatedly encountered the common defense narrative first mentioned early in this book: that victims are, in fact, prostitutes, and that defendants were clients. This formulation criminalized both the defendant and victim as participants in an illicit economy. These narratives imperiled Black women particularly, criminalizing their families and their neighborhoods and objectifying and casting suspicion on their sartorial and beauty standards. Defense attorneys' repeated associations of Blackness and femininity with prostitution demonstrated the modes of subjugating communities into carceral institutions (Kelley 2017). This rhetoric was further inscribed into official court records—yet another way that legal archives fixed race in place (Benjamin 2016)—and calcified theories of Blackness and femininity (Browne 2015). It is also always worth revisiting the fact that, in most cases, victims and defendants were kin, neighbors, or friends. Theories about sexual violence that focus on the social worlds of either individual, the defendant, or the victim-witness often ignore the fact that they are part of the same world. To bring this ethnography to a stopping point, we want to make clear that the "common sense" standards invoked during trial processes reinforced racial stereotypes and criminalized the precarity that made victims in Milwaukee vulnerable to sexual violence in the first place.

In September 2013, we sat in Judge Williams's courtroom listening to L'umoya Smith's testimony. She had been on the stand for what seemed like an eternity. L'umoya sat in the witness chair with her back straight and her head upright, but with each successive question from the attorneys, she slowly crumbled forward, the thick, dark hair of her luxuriant weave cascading in front of the microphone. Her responses were halting, slow, breathy, and labored. The courtroom, open and cavernous, magnified her breath, and we listened as she testified about a harrowing night during which she had been abducted at gunpoint and sexually assaulted. She explained how she fled when her assailants were distracted by another witness who stumbled across the crime scene, a man they shot and injured while she took off into the night. Her breath filled the courtroom, tremulous and deep, thrumming inhalations and exhalations resulting in a sound so full that in our memories we recall very nearly feeling her breathing in our own bodies.

L'umoya, a pseudonym we selected that derives from the Zulu word for "breath," was in many ways the most recognizably traumatized person we had encountered in the courts, personifying the nearly paralytic fear that embodied the trauma of sexual assault for many. L'umoya's testimony unfolded over several hours, the details of her ordeal emerging from the slow incremental questions of both the prosecution and defense counsel. The laborious pace and the halting tempo of L'umoya's trembling testimony, her body posture and draping hair, would never enter the trial transcript. Her affect, and thereby her trauma, were all but erased from court records. The jarring reality of L'umoya's testimony stood in sharp contrast to the tempered discussion by the attorneys and judge before the trial began. During a pretrial motion on the inclusion of DNA evidence from a test of L'umoya's underwear, the prosecutor, ADA Brooks, argued for its exclusion. The trial transcript recorded the prosecutor's concerns:

> [H]is whole defense is she's a prostitute. What he would like the jury to believe is that look, there are four male profiles in her underwear so of course she's a prostitute. And I think that's the inference. If he's not going to say it explicitly, it's implicitly to imply to this jury I'm going to call her a prostitute, and look, she has four other male DNA profiles in her underwear. Again, you don't know if it came from sexual contact or not, but still she's a prostitute.

After further discussion, the attorneys agreed to work out a stipulation so that the underwear evidence was excluded from the trial. Throughout jury selection, defense counsel, DC Cahill, did not address issues related to sex work or illegal activity specifically, but he did poll the jury panel on issues of race, as we presented in chapter 1:

> I bring this up and I almost hate to have to bring up, the issue of race or not. The defendant is obviously Black. You'll find out the person accusing him is Black as well. I'm white. The ADA is white. [The] detective is white as well. I'd like to think race is a dead issue these days. I hope it is but if anybody has an issue with it or problem with it and we kind of need to know that. . . . I have had people raise their hands, really not because they think themselves to be racist, but some were raised in racist homes and they were concerned, things of that sort. It shouldn't be a problem here, but if it is, you know, be sure to let us know.

The jury did not raise their hands to indicate they had a "problem with race," but DC Cahill's invocation of racial identity of both his client and the victim-witness suggested that race was very much a factor in his theory of the case. He appealed to racial characterizations that were deeply gendered, asking the jury not to factor in race against his client. Of course, however, he proceeded to build a firmly entrenched racialized and gendered portrait of L'umoya, one informed by his descriptions of her neighborhood and her movement through local spaces, as well as in his reading of her body and her beauty. After the jury was selected, defense counsel made a Batson Challenge, arguing that too many African American jurors had been struck from the jury, prejudicing his client's chances at a fair trial. This was the first and only Batson Challenge we heard during our observations of sexual assault trials, though it seemed clear to us that many could have been made. Judge Williams released the jury members for a break and then reviewed for the record the grounds for excluding each juror; defense counsel's challenge was unsuccessful. Judge Williams then brought back the 14-member panel, read the jury instructions, and sent them home until the following morning.

ADA Brooks's opening statement described how L'umoya Smith had problems sleeping sometimes, which led to a late-night walk to her mother's apartment and her subsequent kidnapping and sexual assault on her return home from her mother's. Following Brooks, defense counsel made his opening statement: "You're going to get two different versions of the story . . . of what happened." The defendant, DC Cahill argued, was driving around Milwaukee with another friend who "wanted to pick up a prostitute." Defense counsel's description of L'umoya's home and neighborhood, and of L'umoya herself, stood in stark contrast to the prosecution's story. DC Cahill stated that the defendant was searching for a prostitute that night, driving to various intersections around the location of L'umoya's home, including "35th and Lisbon," "North Avenue and 18th," places that he described as "an area in the city that they know where women walk the streets and you can pick someone up if you want to do that sort of thing." He referenced these intersections, specifying for the jury the sex-work "drags" on the West Side and North Side neighborhoods of Milwaukee. He argued: "There is no sexual assault that went on. There was no snatching and grabbing. This was pure and simply a prostitution date. . . . There was no kidnapping, no grabbing."

In addition to her residential precarity, living in a low-income neighborhood, L'umoya's description of her journey to her mother's home revealed familial precarity as well. She testified that, when she arrived at her mother's, she was not allowed to stay because her mom was embroiled in a fight with a friend. L'umoya exposed her own precarity as she described her walk home in the very early morning hours and how she stayed away from dark side streets as she navigated neighborhood space: "We always try to stay on the busy streets." She told the court that there were cars, lights, and police officers that traversed the busy streets and so it felt safer, until a white car slowed and pulled alongside her, followed by the terrifying experience of abduction. As L'umoya continued her testimony, the jurors seemed visibly uncomfortable. In our field notes, we wrote:

> [the jurors] looked all around the courtroom. . . . Some of the jurors have their hands over their mouths, and they look pained and worried. Their faces are sad as they look at the victim on the stand, and their eyes dart from the ADA to the judge to the witness.

We, too, found ourselves writing more slowly—uncomfortable and feeling as if we should not participate in the spectacle of her trauma. We were all being implicated in her suffering demanded by the courts, and it was visceral for everyone.

By the time L'umoya testified about the man who had stumbled into the middle of the crime scene, drawing her attackers' attention away long enough for her to escape, the emotion from the jury felt palpable. The "man," Mr. Jeffers, later testified about his own insomnia and his trip to a 24-hour neighborhood pharmacy to fetch his prescription. It was on his way to the pharmacy that he unknowingly interrupted the sexual assault and was shot in the arm by one of the men. L'umoya's account of Mr. Jeffers interrupting the assault gripped us all. Her voice resounded with wonder at the miraculous appearance of Mr. Jeffers, and she reiterated more than several times how she one day hoped to thank him.

The defendant was also charged with robbery, so ADA Brooks asked L'umoya what she carried in her purse that night. In her words, the list of items was: "Half of my rent money, my and my son's Social Security cards, my ID, my birth certificate, my SNAP card, my phone, and the items I got from my mom's house, all my . . . all my thing[s] that say who I am." She further explained that she had walked to her mother's house to pick up her asthma pump, her son's asthma pump, and pain pills she was taking after a recent miscarriage. Asked when she had the miscarriage, L'umoya quietly responded that "[it] happened to me my whole life." Upon being told she had to speak up so that the jury and the court reporter could hear her, she said: "I just lost a baby before. I just don't want to talk about that[,] please."

Here, a description of the vital items she was carrying on her person—her medications, her identification, and her currency—resist interpretation. Was the possession of half her rent money on her person an indication of her lack of access to traditional banking systems? As ethnographers, we could read it as her exclusion from institutional resources, potentially also as a symptom of residential precarity and suggestive of an unsecured home space. Asthma and miscarriages also stood out as markers of precarities, and in Milwaukee they were forms of morbidity that inordinately overburdened Black women (Creswell et al. 2019; D. Davis 2019). Storing pain pills outside of one's home also seemed par for the course for those living with precarity. The addictive qualities of painkillers made them difficult contraband to maintain in the home. L'umoya's illness, the pain for which she required prescription drugs, and even her neighbor's late-night walk that interrupted the men assaulting her suggested a neighborhood in which illness was rife.

While we as ethnographers recognized the vulnerabilities of L'umoya's neighborhood and of all the residents who lived there, much of defense counsel's cross-examination of L'umoya focused on why she was walking in an area "known for prostitution."

DEFENSE: If you knew that Lisbon was an area of prostitution and you didn't want to be part of that, why walk on Lisbon then that night?
L'UMOYA: Because there was a lot of police out that night.
DEFENSE: What difference does that make?
L'UMOYA: I felt safer and all the streetlights on, and I wasn't going to go down the side street.
DEFENSE: [Y]ou could have avoided Lisbon entirely, couldn't you?
L'UMOYA: Yeah.

In this brief exchange, L'umoya and the defense counsel offered competing insights into the realities of the landscape of 35th and Lisbon Avenue. Defense counsel suggested that only prostitutes traversed this thoroughfare, while L'umoya offered us the local insight of a heavily policed and peopled area that, despite and because of its dense occupation by sex workers, granted some sense of safety. Toward the end of her testimony, DC Cahill questioned L'umoya about her clothing:

DEFENSE: Were you wearing a white tee shirt that night, also?
L'UMOYA: I don't know. I was wearing my underwear and they took most of the stuff.
DEFENSE: You were wearing red pants that night?
L'UMOYA: I don't remember what I had on.
DEFENSE: Do you remember were you wearing multicolored sneakers that night?
L'UMOYA: I don't remember what I had on.
DEFENSE: Did you have blue hair over white hair?
L'UMOYA: Yes.
DEFENSE: Extensions?
L'UMOYA: Yes.
DEFENSE: That was attached to your natural hair, right?
L'UMOYA: Yes.

DEFENSE: And you were wearing—you had pink thong underwear?
PROSECUTOR: OBJECTION. Relevance?

Defense also raised the specter of L'umoya's hair and clothing much later during the trial, questioning the police witnesses who testified about responding to the crime scene:

DEFENSE: Officer, did you have the opportunity to observe what Ms. Smith was wearing on the night you first met her and talked with her?
OFFICER: I did.
DEFENSE: Do you remember what it was?
OFFICER: She had an outer jacket, coat, it was a greenish color, and a white tee shirt. She had multicolored shoes on and colored jeans.
DEFENSE: Red pants? Or were they jeans?

. . .

DEFENSE: Okay. Her hair, did she wear her natural hair, hair extension, or wig?
OFFICER: She had some artificial hair.
DEFENSE: A blue hair or white hair?
OFFICER: That's what I saw.

DC Cahill's questions about hair revealed that he either knew little about hair weaves or he deployed it as a racialized, illicit signature. The red pants were raised once again when he questioned another detective. Unwilling to linger on the red pants, this same detective testified to viewing L'umoya's belt "flapping around," hanging from her belt loops on the surveillance video we mentioned in chapter 4. Weeks after the trial came to an end, ADA Brooks told us that the "greenish" jacket was, in fact, a winter coat emblazoned with a Green Bay Packers insignia. This detail was forgotten by the witnesses after the long passage of time between the events and the trial.

During closing statements, the prosecutor amplified the trauma that L'umoya so clearly evidenced on the stand, insisting that she was no prostitute. Defense counsel, however, again invoked place and beauty standards to suggest that L'umoya was a sex worker because she was passing through a place where sex workers were known to be and was dressed in a way that they would dress. He also drew attention to L'umoya's body size during his closing arguments:

> Some of the things that bothered me in this case with the evidence though, just initially with Ms. Smith's story about how this whole thing happened, how she allegedly gets grabbed off the street and pulled into a car. It was actually sort of the physics of it that kind of bothered me. . . . Remember, she weighs 206 pounds, so she's not a small person for this guy supposedly pulling backwards.

He went on to spend some time reviewing the "physics" of the abduction, contrasting the body weight of the victim and the defendant, even stumbling performatively before the courtroom in a reenactment of the abduction. Unable to elicit the desired testimony from the sensitive crimes detective about the jeans, he used his own language in closing arguments—describing the red "fitted" jeans as so tight they were unlikely to be yanked off L'umoya. The word "fitted" was specifically his addendum to the description, as none of the other witnesses described the jeans that way.

> You know, was this a prostitution date? . . . Ms. Smith is out there at 2 o' clock wearing her white tee shirt, her pea-colored hoodie, her red fitted pants, her sneakers. She's walking the area of Lisbon Avenue where even by her own admission she knows that's a prostitution area herself. She's walking it at 2 o'clock in the morning and she's walking it with this wig on or these extensions, blue hair over white hair attached to her regular hair walking in that area. Now, she tells us "I couldn't sleep and my mom called me to tell me to come get some stuff." Okay. But is that what you do then? You put on your tight red jeans, your blue and white hair extensions for the two-mile hike to your mom's house at 2 o'clock in the morning to pick up some stuff that you don't really need. I mean, could it not wait until the morning until it was at least daylight? She said she didn't like being out there walking alone. Or is she really out there just walking this area, trying to find a prostitution date and make some money? I don't know her circumstances. You know, people don't prostitute for fun. It's for money. . . . But the suggestion was just out go for a stroll at 2 o'clock

in the morning in light of all these other facts, seems a little unusual and seems unlikely. And you know why she wouldn't admit it? I suspect she doesn't want her mom to know about it for sure. Doesn't want the police to know. I mean, prostitution is illegal. Who knows for sure? We can't see in Ms. Smith's mind.

In her rebuttal, ADA Brooks addressed the defense counsel's characterizations, reemphasizing L'umoya's trauma for the jury. It should be noted that, when the defendant was sentenced months after the trial, DC Cahill once again spoke of L'umoya's hair and clothing as relevant to his client's sentence. Having witnessed the spectacle of L'umoya's suffering, as we all did that day, Judge Williams did not take these repeated characterizations lightly. Expounding on his perspective of the trial for the sentencing record, it became clear that he knew of additional details that the jury never heard during the trial. Judge Williams spoke of L'umoya's deep depression and how the victim-witness

> describes it as the most traumatic, horrifying experience of her life, which it would be for any woman. She couldn't function, couldn't leave her home, and she still struggles with being able to leave her home. She kept her child inside the house because she was scared and fearful of something happening to her child.

Judge Williams told the court that L'umoya, even months after the trial, still hid in the closet, crying, "shrouded in the dark." She continued to wrap herself in the hoodie she happened to wear the night of the attack until her young son made her get rid of it. This was not the picture of an alleged sex worker wearing tight red pants and hair extensions, Judge Williams noted, and sentenced the defendant to a total of 35 years—25 years of confinement and 10 years of extended supervision.

During her trial testimony, L'umoya's palpable trauma infected the courtroom, and it visibly moved the jury, courtroom personnel, and those in the gallery, including ourselves. DC Cahill's numerous mentions of L'umoya's "fitted" red pants, blue and white hair extensions, and her familial neighborhood were littered throughout the trial transcripts. Not recorded, however, were the five hours of labored, painful testimony that were ultimately condensed to a few pages. The record circulated through the appeals division, an automatic review that is triggered in all major felony convictions. Though the conviction and sentence were upheld, the court record was consulted, reevaluated, and became part of the legal archive—its precedent undisturbed and the legal logics of U.S. criminal justice reinforced.

While the prostitution defense seemed, in some ways, to be a desperate reach, prosecutors told us this was not uncommon. As we have noted, it was not the only time we encountered the defense during our fieldwork in the courts, but it was raised only in relation to Black women victims. In another case we observed, a defendant used a gun to abduct a middle-class African American victim as she returned home from her full-time job. That defendant was ultimately acquitted when his defense attorney argued that the victim was, in fact, a prostitute. In *State v. Jordan*, a case we analyzed in chapter 2, defense counsel also mentioned transactional sex; when the defendant testified, he told the jury he handed a few "bills" to Mary following what he claimed was consensual sex. As noted, Jordan was also acquitted. In *State v. Anthony*, the case that began this book, defense counsel argued that what the victim-witness, Regina, said was a sexual assault was actually transacted sex as a substitute for rent money. The defense's emphasis on Regina's short denim cutoffs paralleled DC Cahill's continuous invocation of the tight red pants. Though Regina's testimony was not marked by the arresting emotion displayed by L'umoya, her suffering was remarkably comparable and was clearly articulated for the court when she told the prosecutor:

> This is my life. It's my everyday. It's trying to go to work 'cause I don't have a car. I don't have the type of expenses to afford a car so when I leave, I have to watch my back, and I don't stay in the safest neighborhood that somebody would want to stay in . . . everything's gone. I'm not who I used to be. When this all happened, I had long hair. I cut my hair recently. I don't feel like the same [Regina]. My hair was maybe like—I mean, you probably wouldn't understand about hair in a woman, but it's, it was who I am. It was my identity. I just didn't feel pretty no more. I just didn't feel pretty like I used to be. He, he stole everything that was a part of me. I know I wasn't an innocent little girl or anything like that, but all of that, that was left, the joy, the fun, the happiness, who I was, was gone

because—and it was replaced with fear. I don't walk out [of] the house the same anymore. I don't go to work the same anymore. I didn't want to leave the house.

Much like L'umoya, Regina described residential precarity, housing, and financial instability. Though she was relatively dry-eyed, she described the intimate effects of trauma past and present for the court. While L'umoya's long black hair draped over her face during trial, Regina's hair—her "identity"—was cut off, "replaced with fear." Weeks after the trial, Judge Colin discussed the case with us, revealing that Regina had written her a letter stating that the jury "had it wrong." Mr. Anthony was not even Regina's landlord; she did not know who he was. How many court records and trial transcripts now associated Black women with prostitution in Milwaukee? How many neighborhoods were geographically mapped as such "drags" by defense attorneys? And how many more women of color would endure the criminalization of precarity in future trials?

In Milwaukee—a city with a complex and polarized racial history and pervasive residential segregation today—geography itself informs our views of precarity. In the courtroom, a defense attorney can argue that racial prejudice ought not to impact the jury's view of his client while simultaneously suggesting that a Black woman in a particular neighborhood late at night can be read only as a prostitute, her red pants a veritable scarlet letter. Social scientists, too, read landscapes as contexts of racial identity and racialized experience. As ethnographers sitting in courtrooms, listening to witnesses testify about their insomnia, their illnesses and health-seeking efforts, and their own sense of precarity, we saw that the Milwaukee landscape aligned with many of the things we know about the distribution of morbidity, mortality, and violent crime in our communities. Theorists like Tiffany Lethabo King (2019, 48) have reminded us that these geographies are legacies of genocide and slavery and that the inescapability of sexual violence is the "terrible inheritance" of conquest.

We also understand what happens to bodies through the frameworks we have learned from our own lived experiences and our feminist scholarly practices. King, once again, suggested that Black women's bodies are often represented as "suspended states of boundarylessness, gender ambiguity, and intercessory spaces" (King 2019, 117). Initially, caught up in the spectacle of testimony, we responded to the curtain of L'umoya's hair as a marker of her own shame and disgust. Hair is, after all, often associated with abjection in psychoanalytic traditions (Kristeva 1982). When exploring other possibilities for understanding L'umoya's hair, we considered Nayanika Mookherjee's (2015) research on Bengali survivors, or *birangonas*, that drew attention to the role of hair as *purdah*, allowing survivors to move about or to be represented in public space. Hair, in L'umoya's case, might have multiple significations: her protection, her glory, a crown. Black feminist traditions mark hair as a culturally rich bodily sign of power, contestation, and beauty (Banks 2000). But for a defense attorney, the spaces of precarity and the bodies that occupy such spaces are not read as vulnerable or beautiful; instead, they are chastised and vilified. These dialogic encounters in the court of law contribute to a slow accretion of knowledge about Black women in Milwaukee that is forever captured in legal records.

Toward a Feminist Future

By undertaking a rigorous analysis of the many modes of expertise brought to bear on the contemporary sexual assault trial, we have laid bare the epistemological practices and ontological conditions of the court and its impacts on the experiences of adjudicants, community members, court personnel, and witnesses. Proceedings are inflected by local knowledge about race, place, and sexuality. We have shown how juries are primed to anticipate a particular type of trial through *voir dire* and how victim-witnesses belied or conformed to those expectations. We described how police work functioned in the courts, and we drew in the forensic nurse to show how her feminized testimony contrasted with that of the masculine police officer. The forensic nurse mediated the body of evidence into the court but also accounted for the absence of evidence. The forensic scientist performed the role of the expert, harnessing the aura of authority, confidence, and authenticity of a deeply practiced witness. The defendants, when testifying themselves or testified about by other witnesses, were vetted as capable or as failing fathers by attorneys and judges.

To conclude, we want to stress the human costs of the sexual assault trial, including both the freedom of the defendant and the pathway to justice and healing for the victim and others. We highlight the routinized forms of domination in the ways categories of identity—particularly racial and sexual identity—are linked to structures of inequality (Crenshaw 1991). Sexual assault adjudication also produced and reproduced knowledge. As Carol Smart (1989) has noted, law is a site of gender struggle, and legal discourses construct and reconstruct gendered subjects. The sociolegal realm is thus a site for change, an obstacle to change, and a prescription of conventional common-sense notions of difference. Narrative archives, performative expertise, and translated evidence were cemented in the form of transcripts and case law and elevated with the authority of science. Cultural narratives were also transformed, challenged, or reified for the jury. As such, the sexual assault trial sustained and shaped the knowledge and experience of urban space, criminality, race, poverty, sexual violence, and victimhood, forming the very cultural narratives on which the court relies in its ongoing charge to adjudicate and resolve these cases. At times, the formation and reproduction of such cultural narratives was bald in its violence and its subjugation; at other times, it was subtle.

Critically, this book has worked to lift the proverbial curtain on the court, revealing its dispositions and pretenses or what sociolegal scholars call "law in practice." It is about the adjudication of sexual violence—a crime often introduced as particularly emotionally disturbing—but it is also a crime that is rarely prevented or prosecuted. With its monopoly on justice (in the sense that it is an extension of its monopoly on the legitimate use of force), the state designates itself to be the sole arbiter of intervention in cases of sexual violence. But as Ann Russo (2018, 157) asserts in *Feminist Accountability*:

> The current system is not only ineffective, inaccessible, and not a viable source of support or justice for those experiencing harm, but law enforcement, the criminal legal system, and prisons themselves are deeply steeped in and perpetuate oppression and violence.

Russo is one of many scholarly voices who points out that the criminal legal system is not the answer. As we noted in the introduction, scholars and activists have criticized the rise of the punitive state, expanding carceral logics, and the mobilization of criminal legal institutions in response to mainstream antiviolence feminist movements (Kim 2018). Demands for legal reforms and accountability expanded criminal justice responses to sexual and domestic violence, leading to increased criminalization and hyperincarceration of racial and ethnic communities and the subjugation of the poor (Bernstein 2007; Gottschalk 2006). Collective investment in forensic investigation and forensic science contributes to carceral expansion.

These complicated developments in carceral solutions have been sustained by decades of qualified legal reforms. For example, rules of evidence and the passing of rape shield laws have not resulted in case decision-making processes that are less reliant on character, reputation, or questions about the victim's behavior. Most people (though not all) who experience sexual violence want very little to do with law enforcement, the legal system, or penal institutions. We hope this book makes it obvious why so many eschew the solutions offered by the courts. Narrow legal definitions of sexual violence often do not fully encompass survivors' experiences of violence, including the fact that the person who perpetrated the harm is likely a friend, family member, partner, boss, coworker, or other acquaintance. And though the desire for accountability is clear, many survivors do not envision accountability to manifest as sweeping their friends or family into the punitive discipline of the carceral state. We see this in case after case, written in victim impact statements and verbalized as pleas for leniency during sentencing hearings. There are economic reasons, familial reasons, and more that are driving these pleas. Communities of color, immigrants, poor families, queer persons, and transgender persons know this better than most: The state's tools are predicated on violence and subjugation, and once you are subsumed by the state, it is difficult to escape and find other paths to justice. Of course, most sexual assault cases will never make it to court, but for the victims and defendants who do suffer through this adversarial process, they are unlikely to find help processing their trauma, healing, or experiencing anything they recognize as justice. Accountability is too often conflated with punishment and justice within U.S. criminal law, and this book shows the pathways that victims and defendants navigate within the system.

Compelled to participate in criminal justice processes, victims and defendants also become the fodder through which the court reproduces and sustains collective knowledge about sexual violence, race, and gender. Prosecutors and defense attorneys told us time and again that they utilized cultural narratives and developed case theories according to what they believed would resonate most with the common sense of contemporary juries in Milwaukee County. They often reported that their job was to "win the case at all costs" for their client, for the state, and in the name of public protection. Their strategies often entailed reinscribing the most racist and sexist stereotypes about victims and defendants.

In writing this book, we often have been asked what attorneys can do to pursue justice without reinscribing racist, classist, and sexist notions of sexuality and sexual violence. What reforms would we suggest might make the court experience better for victims? This question must be posed in the context of the spectacle of suffering central to our work. These spectacles have manifested in each chapter of this book, for example, as jurors sharing their experience of sexual violence in chapter 1. In chapter 2, we described at length the trauma of victim-witness testimony. In chapter 3, we made clear the ability of police testimony to supplant victim testimony. The indignity and humiliation of a forensic exam, for a modest gain of evidence, underpin the testimony we described in chapter 4. Chapter 5 detailed the spectacle of the forensic scientist's testimony and the racial logics they promote. Finally, chapter 6 focused on fatherhood and the public confessions and admonishments of both the defendant and his family. These spectacles of suffering are intrinsic to the adversarial justice system, and it is hard to think of reformist agendas that can dismantle such legal traditions, neutralize the pernicious stories of racial pathology that become the court's foundation, and treat adjudicants with dignity and respect.

Reforms also do not prevent sexual assault or stop it from happening again. For prosecutors to win "at all costs" means that the costs are borne by the participants—the victim-witness, the defendant, their families and communities—and can be traumatic, deep, and long-lasting. And so we find ourselves seeking other systems of accountability, those that center healing, security, and community. Procriminalization strategies and the optimization of the legal system cannot deliver these alternatives, but there are other possibilities and futures. As Mimi Kim (2018) states, "[T]he critique of mainstream feminist pro-criminalization strategies to address domestic and sexual violence has inspired alternative visions for violence prevention and intervention," including community account-ability and transformative justice. This book, at its end, is not a reform-ist project. And while others may read some aspects of reformism into the text—there are certainly ways to mitigate daily cruelties, injustices, and acts of sexism and racism with which the courts are replete—there is no undoing of the legal archive and decades of precedent on which the court draws in its project of surveilling, disciplining, and punishing.

Rather than detail the work that many feminist scholars—particularly Black feminist, queer, transgender, and antiracist scholars—have done to set out visions for restorative and transformative justice, we end with one final ethnographic scene. We return to the day that 10-year-old Maya's father was sentenced. Neither Maya nor her stuffed animal, Elsa, appeared that day. Maya's mother testified at the sentencing hearing, balancing the impossible task of advocating for her daughter's safety and well-being while also begging for the court's mercy for her partner. She and Maya's father had four children together, and while she did not want him to be near any of them, she was very worried about her ability to support her children on her own. "How am I going to raise these kids?" she asked the judge. The judge nonetheless delivered a lengthy sentence, and Maya's mother would have to move on without him. In the hallway after the sen-tencing, Maya's mother stood with tears in her eyes as the ADA gave her a pep talk. Our field notes dub the tone of the parlay as a "girlfriend" talk, because the white attorney's tone took on some uncharacteristic pepper while her neck wove slightly back and forth in what seemed to be an im-pression of hip-hop sassiness. "Look girl, you don't need him!" the pros-ecutor said, hand on her hip and wagging finger in the air. "You did the right thing and you are going to be fine on your own."

Though the prosecutor was well-meaning, the scene left us unsettled. The prosecutor's easy code-switch into what she perceived as the ges-tural repertoire and vernacular of a Black woman crossed a line. The well-intentioned platitude was, at its root, disingenuous. The prosecu-tor's easy ability to slip into Black vernacular, and her quick ability to slip right back out, were antithetical to the stuckness of Ms. Peeples's very dire situation. Could the prosecutor really promise Maya's mother that she and her four children would be fine? Did the court offer support or reparations? Would Mr. Peeples be able to earn a living and support his family from prison? (The answer to all three questions was no, no, and probably not.) What would happen when Maya's mother had to cover all the family expenses on her own? For there to be better answers to these questions, we must imagine what a transformative or reparative approach to this case could look like. It seems imperative to consider a world in which Maya Peeples does not have to suffer from sexual violence, or the indignities of a forensic examination, or five hours of public testimony in open court, a world in which her story—and not the version of the story held up by medical experts, scientists, and police—can find a hearing. On another scale, Maya's victimization should not feed the system that will continue to criminalize her kin, sexualize her peers, and imperil her community. Completing this book has pushed us to turn toward the work of building a future in which Maya, her mother, and her siblings are not further imperiled by greater precarity and vulnerability. Currently, this is often the outcome of every case adjudicated within Milwaukee's court system. Abolitionists invite us to build a feminist future that replaces carceral solutions with new systems of accountability that center community, healing, and repair, and we invite our readers to build this world with us.

ACKNOWLEDGMENTS

We have accrued many debts of gratitude in writing this book. Though we owe our thanks to many, the flaws in this project are ours alone. These acknowledgements are jointly written because the journey was ours together. A lot of life happened during the research and writing of this book, and we are deeply grateful for the support from family, friends, and colleagues far and wide. We owe an enormous debt of gratitude to the witnesses, defendants, and their families and supporters who we do not name here. The Milwaukee County court personnel—the judges, attorneys, and victim advocates—were patient with our presence and our questions. The forensic scientists and sexual assault nurse examiners of Wisconsin were generous with their time. We admire the court reporters from whom we acquired trial transcripts as deeply devoted professionals without whom this project would not be possible. We also thank Melisa Fousek, our committed interview transcriptionist. Beyond the courts, our local communities supported us and educated us on the ins and outs of sexual assault response in Milwaukee County, including the Aurora Sinai Hospital's Sexual Assault Treatment Center, the Healing Center, the Mayor's Commission on Domestic Violence and Sexual Assault, and the Wisconsin Coalition Against Sexual Assault. We are deeply indebted to the scholarship and activism of women of color, queer, transgender, and antiracist feminists, many of whom are cited here. May we together continue to build toward strategies to end violence.

We thank the National Science Foundation Program in Law and Social Science (Award #1250606) for the funding that supported this research project. Summer Faculty Fellowships and Regular Research Grants from Marquette University gave us the opportunity to refine our questions and plan the full project. Our grants were managed collectively by the talented staff of the Office of Sponsored Research and the Office of the Dean in the College of Arts and Sciences. We especially appreciate Patricia Colloton and Anne Bartelt for going above and beyond to assist us.

The first half of the book was written during our sabbatical year in 2017. Heather's sabbatical was supported by a Way Klingler Sabbatical Award, and Sameena's was funded by the Helen Way Klingler College of Arts and Sciences. A grant from the Center for Peacemaking assisted us in our analysis, and a Jumpstart Research Grant from the Office of Sponsored Research at Marquette University provided the resources for our student Chelsea Pierski to collect data for our pilot study. A Research Experiences for Undergraduates (REU) grant from the National Science Foundation gave us the opportunity to work with Kimberly Nolte, Sophia Torrijos, Bridget Springmire, and Amber Powell. These undergraduate research assistants were invaluable contributors to the project. We are also grateful to the Ronald McNair Scholars Program at Marquette University, which provided training, support, and community to so many of the undergraduate scholars with whom we worked.

Special acknowledgements go to the talented Amber Powell—our friend and incomparable collaborator. Honest, insightful, and inspired, her daily presence in the courts as part of our research team shaped our work in ways that cannot be adequately expressed.

We are grateful to Jean Grow, who suggested we apply for a fellowship from the Women's International Study Center in Santa Fe, New Mexico. We were ecstatic to be awarded the fellowship, as it provided us with critical time to outline this entire book and to get us started in its drafting. We remember our days at the Acequia Madre House with fondness. These were inspiring and healing days as we worked through our notes and our experiences.

Our dear colleagues in the Department of Social and Cultural Sciences at Marquette University workshopped critical sections of the book with us over the years. We would also like to thank Marquette's Center for the Advancement of Humanities Colloquium and colleagues in Marquette University's School of Law who kindly workshopped material with us and generously offered connections and contacts among trial attorneys. We appreciate Rob Smith and the Center for Urban, Research, Teaching & Outreach for providing a home and tools for community-engaged scholars.

Many colleagues beyond Marquette were generous with their time and feedback. We are grateful to have shared space, time, and ideas with Susannah Bartlow, Srimati Basu, Vania Brightman Cox, Dána-

Ain Davis, Christina Hanhardt, Cynthia Howson, Dawn Moore, April Petillo, Ashanté Reese, Shonna Trinch, and Anika Wilson. They all heard the earliest versions of many chapters of the book and provided keen comments and suggestions. Rose Corrigan, Lesley McMillan, Gethin Rees, and Deborah White continue to be the bedrock of Comparative Analysis & International Rape Research Network and provide support and expertise in our small circle of researchers of sexual violence. We are also grateful for the feedback and receptivity of colleagues and participants at the annual meetings of the Law and Society Association; American Anthropological Association; American Sociological Association; American Society of Criminology; National Women's Studies Association; Society for Applied Anthropology; and Sociologists for Women in Society. We appreciate the leadership of the International Association of Forensic Nursing and the time, energy, and insight of Jacqui Callari-Robinson. The Honorable Audrey Skwierawski opened many doors to us before she joined the bench.

We were honored to deliver the Huth Lecture at the University of Dayton in the Department of Sociology, Anthropology, and Social Work. Simanti Dasgupta and Jamie Small were excellent hosts and interlocutors, as were their colleagues and students; their feedback was instrumental in reshaping chapter 6. João Biehl and Amy Krauss were wonderful hosts and organizers of the conference on "Law and Reproductive Health in an Unjust World" at Princeton University, where they responded to a talk based on chapter 4. Parts of chapter 4 have appeared in print in "Normalizing Sexually Violated Bodies: Sexual Assault Adjudication, Medical Evidence, and the Legal Case," in *The Ethnographic Case*, published by Mattering Press. The graduate students and faculty of the Department of Anthropology at Johns Hopkins University were equally generous in their feedback at the "Enacting Aspirations" conference, where they engaged with long sections of the conclusion. Nicole Gonzalez Van Cleve was a lively interlocutor when we invited her to join us at Marquette as Metcalfe Chair and McGee Lecturer, and we are grateful to her for her insights.

Our editor, Jennifer Hammer, has been a staunch supporter and advocate. We are grateful for her suggestions and those of four anonymous reviewers that helped to shape our work. We also extend our thanks to all of the staff of New York University Press who played a role in bringing this book into the world, including Veronica Knutson. We are so thankful to Mafalda Mondestin for her inspiring artwork that graces the cover and helped us to see the end of this project.

There are many friends who put in a lot of energy and care to keep us in good spirits as we weathered the storms of this project: Jane Peterson, Ericka Tucker, Drew Tomkins, Julia Azari, Todd Osterman, Kelsey Jillette, Amrita Ibrahim, Adil Qureshi, Don Selby, Noelle Brigden, Amber Wichowsky, Sam Harshner, Nakia Gordon, Ermitte Saint-Jacques, and Fleming Daugaard-Hansen. We also thank pets past (Taz) and present (Fyodor and Otis).

Sameena is grateful to all her siblings, Ayna, Kedy, Jeanremi, Lisa, Rashad, Sayila, and Martine, to her sister-friends Alison, Veronica, and Lindsay, and to her parents, Nasira and Abdus-Sattar, and in-laws, the Edmes and the Verellas. She also wants to thank Ibrahim and Tipan, who were patient and tolerant and dealt with the ups and downs of her presences and absences and fed her in loving ways throughout the journey. Heather is indebted to her family, Denise, Stephen, and Benjamin, to her sisters, Emalie, Erin, Jeanette, Tess, and Carrie, and to her family-in-law, the McCarthys and the Stanns. She is forever most grateful for James and Kevin, who provided enduring strength, love, laughter, imagination, and sustenance on every level.

Sameena and Heather are deeply indebted to each other. We traveled together, sharing meals, stories, laughter, and tears. This book, and our continued work together, are based in both friendship and respect that have been nurtured with compassion and humility. Our scholarship is better because of each other, and the world is better for feminist friendships that pave pathways of survival into our collectively unknown futures.

NOTES

INTRODUCTION

1 Jenna Sachs, "Chief Judge Says Milw. Co. GPS Monitoring System Is Over Capacity," Fox 6 Now Milwaukee, October 31, 2013, www.fox6now.com.

2 We use the term "Latino/a" to reflect the different gender presentations of adjudicants, but we do not use the term "Latinx," as it has not been widely adopted by our research participants. We also do not use the term "Latine" because our interlocutors all presented within the framework of gender binaries. We reserve these terms for inclusion of nonbinary individuals as well as those who self-select to use the term. We use either Latino or Latina in the singular when describing a particular individual.

3 City of Milwaukee, "Demographics and Data," Milwaukee City Wide Policy Plan, 9–24, http://city.milwaukee.gov.

4 Gina Barton and Becky Vevea, "Police Launch Investigation into Inaction Complaints," *Milwaukee Wisconsin Journal Sentinel*, July 7, 2010, http://archive.jsonline.com. Gina Barton. "Police to Improve Sensitive Training," *Milwaukee Wisconsin Journal Sentinel*, July 9 2010, http://archive.jsonline.com.

5 Erin Toner, "Did Missing DNA Thwart Hunt for Serial Killer?" *All Things Considered*, National Public Radio, September 11, 2009, www.npr.org.

6 John Diedrich, "Police Suspect Serial Killer in Deaths of 6 Milwaukee Women Over 21 Years," *Milwaukee Wisconsin Journal Sentinel*, May 18, 2009, http://archive.jsonline.com.

7 Wisconsin State Legislature, "Chapter 940: Crimes Against Life and Bodily Security. Section 940.225. Sexual Assault," https://docs.legis.wisconsin.gov.

8 (1) First Degree Sexual Assault. Whoever does any of the following is guilty of a Class B felony: (a) Has sexual contact or sexual intercourse with another person without consent of that person and causes pregnancy or great bodily harm to that person. (b) Has sexual contact or sexual intercourse with another person without consent of that person by use or threat of use of a dangerous weapon or any article used or fashioned in a manner to lead the victim reasonably to believe it to be a dangerous weapon. (c) Is aided or abetted by one or more other persons and has sexual contact or sexual intercourse with another person without consent of that person by use or threat of force or violence.

9 "Sexual Intercourse" includes the meaning assigned under s. 939.22 (36) as well as cunnilingus, fellatio or anal intercourse between persons or any other intrusion, however slight, of any part of a person's body or of any object into the genital or anal opening either by the defendant or upon the defendant's instruction. The emission of semen is not required.

Reference to 939. 22 (36) yields the previous definition that "'Sexual inter-course' requires only vulvar penetration and does not require emission," and penetration is further defined in the jury instructions as any penetration of the genitals, however so slight, a formulation common across many U.S. jurisdictions.

(b) "Sexual Contact" means any of the following:

1. Any of the following types of intentional touching, whether direct or through clothing, if that intentional touching is either for the purpose of sexually degrading; or for the purpose of sexually humiliating the complainant or sexually arousing or gratifying the defendant or if the touching contains the elements of actual or attempted battery under s. 940.19 (1):

a. Intentional touching by the defendant or, upon the defendant's instruction, by another person, by the use of any body part or object, of the complainant's intimate parts.

b. Intentional touching by the complainant, by the use of any body part or object, of the defendant's intimate parts or, if done upon the defendant's instructions, the intimate parts of another person.

2. Intentional penile ejaculation of ejaculate or intentional emission of urine or feces by the defendant or, upon the defendant's instruction, by another person upon any part of the body clothed or unclothed of the complainant if that ejaculation or emission is either for the purpose of sexually degrading or sexually humiliating the complainant or for the purpose of sexually arousing or gratifying the defendant.

10 (1) First Degree Child Sexual Assault: Whoever does the following is guilty of Class A felony: (a) Has sexual contact or sexual intercourse with a person who has not attained the age of 13 years and causes great bodily harm to the person. Class B felony (b) Has sexual intercourse with a person who has not attained the age of 12 years or (c) Has sexual intercourse with a person who has not attained the age of 16 year by use or threat of force or violence. (2) Second Degree Sexual Assault: Whoever has sexual contact or intercourse with a person who has not attained the age of 16 years is guilty of a Class C felony.

11 Wisconsin Department of Justice, "UCR Sex Offense Data," www.doj.state.wi.us.

12 On average, only about 60–65 percent of all sexual victimizations are reported to law enforcement nationally. Lynn Langton, Marcus Berzofsky, Christopher Krebs, and Hope Smiley-McDonald. "Victimizations Not reported to the Police, 2006–2010," NCJ 238536, U.S. Department of Justice, Bureau of Justice Statistics, August 2012, 1–17, https://bjs.gov/content.

13 Federal policy and national media attention have brought forensic examination to the forefront (National Research Council 2009; Tofte 2009). A 2009 Human Rights Watch report on rape kit processing backlogs in Los Angeles County drew renewed attention to the plight of rape victims across the United States (Tofte 2009). These backlogs exist despite legislative efforts. For example, Wisconsin congressional Representative Jim Sensenbrenner was the primary sponsor of

the Debbie Smith Act, which was passed as part of the Justice for All Act in 2004. The Debbie Smith Act provided extra funding for the processing of DNA rape kit samples in various local and state crime laboratories. The act also addressed the lack of available and trained DNA technicians by funding SANE programs and certification programs and training of law enforcement and court personnel on how to present DNA evidence in the courtroom. In the 2008 reeauthorization in 2008, appropriations for DNA analysis grant programs were extended to fiscal year 2014. This coincided with the recent January 2009 Violence Against Women Act compliance date requiring all U.S. states to meet an individual's demand for a sexual assault forensic examination regardless of whether the complainant files a police report.

14 Kelly Moe Litke, Ian Henderson, Rose Hennessy, Peter Fiala, Stephen Montagna, and Jerrett Jones, "The Burden of Sexual Violence in Wisconsin," Wisconsin Coalition Against Sexual Assault, 2010, 1–102, https://www.wcasa.org.

15 Wisconsin Court System, "Circuit Court Statistics," Publications: Guides, Reports, Newsletters, etc., www.wicourts.gov.

16 Wisconsin State Public Defenders, "SPD Facts-At-A-Glance," About the SPD, www.wispd.org.

3. THE LOW AND THE HIGH

1 In 2014, men made up about 90 percent of all police in the United States. For more details, see the Federal Bureau of Investigation, "Police Employee Data," 2014 Crime in the United States, Criminal Justice Information Services Division, https://ucr.fbi.gov.

2 Daubert hearings emerged from case law and set a higher standard for the inclusion of scientific expertise during trials. The Daubert standard replaced the earlier Frye standard. Though the case law has shifted, in practice, Daubert hearings to challenge the inclusion of forensic evidence were very rare during our field research.

3 It is impossible to anonymize the case and conviction of Michael Vagnini, and thus we did not assign a pseudonym here. The Milwaukee press reported on the case for months and continue to cover federal charges and damages awarded to victims years later.

4 For example, the radio series *This American Life* broadcast an episode titled "Cops See It Differently [Parts One and Two]."

5 It is worth noting that the full phrase is "one bad apple spoils the barrel" and therefore does imply broader cultural problems within an organization.

6. THE GOOD FATHER

1 A few months later, however, another child pornography case before the same judge resulted in him stating how annoyed he was to have to give the mandatory-minimum five-year sentence. He complained, on the record, that his ability to exercise his discretion had been limited by the legislature. In his opinion, this case did not warrant such a severe sentence.

BIBLIOGRAPHY

Adam, Vincanne. 2016. *Metrics: What Counts in Global Health*. Durham: Duke University Press.

Alcoff, Linda. 2018. *Rape and Resistance: Understanding the Complexities of Sexual Violation*. Cambridge: Polity Press.

Alcoff, Linda, and Laura Gray. 1993. "Survivor Discourse: Transgression or Recuperation?" *Signs* 18: 260–90.

Alexander, Elizabeth. 1994. "'Can you be BLACK and Look at This?' Reading the Rodney King Video(s)." *Public Culture* 7(1): 77–94.

Alexander, Michelle. 2010. *The New Jim Crow: Mass Incarceration in the Age of Colorblindness*. New York: The New Press.

Anderson, Stephen, Gillian Cohen, and Stephanie Taylor. 2000. "Rewriting the Past: Some Factors Affecting the Variability of Personal Memory." *Applied Cognitive Psychology* 14(5): 435–54.

Balkin, J. M. 1993. "Understanding Legal Understanding: The Legal Subject and the Problem of Legal Coherence." *Yale Law Journal* 103: 105–76.

Banks, Ingrid. 2000. *Hair Matters: Beauty, Power, and Black Women's Consciousness*. New York: New York University Press.

Baskin Deborah and Ira Sommers. 2010. "The Influence of Forensic Evidence on the Case Outcomes of Homicide Incidents." *Journal of Criminal Justice* 38(6): 1141–49.

Basu, Srimati. 2015. *The Trouble with Marriage: Feminists Confront Law and Violence in India*. Berkeley: University of California Press.

Baxi, Pratiksha. 2014. *Public Secrets of Law: Rape Trials in India*. New Delhi: Oxford University Press.

———. 2005. "The Medicalisation of Consent and Falsity: The Figure of the *Habitué* in Indian Rape Law." In *The Violence of Normal Times: Essays on Women's Lived Realities*, ed. K. Kannabiran, chap. 2. New Delhi: Women Unlimited.

Beauvoir, Simone. 1969. *The Woman Destroyed*. Translated by P. O'Brien. New York: Pantheon.

Behar, Ruth. 1997. *The Vulnerable Observer: Anthropology That Breaks Your Heart*. Boston: Beacon Press.

Beichner, Dawn, and Cassia Spohn. 2005. "Prosecutorial Charging Decisions in Sexual Assault Cases: Examining the Impact of a Specialized Prosecution Unit." *Criminal Justice Policy Review*. 16: 461–98.

Bell, Monica. 2017. "Police Reform and the Dismantling of Legal Estrangement." *Yale Law Journal* 126: 2054–2150.

Benjamin, Ruha. 2016. "Catching Our Breath: Critical Race STS and the Carceral Imagination." *Engaging Science, Technology, and Society* 2: 145–56.

Bernstein, Elizabeth. 2007. "The Sexual Politics of the 'New Abolitionism.'" *Differences* 18(3): 128–51.

Berliner, Lucy. 2003. "Making Domestic Violence Victims Testify." *Journal of Interpersonal Violence* 18(6): 666–68.

Bevacqua, Maria. 2000. *Rape on the Public Agenda: Feminism and the Politics of Sexual Assault*. Boston: Northeastern University Press.

Blinka, Daniel. 2014. *A Primer on the New Evidence Rules Governing Lay and Expert Opinion*. Milwaukee: Marquette University School of Law. www.wispd.org.

——. 2010. "Why Modern Law Lacks Credibility." *Buffalo Law Review* 58: 357.

Bogira, Steve. 2005. *Courtroom 302: A Year Behind the Scenes in an American Criminal Courthouse*. New York: Knopf/Random House.

Bohner, Gerd. 1998. *Vergewaltigungsmythen* [Rape Myths]. Landau, Germany: Verlag Empirische Pädagogik.

Braun, Virginia, and Celia Kitzinger. 2001. "'Snatch,' 'Hole,' or 'Honey Pot'? Semantic Categories and the Problem of Non-specificity in Female Genital Slang." *Journal of Sex Research* 38(2): 146–58.

Braun, Virginia, and Sue Wilkinson. 2001. "Socio-cultural Represprentations of the Vagina." *Journal of Reproduction and Infant Psychology* 19(1): 17–32.

Brison, Susan. 2002. *Aftermath: Violence and the Remaking of a Self*. Princeton: Princeton University Press.

Brodeur, Jean-Paul. 2010. *The Policing Web*. New York: Oxford University Press.

Browne, Simone. 2015. *Dark Matters: On the Surveillance of Blackness*. Durham: Duke University Press.

Bruner, Jerome. 2002. *Making Stories: Law, Literature, Life*. Cambridge: Harvard University Press.

Bunt, Laura. 2008. "A Quest for Justice in Cuzco, Peru: Race and Evidence in the Case of Mercedes Ccorimanya Lavilla," *Political and Legal Anthropology Review* 31(2): 286–302.

Burns, Robert. 1999. *A Theory of the Trial*. Princeton: Princeton University Press.

Campbell, Rebecca, Deborah Bybee, Kevin Ford, Debra Patterson, and Jamie Ferrel. 2009. *A Systems Change Analysis of SANE Programs: Identifying the Mediating Mechanisms of Criminal Justice System Impact*. Washington, D.C.: National Institute of Justice.

Campbell, Rebecca, Debra Patterson, Deborah Bybee, and Emily R. Dworkin. 2009. "Predicting Sexual Assault Prosecution Outcomes: The Role of Medical Forensic Evidence Collected by Sexual Assault Nurse Examiners." *Criminal Justice and Behavior* 36(7): 712–27.

Campbell, Sue. 2003. *Relational Remembering: Rethinking the Memory Wars*. Lanham, MD: Rowman & Littlefield.

Canguilhem, Georges. 1991. *The Normal and the Pathological*. Boston: Zone Books.

Carpenter, Laura. 2005. *Virginity Lost: An Intimate Portrait of First Sexual Experiences*. New York: New York University Press.

Carr, Summerson. 2010. *Scripting Addiction: The Politics of Therapeutic Talk and American Sobriety*. Princeton: Princeton University Press.

Choo, Hae Yeon, and Myra Marx Ferree. 2010. "Practicing Intersectionality in Sociological Research: A Critical Analysis of Inclusions, Interactions and Institutions in the Study of Inequalities." *Sociological Theory* 28(2): 129–49.

Code, Lorraine. 1995. *Rhetorical Spaces: Essays on Gendered Locations*. New York: Routledge.

Cole, Simon, and Rachel Diosa-Villa. 2009. "Investigating the 'CSI Effect' Effect: Media and Litigation Crisis in Criminal Law." *Stanford Law Review* 61(6): 1335–74.

———. 2007. "CSI and Its Effects: Media, Juries, and the Burden of Proof." *New England Law Review* 41(3): 435–70.

Cole, Simon, and Michael Lynch. 2006. "The Social and Legal Construction of Suspects." *Annual Review of Law and Social Science* 2: 39–60.

Collins, Patricia Hill. 2004. *Black Sexual Politics: African Americans, Gender, and the New Racism*. New York: Routledge.

———. 1990. *Black Feminist Thought: Knowledge, Consciousness, and the Politics of Empowerment*. New York: Routledge.

Connell, R.W., and James Messerschmidt. 2005. "Hegemonic Masculinity: Rethinking the Concept." *Gender and Society* 19(6): 829–59.

Corrigan, Rose. 2013a. *Up Against a Wall: Rape Reform and the Failure of Success*. New York: New York University Press.

———. 2013b. "The New Trial By Ordeal: Rape Kits, Police Practices and the Unintended Effects of Policy Innovation." *Law and Social Inquiry* 38(4): 920–49.

———. 2006. "Making Meaning of Meghan's Law." *Law and Social Inquiry* 31(2): 267–312.

Cossins, Anne. 2010. "Time Out For Longman: Myths, Science and the Common Law." *Melbourne University Law Review* 34: 69–105.

Cover, Robert. 1983. "The Supreme Court 1982 Term: *Nomos* and Narrative." *Harvard Law Review* 97: 4–68.

Crenshaw, Kimberlé. 1991. "Mapping the Margins: Intersectionality, Identity Politics, and Violence Against Women of Color." *Stanford Law Review* 43(6): 1241–99.

Creswell, Paul D., Christy Vogt, Megan Christenson, and Carrie Tomasallo. 2019. "Health Disparities in Hospitalization for Wisconsin." Department of Health Services. Division of Public Health. Bureau of Environmental and Occupational Health.

Das, Veena. 2007. "Commentary: Trauma and Testimony: Between Law and Discipline." *Ethos* 35(3): 3303–35.

———. 2003. "Trauma and Testimony: Implications for Political Community." *Anthropological Theory* 3(3): 293–307.

———. 2000. "The Act of Witnessing: Violence, Poisonous Knowledge and Subjectivity." In *Violence and Subjectivity*, ed. V. Das, A. Kleinman, M. Ramphele, and P. Reynolds, 205–25. Berkeley: University of California Press.

Daston, Lorrain. 1992. "Objectivity and the Escape from Perspective." *Social Studies of Science* 22(4): 597–618.

Daston, Lorraine, and Peter Galison. 1992. "The Image of Objectivity." *Representations* 40: 81–128.

Davis, Angela J., John Chisholm, and David Noble. 2019. *Race and Prosecution*. New York: Institute for Innovation in Prosecution at John Jay College.

Davis, Dána-Ain. 2019. *Reproductive Injustice: Racism, Pregnancy and Premature Birth*. New York: New York University Press.

Desmond, Matthew, Andrew Papachristos, and David Kirk. 2016. "Police Violence and Citizen Crime Reporting in the Black Community." *American Sociological Review* 81(5): 857–76.

DiMaggio, Paul. 1997. "Culture and Cognition." *Annual Review of Sociology* 23: 263–287.

Donovan, Roxanne, and Michelle Williams. 2002. "Living at the Intersection: The Effects of Racism and Sexism on Black Rape Survivors." *Women & Therapy* 25(3–4): 95–105.

Donzelot, Jacques. 1977. *The Policing of Families*. New York: Random House.

Dowd Hall, Jacquelyn. 1993. *Revolt Against Chivalry: Jessie Daniel Ames and the Women's Campaign Against Lynching*. New York: Columbia University Press.

Dougherty, Molly C., and Toni Tripp-Reimer. 1985. "The Interface of Nursing and Anthropology." *Annual Review of Anthropology* 14: 219–41.

Du Mont, Janice, and Deborah Parnis. 2003. "Forensic Nursing in the Context of Sexual Assault: Comparing the Opinions and Practices of Nurse Examiners and Nurses." *Applied Nursing Research* 16(3): 173–83.

———. 2000. "Sexual Assault and Legal Resolution: Querying the Medical Collection of Forensic Evidence." *Medicine and Law* 19(4): 779–92.

Du Mont, Janice, and Deborah White. 2007. *The Uses and Impacts of Medico-legal Evidence in Sexual Assault Cases: A Global Review*. World Health Organization Sexual Violence Research Initiative. Geneva, Switzerland: WHO Press.

Editorial Board. "Rekia Boyd Shooting Was 'Beyond Reckless,' So Cop Got a Pass." *Chicago Tribune*. April 22, 2015. www.chicagotribune.com/opinion/editorials/ct-cop-verdict-servin-edit-0423-20150422-story.html.

Ehrlich, Susan. 2001. *Representing Rape: Language and Sexual Consent*. London: Routledge.

Ellison, Louise, and Vanessa E. Munro. 2009. "Of 'Normal Sex' and 'Real Rape': Exploring the Use of Socio-sexual Scripts in (Mock) Jury Deliberation." *Social and Legal Studies* 18(3): 291–312.

Emerson, Robert, Rachel Fretz, and Linda Shaw. 2011. *Writing Ethnographic Fieldnotes*. Chicago: University of Chicago Press.

Epstein, Rebecca, Jamilia Blake, and Thalia González. 2014. *Girlhood Interrupted: The Erasure of Black Girls' Childhood*. Washington, D.C.: Georgetown Law Center on Poverty and Inequality.

Estrich, Susan. 1987. *Real Rape*. Cambridge, MA: Harvard University Press.

Ewick, Patricia, and Susan Silbey. 1998. *The Common Place of Law: Stories From Everyday Life*. Chicago: University of Chicago Press.

Feinstein, Rachel. A. 2019. *When Rape Was Legal: The Untold History of Sexual Violence During Slavery*. New York: Routledge.

Feldberg, Georgina. 1997. "Defining the Facts of Rape: The Uses of Medical Evidence in Sexual Assault Trials." *Canadian Journal of Women and the Law* 9: 89–114.

Flood, Dawn R. 2012. *Rape in Chicago: Race, Myth and the Courts*. Urbana: University of Illinois Press.

Foucault, Michel. 1980. *The History of Sexuality*, Volume 1: *An Introduction*. Translated by R. Hurley. New York: Pantheon.

———. 1978. "About the Concept of the 'Dangerous Individual' in 19th-Century Legal Psychiatry." Translated by Alain Baudot and Jane Couchman. *International Journal of Law and Psychiatry* 1: 1–18.

———. 1973. *The Archaeology of Knowledge and the Discourse on Language*. Translated by S. Smith. New York: Pantheon.

Frederickson, George. M. 1971. *The Black Image in the White Mind: The Debate on Afro-American Character and Destiny, 1817–1914*. Middletown, CT: Wesleyan University Press.

French, Sandra L. 2003. "Reflections on Healing: Framing Strategies Utilized by Acquaintance Rape Survivors." *Journal of Applied Communication* 31(4): 298–319.

Frese, Bettina, Miguel Moya, and Jesús L. Megías. 2004. "Social Perception of Rape: How Rape Myth Acceptance Modulates the Influence of Situational Factors." *Journal of Interpersonal Violence* 19(2): 143–61.

Gavey, Nicola. 2005. *Just Sex? The Cultural Scaffolding of Rape*. New York: Routledge.

Girardin, Barbara, Diana Faugno, Patty Seneski, Laura Slaughter, and Margaret Whelan. 1997. *The Color Atlas of Sexual Assault*. Philadelphia: Mosby Press.

Gonzalez Van Cleve, Nicole. 2016. *Crook County: Racism and Injustice in American's Largest Criminal Court*. Stanford: Stanford University Press

Gottschalk, Marie. 2006. *The Prison and the Gallows: The Politics of Mass Incarceration in America*. Cambridge: Cambridge University Press.

Greer, Danielle M., Dennis J. Baumgardner, Farrin D. Bridgewater, David A. Frazer, Courtenay L. Kessler, Erica S. LeCounte, Geoffrey R. Swain, and Ron A. Cisler. 2013. *Milwaukee Health Report 2013: Health Disparities in Milwaukee by Socioeconomic Status*. Milwaukee: Center for Urban Population.

Guha, Ranajit. 1988. "The Prose of Counter-Insurgency." In *Selected Subaltern Studies*, ed. R. Guha and G. Spivak, 45–86. Oxford: Oxford University Press.

Haaken, Janice. 1999. "Heretical Texts: The Courage to Heal and the Incest Survivor Movement." In *New Versions of Victims: Feminists Struggle with the Concept*, ed. S. Lamb, 13–41. New York: New York University Press.

Harding, Sandra. 2004. *The Feminist Standpoint Theory Reader: Intellectual and Political Controversies*. New York: Routledge.

Harper, Ian, Tobias Kelly, and Akshay Khanna, eds. 2015. *The Clinic and the Court: Law, Medicine and Anthropology*. Cambridge: Cambridge University Press.

Henslin, James M., and Mae A. Biggs. 1971. "Dramaturgical Desexualization: The Sociology of the Vaginal Examination." In *Studies in the Sociology of Sex*, ed. J. M. Henslin, 243–72. New York: Appleton-Century Crofts.

Hinton, Elizabeth. 2016. *From the War on Poverty to the War on Crime: The Making of Mass Incarceration in America*. Cambridge, MA: Harvard University Press.

Hlavka, Heather. 2017. "Speaking of Stigma and the Silence of Shame." *Men and Masculinities* 20(4): 482–505.

———. 2014. "Normalizing Sexual Violence: Young Women Account for Harassment and Abuse." *Gender and Society* 28(3): 337–58.

———. 2013. "Legal Subjectivity Among Youth Victims of Sexual Abuse." *Law & Social Inquiry* 39(1): 31–61.

Hlavka, Heather, and Sameena Mulla. 2020. "Thinking Forensically: The Nomos of Sexual Violence." In *Research Handbook of Socio-legal Studies of Medicine and Health*, ed. M. Jacob and A. Kirkland, 232–54. Cheltenham, UK: Edward Elgar.

———. 2018. "'That's How She Talks': Animating Text Message Evidence in the Sexual Assault Trial." *Law and Society Review* 52(2): 401–35.

Hochschild, Arlie. 1983. *The Managed Heart: Commercialization of Human Feeling*. Berkeley: University of California Press.

Holstein, James, and Jaber Gubrium, eds. 2008. *Handbook of Constructionist Research*. New York: Guilford Press.

Hornberger, Julia. 2011. *Policing and Human Rights*. Oxford: Routledge.

Hughes, Everett C. 1958. "Good People and Dirty Work." *Social Problems* 10(1): 3–11.

Hyde, Alan. 1997. *Bodies of Law*. Princeton: Princeton University Press.

IAFN (International Association of Forensic Nursing). 2007. "Summary of IAFN's International Initiatives and Next Steps for Moving Forward Internationally." Baltimore: White Paper.

Innocence Project. 2017. "Strengthening Forensic Science Includes Supporting Forensic Laboratory Funding." Madison: The Innocence Project. www.innocenceproject.org/strengthening-forensic-science-includes-supporting-forensic-laboratory-funding.

Irigaray, Luce. 1996. "This Sex Which Is Not One." In *Feminism and Sexuality: A Reader*, ed. S. Jackson and S. Scott, 79–83. Edinburgh: Edinburgh University Press.

Jasanoff, Sheila. 1995. *Science at the Bar: Law, Science, and Technology in America*. Cambridge, MA: Harvard University Press.

Jordanova, Ludmilla. 1989. *Sexual Visions: Images of Gender in Science Between the Eighteenth and Twentieth Centuries*. Madison: University of Wisconsin Press.

Kapsalis, Terri. 1997. *Public Privates: Performing Gynecology from Both Ends of the Speculum*. Durham: Duke University Press.

Kelley, Robin D. G. 2017. "On Violence and Carcerality." *Signs: Journal of Women in Culture and Society* 42(3): 590–600.

Kim, Mimi E. 2018. 2020. "The Carceral Creep: Gender-Based Violence, Race, and the Expansion of the Punitive State, 1973–1983." *Social Problems* 67: 251–69.

———. "From Carceral Feminism to Transformative Justice: Women-of-color and Alternatives to Incarceration." *Journal of Ethnic and Cultural Diversity in Social Work* 27(3): 219–33.

King, Tiffany Lethabo. 2019. *The Black Shoals: Offshore Formations of Black and Native Studies*. Durham: Duke University Press.

Kirk, David, and Mauri Matsueda. 2011. "Legal Cynicism, Collective Efficacy, and the Ecology of Arrest." *Criminology* 49(2): 334–471.

Kleinman, Arthur. 1988. *The Illness Narratives: Suffering, Healing and the Human Condition*. New York: Basic Books.

Konradi, Amanda. 2007. *Taking the Stand: Rape Survivors and the Prosecution of Rapists*. Westport, CT: Praeger.

———. 1997. "Too Little, Too Late: Prosecutors' Pre-Court Preparation of Rape Survivors," *Law and Social Inquiry* 22(1): 1–54.

Kowalik, Jeannette. 2018. "City of Milwaukee 2015–2017 Infant Mortality Rate (IMR): Data Brief." Milwaukee: City of Milwaukee Health Department.

Kristeva, Julia. 1982. *Powers of Horror: An Essay on Abjection*. New York: Columbia University Press.

Kruse, Corinna. 2016. *The Social Life of Forensic Evidence*. Oakland: University of California Press.

Kuhn, Thomas. 1962. *The Structure of Scientific Revolutions*. Chicago: University of Chicago Press.

Lamb, Sharon, ed. 1999. *New Versions of Victims: Feminists Struggle with the Concept.* New York: New York University Press.

Larsson, Maria, and Annika Melinder. 2007. "Underestimated Sensations: Everyday Odour Memory in Clinical and Forensic Settings." In *Everyday Memory*, ed. S. Magnussen and T. Helstrup, 93–110. Hove, UK, and New York: Psychology Press.

Latour, Bruno, and Steve Woolgar. 1979. *Laboratory Life: The Construction of Scientific Facts*. Princeton: Princeton University Press.

Laws, Sophie 1987. "Down There—Using Speculums for Self-Examination." In *Women's Health: A Spare Rib Reader*, ed. S. O'Sullivan, 8–14. London: Pandora.

Lazarus-Black, Mindie. 2007. *Everyday Harm: Domestic Violence, Court Rites, and Cultures of Reconciliation*. Urbana: University of Illinois Press.

Lees, Sue. 1996. *Carnal Knowledge: Rape on Trial*. London: Women's Press.

Levine, Marc V. 2012. "Race and Male Employment in the Wake of the Great Recession: Black Male Employment Rates in Milwaukee and the Nation's Largest Metro Areas, 2010." *Center for Economic Development Publications*. 20. https://dc.uwm.edu/ced_pubs/20.

Lisak, David, and P. M. Miller. 2002. "Repeat Rape and Multiple Offending Among Undetected Rapists." *Violence and Victims* 17: 73–84.

Lonsway, K. A. 2010. "Trying to Move the Elephant in the Living Room: Responding to the Challenge of False Rape Reports." *Violence Against Women* 16(12): 1356–71.

Lowery, Wesley, Carol D. Leonnig, and Mark Berman. "Even Before Michael Brown's Slaying in Ferguson, Racial Questions Hung Over Police." *Washington Post*, August 13, 2014. www.washingtonpost.com/politics/even-before-teen-michael-browns-slaying-in-mo-racial-questions-have-hung-over-police/2014/08/13/78b3c5c6-2307-11e4-86ca-6f03cbd15c1a_story.html?noredirect=on.

Lynch, Michael, Simon Cole, Ruth McNally, and Kathleen Jordan. 2008. *Truth Machine: The Contentious History of DNA Fingerprinting.* Chicago: University of Chicago Press.

MacKinnon, Catharine A. 1979. *Sexual Harassment of Working Women: A Case of Sex Discrimination.* New Haven: Yale University Press.

Maier, Shana L. 2012. "Sexual Assault Nurse Examiners' Perceptions of the Revictimization of Rape Victims." *Journal of Interpersonal Violence* 27(2): 287–315.

Martin, Emily. 1991. "The Egg and the Sperm: How Science Has Constructed a Romance Based on Stereotypical Male-Female Roles." *Signs* 16(3): 485–501.

Martin, Jeffrey. 2018. "Police and Policing." *Annual Review of Anthropology.* 47: 133–48.

Martin, Patricia Yancey. 2005. *Rape Work: Victims, Gender, and Emotions in Organization and Community Context.* New York: Routledge.

Martinez, Brandon, Nick Peterson, and Marisa Omari. 2019. "Time, Money, and Punishment: Institutional Racial-Ethnic Inequalities in Pretrial Detention and Case Outcomes." *Crime and Delinquency* 66(6/7): 837–63.

Massey, Douglas, and Nancy Denton. 1993. *American Apartheid: Segregation and the Making of the Underclass.* Cambridge, MA: Harvard University Press.

Matthews, Sandra, and Laura Wexler. 2000. *Pregnant Pictures.* New York and London: Routledge.

Matoesian, Gregory. 1993. *Reproducing Rape: Domination Through Talk in the Courtroom.* Chicago: University of Chicago Press.

May, Ruben B., and Mary Pattillo-McCoy. 2000. "Do You See What I See? Examining a Collaborative Ethnography." *Qualitative Inquiry* 6(1): 65–87.

Merry, Sally Engle. 2016a. *The Seductions of Quantification: Measuring Human Rights, Gender Violence, and Sex Trafficking.* Chicago: University of Chicago Press.

——. 2016b. "Postscript to Legal Vernacularization and Transnational Culture: The Ka Hoʻokolokolonui Kanaka Maoli, Hawaiʻi." *Political and Legal Anthropology Review* 19(1): 67–82.

——. 1996. "Legal Vernacularization and Ka Hoʻokolokolonui Kanaka Maoli, The People's International Tribunal, Hawaiʻi 1993." *Political and Legal Anthropology Review* 19(1): 67–82.

McGrath, Roberta. 2002. *Seeing Her Sex: Medical Archives and the Female Body.* Manchester, UK: Manchester University Press.

Miller, Jody. 2008. *Getting Played: African American Girls, Urban Inequality, and Gendered Violence.* New York: New York University Press.

Mookherjee, Nayanika. 2015. *The Spectral Wound: Sexual Violence, Public Memories, and the Bangladesh War of 1971.* Durham: Duke University Press.

Moore, Dawn, and Rashmi Singh. 2018. "Seeing Crime, Feeling Crime: Visual Evidence, Emotions, and the Prosecution of Domestic Violence." *Theoretical Criminology* 22(1): 116–32.

Moynihan, Daniel Patrick. 1965. *The Negro Family: The Case for National Action.* Washington, D.C.: U.S. Department of Labor.

Muhammad, Khalil Gibran. 2010. *The Condemnation of Blackness: Race, Crime and the Making of Modern Urban America.* Cambridge, MA: Harvard University Press.

Mulla, Sameena. 2016. "Sensing Sexual Assault: Evidencing Truth Claims in the Forensic Sensorium." In *Sensing Law*, ed. S. Hamilton et al., 195–214. New York: Routledge.

———. 2014. *The Violence of Care: Rape Victims, Forensic Nurses and Sexual Assault Intervention.* New York: New York University Press.

———. 2011. "Facing Victims: Forensics, Visual Technologies, and Sexual Assault Victims." *Medical Anthropology* 30(3): 271–94.

Mulla, Sameena, and Heather Hlavka. 2011. "Gendered Violence and the Ethics of Social Science Research." *Violence Against Women* 17(12): 1509–20.

National Forensic Science Technology Center (NFSTC). 2018. "Wisconsin State Crime Laboratory Bureau Needs Assessment Report." Prepared for Office of the Attorney General, Wisconsin Department of Justice. Largo: NFSTC at Florida International University. https://wispd.org/images/WSCLBNeedsAssesment.pdf.

National Research Council. 2009. *Strengthening Forensic Science in the United States: A Path Forward.* Committee on Identifying the Needs of the Forensic Science Community. Washington, D.C.: U.S. Department of Justice.

Nelson, Alondra. 2016. *The Social Life of DNA: Race, Reparations and Reconciliation After the Genome.* Boston: Beacon Press.

Nelson, Diane. 2015. *Who Counts? The Mathematics of Death and Life After Genocide.* Durham: Duke University Press.

Nordstrom, Carolyn. 1996. "Rape: Politics and Theory in War and Peace." *Australian Feminist Studies* 11(23): 147–62.

Nugent-Borakove, M. Elaine, Patricia Fanflick, David Troutman, Nicole Johnson, Ann Burgess, and Annie O'Connor. 2006. *Testing the Efficacy of SANE/SART Programs: Do They Make a Difference in Sexual Assault Arrest and Prosecution Outcomes?* Prepared for U.S. Department of Justice. Document No. 214252. https://www.ojp.gov/pdffiles1/nij/grants/214252.pdf.

Peterson, Ruth, and Lauren Krivo. 2010. *Divergent Social Worlds: Neighborhood Crime and the Racial Spatial Divide.* New York: Russell Sage Press.

Petrack, Jenny, and Barbara Hedge. 2002. *The Trauma of Sexual Assault: Treatment, Prevention and Practice.* West Sussex, UK: Wiley.

Pipe, Margaret-Ellen, Michael Lamb, Yael Orbach, and Ann-Christin Cederborg, eds. 2007. *Child Sexual Abuse: Disclosure, Delay and Denial.* London: Lawrence Erlbaum.

Plummer, Deborah. 1995. "Patterns of Racial Identity Development of African Americal Adolescent Males and Females." *Journal of Black Psychology* 21(2): 168–80.

Polletta, Francesca, Pang Ching Bobby Chen, Beth Gharrity Gardner, and Alice Motes. 2011. "The Sociology of Storytelling." *Annual Review of Sociology* 37: 109–30.

Poole, Deborah. 2004. "Between Threat and Guarantee: Justice and Community in the Margins of the Peruvian State." In *Anthropology in the Margins of the State*, ed. D. Poole and V. Das, 35–66. Santa Fe: SAR Press.

Polcyn, Bryan. "Nearly a Thousand Rape Kits Sit Untested by Crime Labs," Fox 6 News (Milwaukee), July 25, 2010.

Porter, Theodore. 1995. *Trust in Numbers: The Pursuit of Objectivity in Science and Public Life*. Princeton: Princeton University Press.

Powell, Amber, Heather Hlavka, and Sameena Mulla. 2017. "Intersectionality and Credibility in Child Sexual Assault Trials." *Gender and Society* 31(4): 457–80.

Presser, Lois. 2013. *Why We Harm*. New Brunswick, NJ: Rutgers University Press.

Quinlan, Andrea. 2017. *The Technoscientific Witness of Rape: Contentious Histories of Law, Feminism and Forensic Science*. Toronto : University of Toronto Press.

Reavey, Paula, and Steven Brown. 2006. "Transforming Past Agency and Action in the Present: Time, Social Remembering and Child Sexual Abuse." *Theory & Psychology* 16(2): 179–202.

Rees, Gethin. 2015. "Contentious Roommates? Spatial Constructions of the Therapeutic Evidential Spectrum in Medico-legal Work." In *The Clinic and the Court: Medicine, Law and Anthropology*, ed. I. Harper, T. Kelly and A. Khanna, 141–62. Cambridge: Cambridge University Press.

———. 2012. "Whose Credibility Is It Anyway? Professional Authority and Relevance in Forensic Nurse Examinations of Sexual Assault Survivors." *Review of European Studies* 4(4): 110–12.

———. 2011. "'Morphology Is a Witness Which Doesn't Lie': Diagnosis by Similarity Relation and Analogical Inference in Clinical Forensic Medicine." *Social Science and Medicine* 73(6): 866–72.

———. 2009. "Constructing Incontrovertible Evidence: How Forensic Medical Examiners Disseminate, Constrain and Sustain Shared Visions and Practices." Constructing Evidence in Legal *Settings*. Conference Paper. Annual Meeting of the Society for the Social Studies of Science, October 28–31, 2009, Washington, D.C.

Ridgeway, Cecilia, and Tamar Kricheli-Katz. 2013. "Intersecting Cultural Beliefs in Social Relations: Gender, Race, and Class Binds and Freedoms." *Gender & Society* 27(3): 294–318.

Rios, Victor. 2011. *Punished: Policing the Lives of Black and Latino Boys*. New York: New York University Press.

Richie, Beth. 2012. *Arrested Justice: Black Women, Violence, and America's Prison Nation*. New York: New York University Press.

Richland, Justin. 2008. *Arguing with Tradition: The Language of Law in Hopi Tribal Court*. Chicago: University of Chicago Press.

Roberts, Dorothy. 2011. *Fatal Invention: How Science, Politics, and Big Business Recreate Race in the Twenty-First Century*. New York: The New Press.

Roberts, Dorothy. 1997. *Killing the Black Body: Race, Reproduction, and the Meaning of Liberty*. New York: Vintage Books.

Rosenberg, Karen, and Judith Howard. 2008. "Finding Feminist Sociology: A Review Essay." *Signs* 33(3): 675–96.

Rushing, Andrew Benton. 1993. "Surviving Rape: A Morning/Mourning Ritual." In *Theorizing Black Feminisms*, ed. S. James and A. Busia, 127–40. New York: Routledge.

Russo, Ann. 2018. *Feminist Accountability: Disrupting Violence and Transforming Power*. New York: New York University Press.

Salamon, Gayle. 2018. *The Life and Death of Latisha King: A Critical Phenomenology of Transphobia*. New York: New York University Press.

Sampson, Robert. 2009. "Racial Stratification and the Durable Tangle of Neighborhood Inequality." *Annals of the American Academy of Political and Social Science* 621: 260–80.

Sanday, Peggy Reeves. 1996. *A Woman Scorned: Acquaintance Rape on Trial*. New York: Doubleday.

Schafran, Lynn Hecht. 1995. "Credibility in the Courts: Why is There a Gender Gap?" *Judges' Journal* 34(1): 40–41.

Schlesinger, Traci. 2005. "Racial and Ethnic Disparity in Pretrial Criminal Processing." *Justice Quarterly* 22(2): 170–92.

Schweitzer, N. J., and Michael Saks. 2006. "CSI Effect: Popular Fiction About Forensic Science Affects the Public's Expectations about Real Forensic Science." *Jurimetrics* 47: 357–64.

Schumm, Jeffrey. M. 2000. "Guidance to the 'Gatekeepers' Regarding Admissibility of Nonscientific Evidence: An Analysis of *Kumho Tire Co. v. Carmichael*." *Florida State University Law Review* 27(4): 865–95.

Shelbourne, Talis. 2019. "Hundreds Gather to Celebrate the Life of Dontre Hamilton Five Years After His Death," *Milwaukee Journal Sentinel*, April 27, 2019.

Shelton, Donald E., Young S. Kim, and Gregg Barak. 2006. "Study of Juror Expectations and Demands Concerning Scientific Evidence: Does the '*CSI* Effect' Exist?" *Vanderbilt Journal of Entertainment and Technology*, 9(2): 331–68.

Skolnick, Jerome. 2002. "Corruption and the Blue Code of Silence." *Police Practice and Research* 3(1): 7–19.

Small, Jamie. 2019. "Constructing Sexual Harm: Prosecutorial Narratives of Children, Abuse, and the Disruption of Heterosexuality." *Gender and Society* 33(4): 560–82.

Smart, Carol. 1989. *Feminism and the Power of Law*. New York: Routledge.

Smith, David. 2008. "An Athapaskan Way of Knowing: Chipewyan Ontology." *American Ethnologist* 25(3): 412–32.

Smith, Dorothy. 1990. *The Conceptual Practices of Power: A Feminist Sociology of Knowledge*. Toronto: University of Toronto Press.

Smith, Olivia. 2018. *Rape Trials in England and Wales: Observing Justice and Rethinking Rape Myths*. London: Palgrave Macmillan.

Sommers, Ira, and Deborah Baskin. 2011. "Influence of Forensic Evidence on the Case Outcomes of Rape Incidents." *Justice System Journal* 32(3): 314–34.

Sommerville, Diane. 1995. "The Rape Myth in the Old South Reconsidered." *Journal of Southern History* 61(3): 481–518.

Soss, Joe, and Vesla Weaver. 2017. "Police Are Our Government: Politics, Political Science, and the Policing of Race-Class Subjugated Communities." *Annual Review of Political Science* 20: 565–91.

Spohn, Cassia, and Julie Horney. 1993. "Rape Law Reform and the Effect of Victim Characteristics on Case Processing." *Journal of Quantitative Criminology* 9: 383–409.

Stanko, Elizabeth. 1985. *Intimate Intrusions: Women's Experience of Male Violence*. New York and London: Routledge.

Staller, Karen M., and Frank E. Vandervort, 2010. "Child Sexual Abuse: Legal Burdens and Scientific Methods." In *Seeking Justice in Child Sexual Abuse: Shifting Burdens and Sharing Responsibilities*, ed. K. M. Staller and K. C. Faller, 1–32. New York: Columbia University Press.

Swidler, Ann, 1986. "Culture in Action: Symbols and Strategies." *American Sociological Review* 5(1): 273–86.

Tallbear, Kim. 2013. *Native American DNA: Tribal Belonging and the False Promise of Genetic Science*. Minneapolis: University of Minnesota Press.

Taslitz, Andrew. 1999. *Rape and the Culture of the Courtroom*. New York: New York University Press.

Taylor, Natalie, and Jacqueline Joudo. 2005. "The Impact of Pre-recorded Video and Closed Circuit Television Testimony by Adult Sexual Assault Complainants on Jury Decision-Making: An Experimental Study." Research and Public Policy Series, No. 68. Canberra: Australian Institute of Criminology.

Temkin, Jennifer. 2010. "'And Always Keep A-Hold of Nurse, for Fear of Finding Something Worse': Challenging Rape Myths in the Courtroom." *New Criminal Law Review* 13(4): 710–34.

———. 2000. "Prosecuting and Defending Rape: Perspectives from the Bar." *Journal of Law and Society* 27(2): 219–248.Temkin, Jennifer, and Barbara Krahé. 2008. *Sexual Assault and the Justice Gap: A Question of Attitude*. Oxford: Hart Publishing.

Tofte, Sarah. 2009. *Testing Justice: The Rape Kit Backlog in Los Angeles City and County*. New York: Human Rights Watch.

Traweek, Sharon. 1988. *Beamtimes and Lifetimes: The World of High Energy Physicists*. Cambridge, MA: Harvard University Press.

Trinch, Shonna. 2003. *Latinas' Narratives of Domestic Abuse: Discrepant Versions of Violence*. Amsterdam: John Benjamins.

Vielmetti, Bruce. "Ex-Milwaukee Officer Gets 26 Months in Prison for Strip, Cavity Searches," *Milwaukee Journal Sentinel*, June 21, 2013. http://archive.jsonline.com/news/crime/ex-milwaukee-officer-gets-26-months-in-prison-for-strip-cavity-searches-b99389482z1-212486141.html.

Voss, James, and Julie Van Dyke. 2001. "Narrative Structure, Information Certainty, Emotional Content, and Gender as Factors in a Pseudo Jury Decision-Making Task." *Discourse Processes* 32(2–3): 215–43.

Weheliye, Alexander. 2014. *Habeas Viscus: Racializing Assemblages, Biopolitics, and Black Feminist Theories of the Human*. Durham: Duke University Press.

Wenders, Jonathan. 2008. *Policing and the Poetics of Everyday Life*. Urbana: University of Illinois Press.

Whalley, Elizabeth, and Colleen Hackett. 2017. "Carceral Feminisms: The Abolitionist Project and Undoing Dominant Feminisms." *Contemporary Justice Review* 20(4): 456–73.

White, Deborah, and Janice Du Mont. 2009. "Visualising Sexual Assault: An Exploration of the Use of Optical Technologies in the Medico-Legal Context." *Social Science and Medicine* 68(1): 1–8.

Wilkie, Laurie. 2003. *The Archaeology of Mothering: An African-American Midwife's Tale*. New York: Routledge.

Williams, Christopher R. 2004. "Anarchic Insurgencies: The Mythos of Authority and the Violence of Mental Health." In *Psychological Jurisprudence: Critical Explorations in Law, Crime and Society*, ed. B. Arrigo, 43–74. Albany: State University of New York Press.

Williams, Erica Lorraine. 2013. *Sex Tourism in Bahia: Ambiguous Entanglements*. Urbana: University of Illinois Press.

Wilson, William Julius. 2009. *More Than Just Race: Being Poor and Black in the Inner City*. New York: W. W. Norton.

———. 1996. *When Work Disappears: The World of the New Urban Poor*. New York: Knopf.

Yllö, Kersti, and M. Gabriela Torres, eds. 2016. *Marital Rape: Consent, Marriage, and Social Change in Global Context*. New York: Oxford University Press.

Yudice, George. 1991. "Testimonio and Postmodernism." *Latin American Perspectives* 18(3): 15–31.

INDEX

Page numbers in *italics* refer to figures.

ABOUT THE AUTHORS

HEATHER R. HLAVKA is Associate Professor of Criminology and Law Studies in the Department of Social and Cultural Sciences at Marquette University. Her work is published in journals including *Gender & Society, Law & Society Review, Law & Social Inquiry, Men & Masculinities, and Violence Against Women.*

Before she joined the Department of Women's, Gender, and Sexuality Studies at Emory University in 2021, SAMEENA MULLA was Associate Professor of Anthropology in the Department of Social and Cultural Sciences at Marquette University. She is the author of *The Violence of Care: Rape Victims, Forensic Nurses and Sexual Assault Intervention,* which won the Society for Applied Anthropology and the American Anthropological Association's Margaret Mead Award.